WHETHER   D0562215

San Francisco saloon of THE TIME OF YOUR LIFE, with its strangely assorted group of thoroughly unforgettable characters,

or in the lonely jail cell with the trapped hard-luck gambler of HELLO OUT THERE,

or in the poignant relationship of the aged trumpeter, the failed poet and the wide-eyed young boy of MY HEART'S IN THE HIGHLANDS,

or in the tragicomedy of the middle-aged spinster and her imaginary-lover-turned-real of LOVE'S OLD SWEEET SONG,

or in the magically enchanting family circle of THE BEAUTIFUL PEOPLE,

the talent that catapulted William Saroyan to sudden spectacular fame and a place among America's foremost playwrights shows itself vividly and indelibly. "Gleeful, heartbreaking, tender and hilarious, probing and elusive."—thus the New York Post described THE TIME OF YOUR LIFE, winner of both the Drama Critics' Circle Award and the Pulitzer Prize. It is a judgment which lends itself to the whole of this marvelous writer's work.

BANTAM WORLD DRAMA EDITIONS

AFTER THE FALL
by Arthur Miller

•

THE CRUCIBLE
by Arthur Miller

•

CYRANO DE BERGERAC
by Edmond Rostand

•

THE ENTERTAINER
by John Osborne

•

EPITAPH FOR GEORGE DILLON
by John Osborne and Anthony Creighton

•

FOUR GREAT PLAYS
BY IBSEN

•

INCIDENT AT VICHY
by Arthur Miller

•

TEN PLAYS BY EURIPIDES
edited by Moses Hadas

•

THREE PLAYS
by Thornton Wilder

•

THE TIME OF YOUR LIFE AND OTHER PLAYS
by William Saroyan

•

A VIEW FROM THE BRIDGE
by Arthur Miller

THE TIME OF YOUR LIFE AND OTHER PLAYS

·

BY WILLIAM SAROYAN

·

With an Introduction by the Author

THE TIME OF YOUR LIFE AND OTHER PLAYS
A Bantam World Drama edition published May 1967

Acknowledgments

Three Plays (Love's Old Sweet Song, The Time of Your Life, My Heart's in the Highlands) *Copyright 1940 by William Saroyan.*
The Beautiful People *Copyright 1941 by William Saroyan. Acting Edition Copyright 1942 by Samuel French.*
Love's Old Sweet Song *Copyright 1940 by William Saroyan. Acting Edition Copyright 1941 by Samuel French.*
My Heart's in the Highlands *Copyright 1939 by William Saroyan. Acting Edition Copyright 1941 by Samuel French.*
The Time of Your Life *Copyright 1939 by William Saroyan. Copyright assigned to James Cagney and William Cagney. Acting Edition Copyright 1941 by Samuel French.*
Hello Out There *Copyright 1941 by William Saroyan. Copyright assigned to Huntington Hartford doing business as Huntington Hartford Enterprises. Acting Edition Copyright 1949 by Samuel French.*
The Collected Plays of William Saroyan *Copyright © 1966 by William Saroyan.*

Library of Congress Catalog Card Number: 67–17774

Bantam Books are published by Bantam Books, Inc., a subsidiary of Grosset & Dunlap, Inc. Its trade-mark consisting of the words "Bantam Books" and the portrayal of a bantam, is registered in the United States Patent Office and in other countries. Marca Registrada. Bantam Books, Inc., 271 Madison Avenue, New York, N.Y. 10016.

PRINTED IN THE UNITED STATES OF AMERICA

Contents

Introduction
1

MY HEART'S IN THE HIGHLANDS
17

THE TIME OF YOUR LIFE
65

LOVE'S OLD SWEET SONG
157

THE BEAUTIFUL PEOPLE
227

HELLO OUT THERE
273

Introduction

The plays referred to in the title of this book are *My Heart's in the Highlands, The Time of Your Life, Love's Old Sweet Song, The Beautiful People,* and *Hello Out There.*

The order is chronological, both in the writing of the plays, and in their appearance on Broadway.

The time involved is from 1939 to 1943, about five years which arrived and departed a rather long time ago when it comes to matters of theatrical action on Broadway where impressions are quickly made and quickly forgotten. But several other of my plays appeared in New York during that same short period of time, namely *Across the Board on Tomorrow Morning* and *Talking To You,* produced and directed by me on one bill, and *Get Away Old Man,* produced and directed by Mr. George Abbott.

I did not choose the plays for this book, but I might as well have done so, for these five plays are in fact the ones I am known by as a playwright. During the years since 1943—almost a quarter of a century—I have written a great many more plays, but I have deliberately kept them from Broadway, with the exception of *The Cave Dwellers,* produced in 1956 or 1957, and I will speak about this boycott in a moment. It isn't terribly important, not even to me, but it may be interesting to the reader, and perhaps even of use to the specialist. A history of the stage is seldom notable for plays written but not produced, although the fact that they were written certainly has some bearing on something.

The publisher has chosen to run the original prefaces to the plays, and I have chosen not to revise them, as young and green as they are. But green is a good color, and being young is not to be avoided, if possible.

Each of the titles says something about the playwright at the time. And if we imagine that a playwright is also always anybody, it tells something about anybody who was there at all, in 1939, not so much under protest, of which there was quite a lot in those days, as with a clear declaration of distrust of the popular values of a culture near bankruptcy: I am here, but if you want to know the truth my heart isn't, my heart is in the highlands; and (severally) I am held here as a small boy in a rattletrap house on a desolate street in a dead town; as a young father-poet, in despair about having his poetry earn his bread; and finally as an old man escaped from the Old People's Home dying of thirst, loneliness, and fear of total failure.

My Heart's in the Highlands is said to be a kind of landmark or turning-point in the American theater, and it doesn't matter very much that I was the first to say so. Why is this play the play it is? The answer is that since I did not know how to write a play, I had no choice but to write this play.

I take the liberty of mentioning only a few of the world-famous playwrights who later wrote plays out of this same personal confidence and thereby brought into focus a new view of the human condition: Beckett, Ionesco, and Pinter. Other playwrights, more conventional, also learned from the play, whether writing for the stage or for films. But I am not going to belabor any of this, although I may say that I certainly had in mind making known to any beginning playwright how he might go about his business in his own way instead of in that fixed way which was believed to be either traditional or profitable. I had in mind starting a new tradition, and I hoped to prove that an unfamiliar style and method could be as appealing and even as profitable as an over-familiar one.

If the playing time of *My Heart's in the Highlands* was too short, only an hour, that of *The Time of Your Life* was too long, so that at least one important part of it was not spoken or performed during the Broadway run: for instance, Joe tells Tom about money near the end of the play, but I was told by the producers that there were commuters who had to catch trains home every night after the show, and so on behalf of the train schedules of these people Joe didn't tell Tom anything about money. Nowadays, though, it is commonplace for plays that need four hours on the boards to get four hours.

In any case, what I'm talking about is the adjustments a playwright is asked to make to something or other for some reason or other. Certainly in the writing itself no playwright should bother about such considerations. Afterwards, he can let it go, if he must. But *The Time of Your Life* was actually not too long at all, even for people who had trains to catch, because that saloon was, in fact, almost the last place in which to remember a world about to go up in smoke. Nobody really knew what was going on or why, but everybody seemed to sense that before anything would get better it would get worse, as of course it soon did. From the vaudeville at the waterfront saloon in San Francisco in 1939 to the dropping of atom bombs on Hiroshima and Nagasaki in 1945 only six years of time were involved. Immediately afterwards, the fear of self-destruction of the human race made a new kind of play and a new kind of song and dance of life imperative in terms of dramatic writing, but anxiety lasted only a dozen years or so, after which relaxation set in, as it always does, so that nostalgia came back to the theater, especially in the big profitable musical branch of it. No harm done, because the prophetic in drama impels an order of propaganda really too boring for the theater, and in any case such propaganda has already been overdone in the daily news.

. *The Time of Your Life* carried forward an order of dramatic freedom that had been announced in *My Heart's in the Highlands*. Come to the theater and have the time of your life, one might presume the title suggests, and so to clarify that aspect of the matter a kind of Credo was written for the play: *In the time of your life, live,* and so forth. Within the Credo is one commandment I have never removed which nevertheless ought not to be there: about killing when it's time to kill. The flaw here is that if there can be a time to kill, then any time can be a time to kill. This unfortunate commandment rounds out the Credo, but it doesn't make any sense.

Now, the thing about the theater that is fascinating to me is that in America, but especially in New York, the theater is a fraud from beginning to end. This is so because presenting a play is an activity involving great numbers of people who are in business and are determined to show a profit, corporate or personal. They have no choice, of course. Getting a play on the boards costs a lot of money, and everybody knows how bitterly money is compelled to protect and enlarge itself. Bankers, almost as contemptible as lawyers and far more than dentists, are the true makers of the American theater, and in fact of American art in general, insofar as the form of art involved needs money to be fulfilled at all—plays, movies, television.

A playwright—a *proven* playwright if you prefer—can write plays, and never again be known as a playwright, so what is a playwright to do? At the beginning, since he has no choice, he gives it a go, as I did.

In December of 1954, about fifteen years after the first performance of *The Time of Your Life*, I wrote a piece, which appeared in *Theatre Arts*, January 1955, thus:

Several years ago when Lawrence Langner's autobiography entitled *The Magic Curtain* was published, I missed the book, as I have so many others. Now, in the September issue of *Theatre Arts* I find several excerpts from that book in which I figure, and I am suddenly half-overwhelmed by a feeling of youth and nostalgia.

I was quite a character in those days, it seems. For instance, I frequently sent out for pears to eat, and ate them. This was actually not eccentricity, however. The market nearest the Boston theater where *The Time of Your Life* was being tried out in the fall of 1939 had no grapes or apples, which I would have preferred. In this manner come the legends and picayune martyrdom as well, for the pears were mushy and punk.

"When the play opened in New Haven," Langner writes, "it was in a state of incredible chaos. Nobody seemed to know what the play was about, including the actors, and a bewildered audience left the theatre and learned from the papers the next day that the drama critics were equally bewildered."

The fact of the matter is that the play had been expertly staged by Robert Lewis, who earlier that year had staged my first play, *My Heart's in the Highlands*. The first performance in New Haven was brilliantly performed by a fine cast. There was no chaos about any of it. The set by Boris Aronson was magnificent. The only trouble with the play on the boards was that it had not been directed by the playwright—myself. A new kind of play impels or even demands a new kind of theatrical method and style, and the playwright himself is most apt to know what the method and style are. As I wrote *The Time of Your Life* I "saw" it on the boards, but in New Haven I saw something entirely different. There was authentic style to the performance, but it just wasn't mine. I believed I had written a very simple folk play—the play of the American saloon. The play I saw seemed to me bogus Russian, and it was very boring.

The chaos Langner speaks of came after the first performance when I made known to him that he had a flop, and an entirely useless one. Certain plays which fail do more for the theater than most plays that succeed, but this was just a flop. I didn't think the situation was hopeless, however. Langner and his partner Theresa Helburn wanted to hire another director when Robert Lewis resigned, but this director wanted the play to be rewritten—to postpone the tryout in Boston for a month or so. I don't believe in that Hollywood approach to theatrical problems. If there is any rewriting to be done, it should be done on the boards, as it was done by Shakespeare, Molière, Lope de Vega and many others.

"A council of war was held and it was decided that Dowling, Saroyan and myself," Langner goes on, "would endeavor to put the play into shape, giving Saroyan billing with Dowling as director. I was soon to learn that Saroyan had never directed a play in his life, had not the slightest idea of how to talk to the actors in such a way that they understood him, and that his method of dealing with them varied from acting their parts himself in the most amateurish manner and requesting them to imitate him, or else bellowing at them."

Let me see if I can review the whole situation and clarify the foregoing remarks. I came to New York from San Francisco in May of 1939 to see a performance of *My Heart's in the Highlands*. I felt that Robert Lewis had done a magnificent job on the whole, although I could not go along with certain conceptions of certain characters, as I told him, urging him and Harold Clurman of the Group Theatre to revise those conceptions and thereby to improve the play. Clurman explained to me in brilliant and rather involved language why I was mistaken. I was not at all convinced, but the play was not changed as I felt it should be. The relationship between the poet and his son was gooey, and anybody knows that the least gooey people in the world are apt to be a poet and his son. I am opposed to the gooey, even when supported by profound explanations on the part of those who are not so opposed.

A short time later I met Eddie Dowling who, as I have said elsewhere, remarked that he would produce any play I might write. Thus challenged to get to work, I went to work and in six days wrote *The Time of Your Life*. I turned it over first to Harold Clurman, however, because I felt morally obliged to do so, since he had produced my first play. Clurman chose not to produce the play. He took some time to tell me why, but I didn't understand anything he said. I understood that he chose not to produce it. I then took the play to Eddie Dowling who chose to produce it. Dowling in turn took it to The Theatre Guild, and The Guild hired Robert Lewis to direct it. Lewis directed it. The play was boring and an unmistakable flop, and it looked as if a lot of money was about to go down the drain. I was determined to prevent my second play from being a flop. I wanted to write more plays and I wanted them to be produced, directed and performed as I believed they ought to be in order to reach people, for whom I wanted to write them. I therefore insisted on taking over.

The Theatre Guild permitted this not so much from confidence as from helplessness. It had no choice. Of course I hadn't directed a play in my life. At some time or another in his life every man hasn't directed a play. At still another time in his life a man decides to direct a play and he directs it. After that, I suppose, he is a director. I told the producers there was no need for the planned schedule of the play to skip a beat. I said the play would have great general appeal by the time it opened in New York. I said it might not be a hit, but it wouldn't be a flop, either. I said it would be a new kind of American play which the public would judge for itself.

Now, my opinion is that I wrote the play, I recast certain important parts (those of Gene Kelly and Celeste Holm), I worked with a new stage designer on a new set, and I directed the play from its first moment to its last— and nobody else did or half-did. To illustrate: the consensus of opinion was that the marble game was a crackpot whim and not required by the story. The producers did not provide the working machine until the first performance in New York, and it took some arguing on my part to get it even then. There had been a marble game on stage all the time, but it had been dead, and it didn't do anything when it was supposed to. The machine did what it was supposed to do in the first New York performance, and neither the critics nor the public felt they did not understand what the machine did, if in fact they bothered to think about understanding it at all. They just happened to like what it did, as I believed they would, because I myself had always been delighted by a marble game that had been beat.

What school of theater did I follow in directing *The Time of Your Life?* Stanislavski? The Hysterical Left-Wing, so popular at that time, so unpopular now? The Precious

Aesthetic? The Screech and Scream? The Rant and Rave? The My Goodness, Aren't We Wonderful, Different, Superior Group School? These schools were great schools, as some of them still are, but they just weren't for me. My school was to get some people who like to act and to give them something to act, and to tell them how their acting could be more effective. I believed every moment of the play should be direct, simple and entertaining. Anything else we might get would be extra, and we got it.

"When we brought the play to New York," Langner writes, "Saroyan was very critical of the Booth Theater, and asked if it might not be possible to push the walls out on either side, in order to accommodate more people, and to improve the sight lines on the sides. As we were opening on the next Wednesday, I informed him that it would not be possible to carry out his wishes in time."

I happen to remember quite clearly what actually happened. During one rehearsal I sat in a side seat and couldn't see the whole playing area on the stage. I asked if tickets were to be sold for the side seats. They were. After a survey I found that perhaps two hundred seats in the auditorium had a poor view of the set. The people who would occupy these seats were entitled to see the whole play, I felt. Langner pointed out that every theater in New York has many seats from which it is impossible to see the whole set. I said those theaters were cheating the public whenever they sold tickets for those seats. I said the first thing a playgoer must be able to do in order to enjoy a play is to see it—every bit of it. I wanted anybody who might pay to see this play to see it. At this point Langner said a remodeling of the theater would not be possible in time for opening night. I went up on the stage and pointed out how, by moving the set in a few feet at each end, everybody in the auditorium would be able to see the whole set and playing area. For some reason Langner was opposed to this simple mechanical adjustment, but I discussed the matter with Watson Barratt, the stage designer, and by opening night the situation was much improved, if not quite perfect.

In 1939 I had believed that The Theatre Guild, operated by Lawrence Langner and Theresa Helburn, was a nonprofit organization. It was no such thing. It was a money-making play-producing agency. I myself did not go to The Theatre Guild with *The Time of Your Life;* Mr. Eddie Dowling did. He was an individual producer of plays, and

I believed that when he accepted the play he would produce it with his own money. When he told me that no
producer puts his own money in the plays he produces
I wanted to know what he does do. I was told that he got
others to put money in the play, and gave them half of the
producer's profits, and kept for himself the other half. For
what, though? For the fact that he was the producer—an
agent, in short. Bankers, lawyers, dentists, and agents. I
despise them all, but they *do* keep the game going, no
doubt about that. And so, fighting them off all the while,
I salvaged my second play. I transformed it from a sure
flop into a kind of hit, even in terms of money. The Theatre
Guild took a good big chunk, Mr. Dowling took another
good big chunk, and I was given my usual little chunk, in
accordance with the terms of the Minimum Basic Contract
provided by the Dramatists' Guild. I thought, "I write
them, I direct them, I fight off their obstructions, and these
rich people get richer. And then, in due course, they write
their memoirs and make me out some kind of arrogant and
rude intruder." I decided that as soon as possible I would
produce my own plays with my own money. "If I'm lucky
and earn a lot of money, I'll start a whole theater and produce both my own plays and the plays of new playwrights."
But after a year I still didn't have enough money, so once
again, this time with my eyes wide open, I turned over to
Mr. Eddie Dowling *Love's Old Sweet Song*. He again went
to The Theatre Guild with it, and so there was a brand new
ball game.

From beginning to end I directed *Love's Old Sweet
Song*, working with perhaps the greatest all-around actor
of the American theater of his day, Mr. Walter Huston.
There were a lot of little kids in the play, one of whom,
named Jules Leni, remains unforgettable. He was the
youngest member of the cast, perhaps no more than three,
dark-eyed, scared, brave, and so sensitive that whenever
there was any kind of commotion in the play he looked
around for sanctuary. And of course there was none. This
compelled me to decide not to have little kids in my plays
in the future, insofar as possible.

In 1941, I had earned money enough at last to produce
a play with my own money, and that play was *The Beautiful People*.

If it wasn't a hit, it wasn't a flop, and it proved a point.

I hired the Belasco Theater for the occasion, hoping that

it would become the home of The Saroyan Theater. But there were far more theatrical things going on in the world that made that expectation unfulfillable. To sum it up, I was drafted into the Army, in spite of a gimpy leg which came from a slipped disc, a duodenal ulcer I didn't even know I had, which I had gotten from the nerve-wracking work I had been doing in the theater for so long, partial deafness, and a totally unsuitable temperament for regimentation.

While I was directing *Across the Board on Tomorrow Morning*, the second production of The Saroyan Theater, a newspaperman from *The Herald Tribune* came to the Belasco Theater and during a pause in the proceedings said, "Are you eager to get into the Army?" To which I truthfully replied, "No, I am a writer. My work is to observe what goes on, and to write about it." We had come to a time so difficult for the nation that lying constituted patriotism, and telling the truth constituted treason. The newspaperman made a story of my reply, and a few days later I was summoned to St. Joseph's in New York where I passed my physical with flying colors, as the saying is. Not only that, kindly friends urged me not to make any more honest remarks, because not only would I be drafted, I would be given the works, and in the Army that means that you either go over the hill, commit suicide, or go mad.

And so in a sense these things happened, one by one, followed by survival. I was badly damaged but I was also determined to believe that I was as good as new. But it wasn't easy to take up where I had been stopped. During the three years I spent in the Army I did no writing, with the exception of an Anglo-American anti-war novel called *The Adventures of Wesley Jackson*, which was written in 1944 in London, and for which at least one direct-commission Hollywood officer felt I should be shot. Publication was held up by various people in the Army and in the Government until after Hiroshima, and when the novel finally did appear it was bitterly attacked by many good and sincere writers and critics, and defended, I am proud to say, by a number of equally good and sincere writers, and by a great many readers, but not by any critics. The book earned no money in America, little enough in England, but was rather successful in Europe, and especially so in Russia. The point is that after the war I was very nearly broke and I had no backlog of work to fall back on, so that when there were taxes to pay I had no money with which to pay them, let alone to start up The Saroyan Theater again.

I have already written somewhere or other that *Hello Out There*, so popular in America and all over the world, I like least of all of my plays, for the reason that its drama is based on an actual event of violence, taken from the news. Such real events are already so dramatic that there is very little a playwright needs to do in order to have himself an exciting play. The personal tragedies of great numbers of unfortunate or unlucky souls destroyed by madness, accident, or crime can easily be exploited in literary and dramatic achievements—if permissions can be cleared with the survivors. But such writing is not for me.

Here, with a few cuts, is a whole chapter from *Here Comes There Goes You Know Who*, published in 1961, which tells about my boycott of Broadway:

In our time, it is simple backwardness for emotionality to be prolonged as a means by which to achieve drama in human relations or in plays.

This truth is not going to be seized upon by enormous numbers of playwrights in anything like a hurry because the usages of emotionality in playwrighting are many, attractive, and convenient. *Have them jump and holler and you've got your play.*

And the reason the playwrights are not going to kick out emotionality is that, apart from not yet knowing enough to do so, they are spoiled by the established theatrical pattern, and the habit of audiences.

And of course the playwright is bullied all over the place by the people who take to the stage, the men and women who for some reason or another become actors and actresses, and insist upon having parts, big parts, juicy parts, easy parts, and *get* them, or else. Either the playwright rewrites a play to suit the big players, or he has no players who can draw a crowd. And a playwright *wants* to draw a crowd, and any kind of a crowd with a willingness to spend money will do.

Well, it won't do. But this does not mean the collapse of the theater, which is in fact no more collapsible than the human personality itself, while the crowd, the mob, the horde, is always collapsible, although transforming the multitude is never easy. It is neither desirable nor necessary for the achievement of success in the theater to be easy: the achievement, that is to say, of instant acceptance of a playwright and of a play.

That is something which in the nature of things should always be difficult.

But the *writing* of a play, the making of a work of art, *should* be easy. It should be as easy as the doing of any other kind of work by any other kind of workman.

It is only the theoretic need, the compulsion, to be instantly accepted that keeps the theater, and all literary art, far behind the rights of children, the reality of them, or to put it another way the demands of the individual in the business of putting up with an unknown amount of personal time, of putting up with one's self, and of putting up with whoever else one knows importantly or unimportantly.

Within itself a play has a right to be easy only in its achievement of effectiveness. To begin with, it has got to be itself, and not a confusion of intentions and expectations based upon the winning of the current ticket-buying horde. The more a playwright strains to win the horde, the less ease he has in the making of a work, and ease is what he needs in order to achieve effectiveness in the work itself, which if it has ease will eventually win a horde in any case, but with this difference: the quality of perceptiveness, of livingness in the horde will have been improved and extended a little, after which of course the work involved, the play, will need to be transcended, just as all of Shakespeare has long needed to be transcended. It doesn't matter that no one so far has had the combination of energy, skill, wit, and health to do so.

Now, this is all very simple stuff. It isn't complicated at all. Shakespeare's drama is achieved by means of the device of emotionality, although in the comedies the order of emotionality is unlike the order that is in the tragedies. He had his horde to satisfy and he did a good job. I do not wish to be considered patronizing to Shakespeare, but it is absolute folly to go on imagining there can be no comparable dramatic force of a new and better order of drama and theater. Emotionality as a device, as in fact the *sole* device, for the achievement of effectiveness in playwrighting is out. It is out, whether we like it or not. It has served its purpose, and it has no purpose any longer.

The kids don't want it, unless the emotionality is fantasy and farce, make-believe pure and simple, for the sheer animal fun of it.

And there *will* come a time when the horde will rejoice in much of Shakespeare as farce, as an exposure of an obsolete form of man in an obsolete procedure of putting up with himself. His scheming, betraying, killing, and dying will be acceptable only as demonstrations of folly in useless but loud and grand action.

Every man is entitled to be continuously alive and in transition, changing if not for the literal better at least for the usages of *recognizing* the change itself, as long as he breathes, and by means of this livingness to find himself, everybody he knows, the world, nature, time, action, and all of his exterior and interior experience dramatic, satisfying, and good.

But isn't man a tragic creature? So what? Suppose he is? He can go right on being tragic, if he is in fact tragic, if the human experience itself is, which is certainly at least still open for a final decision, or more accurately another *temporary* decision which has the appearance of finality. Man is a fluid creature, and the human experience is fluid. In him and in his life there is no vote and no final decision. Every decision is always personal first, and then collective.

Man is an accident, but the element of the deliberate in his accidental reality is now sufficient to permit him to put up with or to seek to correct the wrongs of the accidental that is in him, and to cherish, accept, recognize, employ, extend, enlarge, improve, and thrive upon the accidental *rights* which were also born into him, the principal one of which is to continue, after which the rights are inexhaustibly varied. But he must continue. He must be there, in his accidental abiding place, himself, and he must respect his right to be there as painlessly and as meaningfully as may be.

The plays I write are both funny and earnest without being pompous, pretentious, affected, or excessively ambitious (startled and startling) in themselves. They take for granted that man is (also) unastonishable by the fact of his enormity. They recognize his enormity but do not rant and rave about it.

Now, in 1943 I turned my back on Broadway, but I did not stop writing plays. I simply stopped offering my plays to the machine that was huffing and puffing in the business of getting plays on the boards in front of New Yorkers and people from out of town who had money to spend on tickets. I wrote new plays every year, I have the plays, and they *do* constitute my theater, and they are a part of the real American theater, and of the real world theater, even though they have not been produced, performed, and witnessed.

Such matters are none of my business.

The plays are for the human race, and they will reach the human race, the *concealed* human race, the *still* concealed human race, which is trying to come out from under, as it has been trying for a million years or more. Will it come out from under in the next thousand?

Well, the answer is that it is already out in myself—at my best. The habit of uselessness is strong, however; it persists even after the element of the accidental in one man has enabled him, or driven him, to come out from under. And that doesn't matter, either. We want the human race entire and whole. Man doesn't have to be suddenly something different or brand-new, entirely. Just partly, just in *addition to*. And if I have come out from under, at my best, there are surely others who have as well, by the thousands, most likely, although they may not be writers, communicators, makers of influence, setters of precedents, tellers. They may keep it to themselves, not necessarily out of selfishness or indifference, but for want of a means by which to communicate.

To oversimplify for a moment, it may be said that life stinks, the human experience stinks, every individual stinks, and having said that, from having known the truth of it, the validity of it, you begin to come out from under when you reply to this truth by saying, So what? By saying, Even so. When you know it doesn't matter, when even the toughest truth, the most seemingly final and total, is recognized as also being not anywhere near tough enough on the one hand and on the other irrelevant, and is also not final and not total.

The plays I write come from health, even though I have been sick all my life. Now, whenever I say this, as I frequently do when I am chatting with a doctor, for instance, he misunderstands, and so I expect others to misunderstand, too. I expect anybody to misunderstand, so I'll see if I can make what I mean a little clearer.

We are all of us sick all our lives, but this does not

necessarily mean that mortality itself is only a form of sickness that we have all become adjusted to in varying degrees. That may be the truth, but it's an irrelevant truth.

If we are sick, it follows that there exists the opposite of this, or health, for in the order of things the law of opposites is basic. If *we* are sick, *something* isn't. Or we ourselves are also simultaneously something else, *not* sick, the opposite, healthy. If it is desirable to cease to be sick, or less sick, or at any rate to achieve a balance between the opposites, it is desirable to go after the fulfillment of this possibility. It is desirable not to make ourselves sicker than we are, and it is desirable to try to make ourselves more well than we are, without of course forfeiting the advantages of being more sick than well, which advantages can be considerable. A man sicker than well doesn't forget, for instance, the collective pain and discomfort of everybody, and that *is* an advantage. In the matter of opposites I am on the side of more instead of less, however difficult, increasingly, more is for me to cope with. I am on the side of health instead of sickness, energy instead of dispiritedness, enjoyment instead of distaste, but more than anything else truth instead of falsity, even though I know that all truth is also inevitably false, tentative, tenuous, troublesome. But as you continue to come out from under and to stay out, you move nearer to something more and better than everything else. This state so far is not even *named*, not even by a sign or symbol in mathematics, or in some other form of science. You move nearer to what I shall mistakenly call the Intelligence-of-All, even though I know it is not intelligence, and that nothing we are to conceive may be said to be All. Having come out and being out, you get it entirely, not with mind alone, not with nerves alone, flesh and blood and chemistry and the action of it all in concert alone, you get it entirely, and you get it out, *away* from yourself above all things, and yet inevitably always yourself, too, for you are the one there, moving and transitory. And you can't say that it is *knowing*, either, although it is certainly something of that order. Perhaps it might (also) be said that it is a state of being in which by having become most yourself, which at best is a picayune fragment of the possible total, you have also ceased to be so uselessly yourself alone, and have become delivered from this smallness and uselessness into the vicinity, if vicinity can even suggest it, of unself, or multitudiness, which all the same is you, is yours.

This involvement in an apparent contradictoriness is also unavoidable. The more you are yourself, the fuller you are yourself, the greater the range and variety of the action and elements of yourself, the less you are yourself as formerly.

I write my plays out of that kind of health, and the writing of them has nothing to do with Broadway, with the preferences of the current horde, with theater buildings, with the machinery of production, with real estate, with money, with acceptance, with instant material profit.

I volunteered this introduction to this paperback edition of five of my plays because I felt I ought to address myself to the new reader, to the new student of the theater, and to the new playwright, each of whom is invited in turn to address himself to me.

Paris, July 1966   WILLIAM SAROYAN

My Heart's in the Highlands

To the pure in heart.
To the poet in the world.
To the lowly and great, whose lives are poetry.
To the child grown old, and the child of childhood.
To the heart in the highlands.

Preface

The theater is and always has been a place visited by more or less normal people who, by the grace of God, are out of pain and in a mood to compare their experience in living with the experience of others—with the experience of the people who appear in a play or with the experience of the man who wrote the play. Or both. Or with the experience of the people in the theater, from their response to the play.

There are many reasons for a man to go to a theater and see a play. One man goes to escape dying of boredom. Another goes in order to escape being eager, personally, about all things. To relax and rest and watch others being eager. One man goes to dream. Another goes to be awakened. Another goes because there isn't anything else to do at the time, and many years ahead. Still another goes because it's a social affair—a good chance to put on the fancy clothes and feel fine.

I go to the theater to see still another variation of the world. To see another dimension of human reality. If what I see is false, it's no matter to me, because I *know* it's false. If it's true, fine: I'm delighted. Art comes from the world, belongs to it, can never escape from it. The world is interesting to me. Therefore the theater is interesting to me. I may not like a play, but it can't bore me. This is so because I am a writer.

I know there are others who can take the theater this way. They are not all writers. On the contrary, very often the dullest people in the world are writers—of one sort or another. There are great numbers of people in the world who can't be bored. They are usually the ones who are themselves not bores. Most often, however, what they usually are, are children.

The child race is fresh, eager, interested, innocent, imaginative, healthy and full of faith, where the adult race, more often than not, is stale, spiritually debauched, unimaginative, unhealthy, and without faith.

A number of drama critics sincerely regretted they couldn't understand this simple play, and a number were bored by it. It is perfectly all right with me for any man who must be bored with this play to be bored with it. I believe I understand people well enough to know that a perfectly fine human being could be bored with this play, or be confused by it, or could regard it as preposterous. Or even as preposterous nonsense. He could, by a generous exercise of the imagination, be regarded himself as not insane or dull-witted, either. I would recommend rest, recreation, and reading, however.

If this play can bore a man, I would like to know if any play could escape boring him, or if anything at all could. Here is a play as real as a street corner. As natural as the earth or sidewalk underfoot, the sky overhead. As true as any fable in the literature of the world. Any man who could be bored with this play could be bored with the sudden vision of the Good Lord negotiating a substantial body of water on foot.

The meaning of the play is the meaning of reality itself. It is not a meaning which I or anyone else can express in phrases beginning, "Well, it means—" You simply don't say of any real thing, whether it is the whole world, a city like New York, an ocean, a bird flying, a man dying, or a child entering the world, that it has a meaning. That kind of explaining I leave to those intellectual giants who can explain everything—and understand nothing.

As for the message and moral of the play it is the simplest and oldest in the world:

It is better to be a good human being than to be a bad one. It is just naturally better.

As I see it, the basic trouble with the American theater is that the element of "play" has been completely forgotten by American playwrights and completely left out of their plays. American plays, in fact, are not plays. They are, as a rule, essays at one or another of the many variations of reality, usually sorrowful. As a rule they are dull and depressing. They make a visit to the theater a pleasure only because after the two or two-and-a-half hours of headache, it is delightful to get out into the open air and breathe a moment of plain, unmechanical, worldly reality.

I have a reputation as one who enthusiastically praises and recommends his own work. The reputation is justified. I believe in my work and am eager for others to know about it. I think it will do them good to know about it. If talk of this kind makes a braggart of me, that, I suppose, is something I shall have to continue to be. Nevertheless, all I have ever argued for has been impersonal. My right to be myself is relatively a feeble right for me to quarrel for. In the realm of world events it is not exactly the most important struggle of the day. In the realm of my own life, however, I do not hesitate to say that it is by all odds the most important matter of all. Stop one good man from functioning and you stop all men, which may or may not be Fascism, but is certainly something vicious as far as I am concerned, and something I will not personally tolerate.

The only way I can argue impersonally for integrity and reality, truth and imagination, in art, in living, and in the theater, is to argue specifically—with my own work as a basis for comparison.

The value that comes from my being myself—that is to say, honest, unspoiled and continuously concerned about valid potentialities in living and in art—is a value of some importance to everybody. In the theater, for instance, if I can get by with it (and it is truly something you have to put over, unfortunately), it is likely that others, perhaps more talented, will be encouraged to make the attempt. The result, possibly, will be that the greatest country in the world will become, in art as well as in its day-to-day life, truly the greatest country in the world. As it should be.

I am convinced there is no place in the world like America. It is the first place in the world of its kind, and I for one don't want it to begin to be the last. There never has been such a place. There never has been such a people. Any of us who does not try to do something about it, or make something of it, is a failure—as an artist and as an American. It doesn't make any difference what we do, or how well it is received.

Yet all I know is that I have not so much as made a real beginning. The important truth—the *true* truth—is still in the stage of an expected and hoped-for arrival. I don't want this truth to be forced to arrive somewhere where it won't be able to make itself known. In a factory worker, for instance, who won't be able to tell anybody about it—in a sensibility and mind, that is, which will be innocent but uncommunicative. Just because we're writers doesn't mean that we shall be less than the people of the world. We may be their superiors in technical skill—in being able to articulate what little we know—but we can never afford to be their inferiors in spirit, as we seem to be now.

I would like to see the boys who really know how to write plays really write them, instead of throwing them together out of the shabby devices which they have come to believe are sure-fire. I would like them to remember, for instance, that nothing has ever been more sure-fire than truth and integrity. You can fool all of the people all of the time, but you can fool only the fool in them, which is no great feat of heroism, and nothing to get any blue ribbon for.

To say there is no American theater at all is false, and to some degree silly. To say there is not yet an American theater *equal* to the dramatic materials provided by the American environment and people, however, is very true, and to a small degree profound.

The day-to-day drama of American life following its beautiful destiny is far away from the American drama, wallowing, as it were, in its present unconsciousness, or more correctly going insignificantly mad, or ga-ga, in its busy mechanicalism.

American life is still a total stranger to American dramatic art.

It is about time for ten or eleven (or maybe one or two) experts in the theater—playwrights, directors, actors, scene designers, composers, and others—to introduce American reality to American dramatic art.

I feel confident that the two will get along famously.

A great but simple and more or less dimensionless reality is constant, of course, where there are people and cities, villages, and dwellings. The greater reality, the truer, deeper and more pertinent reality of a people and place, however, can be established—by isolation, emphasis, and magnification—only by men of good will, good vision, and great humanity.

Although these men must be naturals (that is, first writers), I believe they must learn everything good and valuable to be learned from the men in the theater who are technical experts, but, unfortunately, little else.

The present theater is tricky as a consequence of great technical skill being wasted on second-hand material synchronized out of third-rate sensibilities. It doesn't have to remain tricky. Producers with as much sensibility as money are on the scene, and appear to be as willing to gamble on a work of freshness as on a work of artificiality.

This is all anybody who writes plays needs to know.

There is no such thing as experiment. There is only good

and bad art. When a good thing appears to be very new, it is more likely that it is only something that has been forgotten, and is now suddenly remembered. A classic is simply a first work, the beginning of a tradition, and an entry into a fresh realm of human experience, understanding, and expression.

I believe *My Heart's in the Highlands* is a classic.

It was surely impertinent for me to believe that the greater and truer American theater would begin its life after the appearance and influence of this play, but God forgive me, that is what I believed.

I know the play itself is relatively a trifle, but I also know of no one else who hopes for more for the American theater than myself, and plans to do something about fulfilling these hopes personally.

I regret very much that to speak the truth in our day appears to be bad taste. I find, however, that even at the risk of seeming to be a boor I must still say what I truly believe.

I believe that time, with its infinite understanding, will one day forgive me.

WILLIAM SAROYAN

New York, August 1939

MY HEART'S IN THE HIGHLANDS

BY ROBERT BURNS

Farewell to the Highlands, farewell to the North,
The birth-place of valor, the country of worth!
Wherever I wander, wherever I rove,
The hills of the Highlands for ever I love.

   My heart's in the Highlands, my heart is not here,
   My heart's in the Highlands a-chasing the deer,
   A-chasing the wild deer and following the roe—
   My heart's in the Highlands, wherever I go.

Farewell to the mountains high-covered with snow,
Farewell to the straths and green valleys below,
Farewell to the forests and wild-hanging woods,
Farewell to the torrents and loud-pouring floods!

   My heart's in the Highlands, my heart is not here;
   My heart's in the Highlands a-chasing the deer,
   A-chasing the wild deer and following the roe—
   My heart's in the Highlands, wherever I go!

Note

My Heart's in the Highlands was offered as a Group Theatre production at the Guild Theatre in New York City on
April 13, 1939.

This play has grown out of one of my short stories. The
story was called "The Man with the Heart in the Highlands," and was published in December, 1936, in a book
called "Three Times Three." A one-act play bearing the
title of the story was published in *The One-Act Play Magazine*, edited by William Kozlenko, who suggested to me
that the story contained a play, and again in "Contemporary
One-Act Plays," a book published by Scribner's and also
edited by Mr. Kozlenko. After the appearance of the
shorter play, I could not resist the impulse to carry out the
theme to its present completion.

In the production of a play there are many people a
writer admires and wants to thank. A play may or may not
be literature before it is played, but it is certainly not a
play until it is played, and it is most truly a play only *while*
it is being played. The effective playing of a play puts to
work many people. It is a group activity. I wish to express
my gratitude to Harold Clurman, founder and director of
the Group Theatre; Robert Lewis, director of the play;
Herbert Andrews, who did the sets and costumes; Paul
Bowles, who composed the music; Michael Gordon, who
lighted the play; the cast: Jackie Ayers (*The Boy with the
Double-Decker Ice Cream Cone*), Philip Loeb (*Ben
Alexander*), Sidney Lumet (*Johnny*), Art Smith (*Jasper
MacGregor*), William Hansen (*Mr. Kosak*), Hester Sonder-
gaard (*Johnny's Grandmother*), James O'Rear (*Rufe
Apley*), Loren Gage (*Philip Carmichael*), Phil Brown
(*Henry*), Harry Bratsburg (*Mr. Wiley*), Nicholas Conte
(*The Real Estate Agent*), John O'Malley (*The Husband*),
Catheryn Laughlin (*The Wife*), Mae Grimes (*Esther
Kosak*), Peter Leeds (*A Guard*), Charles De Sheim (*An-
other Guard*), and Eda Reis, Eileen Detchon, Undine
Forrest, Charles Henderson, Mary Liles (*Good Friends and
Neighbors*).

THE PEOPLE

JOHNNY
His father, BEN ALEXANDER, *the poet*
Johnny's grandmother
JASPER MAC GREGOR, *the man with the heart in the highlands*
MR. KOSAK, *the grocer*
ESTHER, *his beautiful daughter*
RUFE APLEY, *the carpenter*
PHILIP CARMICHAEL, *the young man from the Old People's Home*
HENRY, *the morning paper route carrier*
MR. WILEY, *the mailman*
MR. CUNNINGHAM, *the real estate agent*
The Young Husband and Wife, and Their Baby
Good Friends and Neighbors
A dog

THE PLACE

A house on San Benito Avenue in Fresno, California.
Mr. Kosak's grocery store.

THE TIME

August and November, 1914.

AN OLD WHITE, *broken-down, frame house with a front porch, on San Benito Avenue in Fresno, California. There are no other houses near by, only a desolation of bleak land and red sky. It is late afternoon of a day in August, 1914. The evening sun is going down.*

JOHNNY, *aged nine, but essentially ageless, is sitting, dynamic and acrobatic, on the steps of the porch, dead to the world and deep in thought of a high and holy order. Far away a train whistle cries mournfully. He listens eagerly, cocking his head on one side like a chicken, trying to understand the meaning of the cry and at the same time to figure out everything. He doesn't quite make it and when the cry ends he stops being eager. A fourteen-year-old boy on a bicycle, eating an ice-cream cone and carrying newspaper bags, goes by on the sidewalk in silence, oblivious of the weight on his shoulders and of the contraption on which he is seated, because of the delight and glory of ice cream in the world.* JOHNNY *leaps to his feet and waves to the boy, smiling in a big humanitarian way, but is ignored. He sits down again and listens to a small overjoyed but angry bird. After making a brief forceful speech of no meaning, the bird flies away.*

From inside the house is heard the somber voice of JOHNNY'S FATHER *reciting poetry of his own composition.*

JOHNNY'S FATHER: The long silent day journeys through the sore solemn heart, and—(*Bitter pause*) And— (*Quickly*) The long silent day journeys through the sore solemn heart, and—(*Pause*) No. (*He roars and begins again*) Crippled and weeping, time stumbles through the lone lorn heart.

> (*A table or chair is pushed over in anger. A groan. Silence*)
>
> (*The boy listens. He gets up and tries to stand on his head, fails, tries again, fails, tries again, and succeeds. While he is standing on his head he hears the loveliest and most amazing music in the world: a*

solo on a bugle. The music is "My Heart's in the
Highlands."

*The bugler, a very old man, finishes the solo in front
of the house. The boy leaps to his feet and runs up
to the old man, amazed, delighted and bewildered)*

JOHNNY: I sure would like to hear you play another song.

MAC GREGOR: Young man, could you get a glass of water for
an old man whose heart is not here, but in the highlands?

JOHNNY: What highlands?

MAC GREGOR: The Scotch Highlands. Could you?

JOHNNY: What's your heart doing in the Scotch Highlands?

MAC GREGOR: My heart's grieving there. Could you get me
a glass of cool water?

JOHNNY: Where's your *mother*?

MAC GREGOR (*Inventing for the boy*): My mother's in Tulsa,
Oklahoma, but her heart isn't.

JOHNNY: Where *is* her heart?

MAC GREGOR (*Loud*): In the Scotch Highlands. (*Soft*) I'm
very thirsty, young man.

JOHNNY: How come the members of your family are always
leaving their hearts in the highlands?

MAC GREGOR (*In the Shakespearean manner*): That's the
way we are. Here today and gone tomorrow.

JOHNNY (*Aside*): Here today and gone tomorrow? (*To
MacGregor*) How do you figure?

MAC GREGOR (*The philosopher*): Alive one minute and
dead the next.

JOHNNY: Where's your *mother's mother*?

MAC GREGOR (*Inventing, but angry*): She's up in Vermont,
in a little town called White River, but her heart isn't.

JOHNNY: Is her poor old withered heart in the highlands,
too?

MAC GREGOR: Right smack in the highlands. Son, I'm dying
of thirst.

*(JOHNNY'S FATHER comes out of the house in a fury,
as if he has just broken out of a cage, and roars at
the boy like a tiger that has just awakened from evil
dreams)*

JOHNNY'S FATHER: Johnny, get the hell away from that poor
old man. Get him a pitcher of water before he falls down
and dies. Where the hell are your manners?

JOHNNY: Can't a fellow try to find out something from a traveler once in a while?

JOHNNY'S FATHER: Get the old man some water, God damn it. Don't stand there like a dummy. Get him a drink, I tell you, before he falls down and dies.

JOHNNY: *You* get him a drink. You're not doing anything.

JOHNNY'S FATHER: Not doing anything? Why, Johnny, you *know* I'm getting a new poem arranged in my mind.

JOHNNY: How do you figure I know? You're just standing there on the porch with your sleeves rolled up.

JOHNNY'S FATHER (*Angry*): Well, you ought to know. (*Roaring*) You're my son. (*Amazed*) If you shouldn't know, who should?

MAC GREGOR (*Blithely*): Good afternoon. Your son has been telling me how clear and cool the climate is in these parts.

JOHNNY (*Bewildered, but eager to learn*): (*Aside*) Holy Moses, I didn't say anything about the climate. Where's he getting that stuff from?

JOHNNY'S FATHER (*The aristocrat, grandly*): How do you do? Won't you come in for a little rest? We should be honored to have you at our table for a bite of supper.

MAC GREGOR (*The realist*): Sir, I'm starving. I shall come right in.

(*He moves to enter the house.* JOHNNY *gets in his way, looking up at him*)

JOHNNY (*The romantic*): Can you play "Drink to Me Only with Thine Eyes"? I sure would like to hear you play that song on the bugle. That song is my favorite. I guess I like that song better than any song in the world.

MAC GREGOR (*The disillusioned*): Son, when you get to be my age you'll know songs aren't important, bread's the thing.

JOHNNY (*The faithful*): Anyway, I sure would like to hear you play that song.

(MAC GREGOR *goes up on the porch and shakes hands with* JOHNNY'S FATHER)

MAC GREGOR (*History in the making*): My name is Jasper MacGregor. I am an actor.

JOHNNY'S FATHER (*Delighted*): I'm mighty glad to make your acquaintance. (*The imperial giver of orders*) Johnny, get Mr. MacGregor a pitcher of water.

(JOHNNY *runs around the house*)

MAC GREGOR (*Dying of thirst, sighing, but telling the truth nevertheless*): Charming boy.

JOHNNY'S FATHER (*Ordinary statement*): Like myself, he's a genius.

MAC GREGOR (*Roaring, from fatigue*): I suppose you're very fond of him?

JOHNNY'S FATHER (*Delighted to be alive*): We are the same person— He is the heart of my youth— Have you noticed his eagerness?

MAC GREGOR (*Delighted to be still alive*): I should say I have.

JOHNNY'S FATHER (*Proudly and with anger*): I'm the same way myself, although older and less brilliant.

(JOHNNY, *running, returns with a pitcher of water which he hands to the old man. The old man throws back his shoulders, lifts his head, his nostrils expand, he snorts, his eyes widen, he lifts the pitcher of water to his lips and drinks all the water in one long swig, while* JOHNNY *and his* FATHER *watch with amazement and admiration. The old man breathes deeply, looks around at the landscape and up at the sky and to the end of San Benito Avenue where the evening sun is going down*)

MAC GREGOR (*Reflection, sadly; weariness, softly*): I reckon I'm five thousand miles from home. Do you think we could eat a little bread and cheese to keep my body and spirit together?

JOHNNY'S FATHER (*Napoleon*): Johnny, run down to the grocer's and get a loaf of French bread and a pound of cheese.

JOHNNY (*The voice of doom*): Give me the money.

JOHNNY'S FATHER (*Statistics, poetic, with pride*): You know I haven't got a *penny*, Johnny. Tell Mr. Kosak to give us credit.

JOHNNY (*The unwilling dutiful son*): He won't do it. He's tired of giving us credit. He says we don't work and never pay our bills. We owe him forty cents.

JOHNNY'S FATHER (*Impatient, irritated*): Go on down there and argue it out with him. You know that's your job.

JOHNNY (*Defending his rights*): He won't listen to reason. He says he doesn't know anything about anything. All he wants is the forty cents.

JOHNNY'S FATHER (*Napoleon*): Go on down there and *make* him give you a loaf of bread and a pound of cheese. (*Gently, pleading, flattering*) You can do it, Johnny.

MAC GREGOR (*Impatient and hungry*): Go on down there and tell Mr. Kosak to give you a loaf of bread and a pound of cheese, son.

JOHNNY'S FATHER: Go ahead, Johnny. You've never failed to leave that store with something or other. You'll be back here in ten minutes with food fit for a King. (*For his own amusement*) Or at least a Duke of some kind.

JOHNNY: I don't know. Mr. Kosak says we are trying to give him the merry run-around. He wants to know what kind of work you do.

JOHNNY'S FATHER (*Furiously*): Well, go ahead and tell him. (*The hero*) I have nothing to conceal. I write poetry, night and day.

JOHNNY (*Giving in at last*): All right, but I don't think he'll be impressed. He says you never go out and look for work. He says you're lazy and no good.

JOHNNY'S FATHER (*Roaring*): You go on down there and tell that great-hearted Slovak he's crazy, Johnny. You go on down there and tell that splendid scholar and gentleman your father is one of the greatest unknown poets living.

JOHNNY: He won't care, Pa, but I'll go. I'll do my best. Haven't we got anything in the house?

JOHNNY'S FATHER (*Mock-tragically, roaring*): Only popcorn. (*To* MAC GREGOR) We've been eating popcorn four days in a row now. Johnny, you've got to get bread and cheese if you expect me to finish that long poem.

JOHNNY: I'll do my best.

MAC GREGOR: Don't take too long, Johnny. I'm five thousand miles from home.

JOHNNY: I'll run all the way, Mr. MacGregor.

JOHNNY'S FATHER (*For the amusement of the good Lord*): If you find any money on the way, remember we go fifty-fifty.

JOHNNY (*Delighted with the comedy*): All right, Pa. (JOHNNY *runs down the street*)

> *The inside of Mr. Kosak's Grocery Store.* MR. KOSAK *is sleeping on his folded arms when* JOHNNY *runs into the store.* MR. KOSAK *lifts his head. He is a fine, gentle, serious man with a big, blond, old-fashioned mustache. He shakes his head trying to waken.*

JOHNNY (*The diplomat, as it were*): Mr. Kosak, if you were in China and didn't have a friend in the world and no money, you'd expect somebody over there to give you a pound of rice, wouldn't you?

MR. KOSAK: What do you want?

JOHNNY: I just want to talk a little. You'd expect some member of the Aryan race to help you out a little, wouldn't you, Mr. Kosak?

MR. KOSAK: How much money you got?

JOHNNY: It's not a question of money, Mr. Kosak. I'm talking about being in China.

MR. KOSAK: I don't know nothing about nothing.

JOHNNY: How would you feel in China that way, Mr. Kosak?

MR. KOSAK: I don't know, Johnny. What would I be doing in *China?*

JOHNNY: Well, you'd be visiting there. You'd be hungry and five thousand miles from home and not a friend in the world. You wouldn't expect *everybody* to turn you away without even a pound of rice, would you, Mr. Kosak?

MR. KOSAK: I guess not, but you ain't in China, Johnny, and neither is your Pa. You or your Pa's got to go out and work sometime in your lives, so you might as well start now. I ain't going to give you no more groceries on credit because I know you won't pay me.

JOHNNY: Mr. Kosak, you misunderstand me. This is 1914, not 1913. I'm not talking about a few groceries. I'm talking about all them heathen people around you in China, and you hungry and dying.

MR. KOSAK: This ain't China. You got to go out and make your living in this country. Everybody's got to work in America.

JOHNNY: Mr. Kosak, suppose it was a loaf of bread and a pound of cheese you needed to keep you alive in the world, would you hesitate to ask a Christian *missionary* for these things?

MR. KOSAK: Yes, I would. I would be ashamed to ask.

JOHNNY: Even if you knew you would give him back *two* loaves of bread and *two* pounds of cheese instead of one loaf and one pound? Even then, Mr. Kosak?

MR. KOSAK: Even then.

JOHNNY: Don't be that way, Mr. Kosak. That's defeatist talk, and you know it. Why, the only thing that would happen to you would be death. You'd *die* out there in China, Mr. Kosak.

MR. KOSAK: I wouldn't care if I would. You and your Pa have got to pay for bread and cheese. Why don't your Pa go out and get a job?

JOHNNY (*Swift abandonment of the intellectual attack for the human one*): Mr. Kosak, how are you?

MR. KOSAK: I'm fine, Johnny. How are you?

JOHNNY: Couldn't be better, Mr. Kosak. How are the children?

MR. KOSAK: They're all fine, Johnny. Stepan is beginning to walk now.

JOHNNY: That's great. How's Angela?

MR. KOSAK: Angela's beginning to sing. How's your Grandmother?

JOHNNY: She's fine. She's beginning to sing too. She says she'd rather be an opera singer than Queen of England. How's your wife Martha, Mr. Kosak?

MR. KOSAK: Oh, swell.

JOHNNY: I can't tell you how glad I am to hear that everything is fine at your house. I know Stepan is going to be a great man some day.

MR. KOSAK: I hope so. I'm going to send him to high school and see that he gets every chance I didn't get. I don't want *him* to have trouble all *his* life, too.

JOHNNY: I have great faith in Stepan, Mr. Kosak.

MR. KOSAK: What do you want, Johnny, and how much money you got?

JOHNNY: Mr. Kosak, you know I didn't come here to buy anything. You know I enjoy a quiet philosophical chat with you every now and then. (*Quickly, pleading*) Let me have a loaf of French bread and a pound of cheese.

MR. KOSAK: You got to pay cash, Johnny.

JOHNNY: And Esther? How is your beautiful daughter Esther?

MR. KOSAK: She's all right, Johnny, but you got to pay cash. You and your Pa are the worst citizens in this county.

JOHNNY: I'm glad Esther's all right, Mr. Kosak. Jasper MacGregor is visiting our house. He's a great actor.

MR. KOSAK: Never heard of him.

JOHNNY: And a bottle of beer for Mr. MacGregor.

MR. KOSAK: I can't give you a bottle of beer.

JOHNNY: Sure, you can.

MR. KOSAK: I can't. I'll let you have one loaf of French

bread and a pound of cheese, but that's all. What kind of work does your Pa do *when* he works, Johnny?

JOHNNY: My father writes poetry, Mr. Kosak. That's the only work my father does. He's one of the greatest writers of poetry in the world.

MR. KOSAK: When does he get any money?

JOHNNY: He *never* gets any money. You can't have your cake and eat it too.

MR. KOSAK: I don't like that kind of work. Why doesn't your Pa work like everybody else, Johnny?

JOHNNY: He works harder than everybody else. My father works twice as hard as the average man.

(MR. KOSAK *hands* JOHNNY *a loaf of French bread and a pound of cheese*)

MR. KOSAK: Well, that's fifty-five cents you owe me, Johnny. I'll let you have some stuff this time, but never again.

JOHNNY (*At the door*): Tell Esther I love her.

(JOHNNY *runs out of the store.* MR. KOSAK *swings at a fly, misses, swings again, misses, and, objecting to the world in this manner, he chases the fly all around the store, swinging with all his might*)

The house. JOHNNY'S FATHER *and the old man are looking down the street to see if* JOHNNY *is coming back with food. His* GRANDMOTHER *is standing on the porch also eager to know if there is to be food.*

MAC GREGOR: I think he's got some food with him.

JOHNNY'S FATHER (*With pride*): Of course he has.

(*He waves at the old lady on the porch who runs into the house to set the table.* JOHNNY *runs to his* FATHER *and* MAC GREGOR)

I knew you'd do it.

MAC GREGOR: So did I.

JOHNNY: He says we got to pay him fifty-five cents. He says he's not going to give us any more stuff on credit.

JOHNNY'S FATHER: That's *his* opinion. What did you talk about?

JOHNNY: First I talked about being hungry and at death's door in China. Then I inquired about the family.

JOHNNY'S FATHER: How is everyone?

JOHNNY: Fine. I didn't find any money, though. Not even a *penny*.

JOHNNY'S FATHER: Oh, that's all right. Money isn't everything.

(*They go into the house*)

> *The living room. They are all at the table after supper.* MAC GREGOR *finds crumbs here and there which he places delicately in his mouth. He looks around the room to see if there isn't something more to eat.*

MAC GREGOR: That green can up there, Johnny. What's in there?

JOHNNY: Marbles.

MAC GREGOR: That cupboard, Johnny. Anything *edible* in there?

JOHNNY: Crickets.

MAC GREGOR: That big jar in the corner there, Johnny. What's delectable in there?

JOHNNY: I got a gopher snake in that jar.

MAC GREGOR: Well, I could go for a bit of boiled gopher snake in a big way, Johnny.

JOHNNY (*Defiantly, protector of animals*): Nothing doing, Mr. MacGregor.

MAC GREGOR: Why not, Johnny? Why the hell not, son? I hear of fine Borneo natives eating snakes and grasshoppers. You haven't got a half dozen fat grasshoppers around, have you, Johnny?

JOHNNY: Only four.

MAC GREGOR: Well, trot them out, son, and after we've had our fill, I'll play "Drink to Me Only with Thine Eyes" for you. I'm mighty hungry, Johnny.

JOHNNY: So am I, but I don't want anybody killing them innocent animals. They got rights the same as anybody else.

JOHNNY'S FATHER (*To* MAC GREGOR): How about a little music? I think the boy would be delighted.

JOHNNY (*Leaping to his feet*): I sure would, Mr. Mac-Gregor.

MAC GREGOR: All right, Johnny. Bread. Bread. My God, how savagely it quarrels with the heart.

(MAC GREGOR *gets up and begins to blow into the*

bugle. He blows louder and more beautifully and mournfully than anybody ever blew into a bugle. Eighteen NEIGHBORS *gather in front of the house and cheer when he finishes the solo: "Drink to Me Only with Thine Eyes"*)

JOHNNY'S FATHER (*Delighted, for amusement*): I want you to meet your public.

(*They go out on the porch*)

The house. The crowd is looking up at JOHNNY'S FATHER, MAC GREGOR *and* JOHNNY.

JOHNNY'S FATHER: Good neighbors, and friends, I want you to meet Jasper MacGregor, the greatest Shakespearean actor of our day. (*Pause*) I believe.

MAC GREGOR (*The actor*): I remember my first appearance in London in 1851 as if it was yesterday. I was a boy of fourteen from the slums of Glasgow. My first part was a courier in a play, the title of which I have unfortunately forgotten. I had no lines to speak, but moved about a good deal, running from officer to officer, and from lover to his beloved, and back again, over and over again.

RUFE APLEY, THE CARPENTER (*Regretfully interrupting the great speech*): How about another song, Mr. MacGregor?

MAC GREGOR: Have you got an egg at your house?

RUFE APLEY: I sure have. I've got a *dozen* eggs at my house.

MAC GREGOR: Would it be convenient for you to go and get one of them dozen eggs? When you return I'll play a song that will make your heart leap with joy and grief.

RUFE APLEY: I'm on my way already.

(*He goes*)

MAC GREGOR (*To the crowd*): My friends, I should be delighted to play another song for you on this golden-throated bugle, but time and distance from home find me weary. If you will be so good as to go, each of you to his home, and return in a moment with some morsel of food, I shall be proud to gather my spirit together and play a song I know will change the course of each of your lives, and change it, mind you, for the better.

(*The people go. The last to go is* ESTHER KOSAK, *who hears the speech out, then runs.* MAC GREGOR, JOHNNY'S FATHER, *and* JOHNNY *sit on the steps and*

remain in silence, and one by one the people return,
bringing food to MAC GREGOR: *an egg, a sausage, a*
dozen green onions, two kinds of cheese, butter, two
kinds of bread, boiled potatoes, fresh tomatoes, a
melon, tea, and many other good things to eat)

Thank you, my friends, thank you.

> (*He stands solemnly, waiting for absolute silence,*
> *straightens himself, looks about him furiously, lifts*
> *the bugle to his lips and is irritated by the swift and*
> *noisy return of* ESTHER KOSAK, *bringing an eggplant.*
> *When there is silence, he plays "My Heart's in the*
> *Highlands, My Heart is not Here." The people*
> *weep, kneel, sing the chorus, and go away.* MAC-
> GREGOR *turns to the father and son)*

(*Grandly*) Sir, if it is all the same to you I should like
to dwell in your house for a long time to come.

JOHNNY'S FATHER (*Delighted and amazed*): Sir, my house
is your house. (*They go into the house*)

> *The living room. Eighteen days later,* MAC GREGOR
> *is lying on the floor, face up, asleep.* JOHNNY *is*
> *walking about quietly in the room, looking at every-*
> *body. His* FATHER *is at the table, writing poetry.*
> *His* GRANDMOTHER *is sitting in the rocking chair,*
> *rocking. There is a knock on the door. Everybody*
> *but* MAC GREGOR *jumps up and runs to it.*

JOHNNY'S FATHER (*At the door*): Yes?

YOUNG MAN: I am looking for Jasper MacGregor, the actor.

JOHNNY'S FATHER: What do you want?

JOHNNY: Well, ask him in anyway, Pa.

JOHNNY'S FATHER: Yes, of course. Excuse me. Won't you
please come in?

> (*The* YOUNG MAN *enters*)

YOUNG MAN: My name is Philip Carmichael. I am from the
Old People's Home. I have been sent to bring Mr. Mac-
Gregor home.

MAC GREGOR (*Wakening and sitting up*): Home? Did
someone mention home? (*Roaring*) I'm five thousand
miles from home, always have been, and always will be.
Who is this young man?

YOUNG MAN: Mr. MacGregor, I'm Philip Carmichael, from

the Old People's Home. They've sent me to bring you back. We are putting on our annual show in two weeks and need you for the leading role.

MAC GREGOR (*Getting up with the help of* JOHNNY'S FATHER *and* JOHNNY): What kind of a part is it? I can't be playing young adventurers any longer.

YOUNG MAN: The part is King Lear, Mr. MacGregor. It is perfect for you.

MAC GREGOR (*The actor, with a job again*): Good-by, my beloved friends.

(*He returns from the porch*)

In all the hours of my life, in all the places I have visited, never and nowhere have I had the honor and pleasure to commune with souls loftier, purer, or more delightful than yours. Good-by.

(*The* OLD MAN *and the* YOUNG MAN *leave the house.*

There is a moment of silence, full of regret and loneliness)

JOHNNY'S FATHER (*Hungry, loudly*): Johnny, go on down to Mr. Kosak's store and get a little something to eat. I know you can do it, Johnny. Get ANYTHING.

JOHNNY (*Hungry, loudly, and angry*): Mr. Kosak wants eighty-five cents. He won't give us anything more without money.

JOHNNY'S FATHER: Go on down there, Johnny. You know you can get that fine Slovak gentleman to give us a little something to eat.

JOHNNY (*With despair*): Aw, Pa.

JOHNNY'S FATHER (*Amazed, roaring*): What? You, *my son*, in a mood like that. Come on. I fought the world this way before you were born. After you were born we fought it together, and we're going to go on fighting it. The people love poetry but don't know it, that's all. Nothing is going to stop us, Johnny. Go on down there now and get us something to eat.

JOHNNY: All right, Pa. I'll do my best.

(*He runs to the door*)

The house. It now has a large sign: "For Rent."

It is a moment before daybreak of a day early in

November, 1914. There is a suggestion of Winter coming. High in the sky a flock of geese flying south make their call. JOHNNY *is sitting on the steps of the front porch with his chin in his hand. He hears the geese, listening carefully, leaps to his feet and looks into the sky for them. The sound decreases, then ends.* JOHNNY *goes back to the steps of the porch and sits down. As the sun rises, a big solemn smile comes over his face. He looks out of the corner of his eye at the morning's light as if it were a quiet friend with whom he was on terms of perfect understanding. As the light increases, this play between* JOHNNY *and the sun grows, like a theme of music, bringing him to his feet, turning his face to the light. He lifts his arms, and very solemnly begins turning somersaults. He then runs around the house lickety-split and returns on the other side, almost dancing.*

A freight train goes by not far enough away not to make the earth tremble.

The light of morning increases.

A newspaper route carrier arrives on foot, whistling.

He is the typical small-town morning route carrier: about thirteen years old. He is in that somber and dignified state which comes over men who have done their work. His paper bags are empty. Night is over. His daily wage has been earned. The papers have been left at the doors of the readers. Another day has come to the world. He has walked two hours through dark streets to morning. The song he is whistling is soft and full of understanding. It is a song of his own composition, a morning song.

JOHNNY (*Running down the steps*): Hello.
THE BOY (*Stopping*): Hello.
JOHNNY: What was that song?
THE BOY: What song?
JOHNNY: That you were whistling?
THE BOY: Was I whistling?
JOHNNY: Sure. Didn't you know?
THE BOY: I guess I'm always whistling.
JOHNNY: What was it?

THE BOY: I don't know.

JOHNNY: I wish I could whistle.

THE BOY: Anybody can whistle.

JOHNNY: I can't. How do you do it?

THE BOY: There's no *how* to it. You just whistle.

JOHNNY: How?

THE BOY: Like this. (*He whistles a moment, obviously improvising, a tour de force of technique*)

JOHNNY (*With admiration*): I wish I could do that.

THE BOY (*Pleased and eager to make an even better impression*): That was nothing. Listen to this.

> (*He gives the melody a sort of counterpoint, two tones, and a bit of syncopation*)

JOHNNY: Can't you teach me to do that?

THE BOY: You can't teach whistling. You just do it. This is another way.

> (*He whistles a little melody, the loud newsboy's style, but keeps it soft*)

JOHNNY (*Trying to whistle*): Like that?

THE BOY: That's the way to *start*. Keep it up and after a while your mouth'll take the right shape and you'll be whistling before you know it.

JOHNNY: Honest?

THE BOY: Sure.

JOHNNY: Is your mother dead?

THE BOY: How did you know?

JOHNNY: My mother's dead too.

THE BOY: Yeah?

JOHNNY (*With a sigh*): Yeah. She died.

THE BOY: I don't remember my mother. Do you remember your mother?

JOHNNY: I don't exactly remember her. Sometimes I dream about her, though.

THE BOY: I used to, too.

JOHNNY: Don't you any more?

THE BOY (*Disillusioned*): Naaaah. What good does that do you?

JOHNNY: My mother sure is beautiful.

THE BOY: Yeah, I know. I remember. You got a father?

JOHNNY (*Proudly*): Oh, sure. He's in the house *now*, sleeping.

THE BOY: My *father's* dead, too.

JOHNNY: Your *father*, too?

THE BOY (*Matter-of-fact*): Yeah.

> (*They begin bouncing an old tennis ball back and forth to each other*)

JOHNNY: Haven't you got anybody?

THE BOY: I got an aunt, but she ain't really my aunt. I was brought up in an orphanage. I'm adopted.

JOHNNY: What's an orphanage?

THE BOY: That's a kind of a place where kids that ain't got any mothers and fathers live until somebody adopts them.

JOHNNY: What do you mean, adopts?

THE BOY: Somebody who wants a boy or girl comes to the orphanage and looks everybody over and goes away with whoever they like. If they pick you, you go and stay with them.

JOHNNY: Do you like that?

THE BOY: It's all right.

> (THE BOY *puts away the ball*)

JOHNNY: What's your name?

THE BOY: Henry. What's yours?

JOHNNY: Johnny.

THE BOY: Do you want a paper? There's a War in Europe.

JOHNNY: I haven't got any money. We aren't rich. We don't work. My father writes poetry.

THE BOY (*Giving* JOHNNY *the extra*): Oh, that's all right. Don't you *ever* have any money?

JOHNNY: Sometimes. I found a quarter once. It was lying on the sidewalk, right in front of me. Once my father got a check for ten dollars from New York, too. We bought a chicken and a lot of stamps and paper and envelopes. The chicken wouldn't lay eggs, though, so my grandmother killed it and cooked it for us. Did you ever eat chicken?

THE BOY: Sure. I guess I've eaten chicken six or seven times.

JOHNNY: What are you going to do when you grow up?

THE BOY: Shucks. I don't know. I don't know what I'll do.

JOHNNY (*Proudly*): I'm going to be a poet, like my father. He said so.

THE BOY: I guess I'll carry a paper route for a while.

> (*He moves to go*)

Well. So long.

JOHNNY: Won't you come here again?

THE BOY: I go by here every morning about this time. I ain't never seen you up before, though.

JOHNNY (*Smiling*): I had a dream and then I woke up and didn't want to sleep any more. I wanted to get up and come out here. I saw my mother.

THE BOY: Maybe I'll see you again some morning when you can't sleep.

JOHNNY: I hope so. So long.

THE BOY: So long. Just keep trying and you'll be whistling before you know it.

JOHNNY: Thanks.

> (THE BOY *goes, whistling.* JOHNNY *tosses the folded paper up on the porch, and sits down again on the steps.*
>
> *His* GRANDMOTHER *comes out on the porch with a broom and begins to sweep*)

JOHNNY'S GRANDMOTHER (*In Armenian, which is the only language she speaks, with the exception of Turkish, Kurdish, and a little Arabic, which nobody around seems to know*): How are you, my heart?

JOHNNY (*Who understands Armenian, but hardly ever speaks it; in English*): Fine.

JOHNNY'S GRANDMOTHER: How's your Papa?

JOHNNY: I don't know. (*Calling loudly to his father*) Oh, Pa. How are you? (*Pause. Louder*) Pa. (*Pause. Silence*) I guess he's sleeping.

JOHNNY'S GRANDMOTHER: Is there any money?

JOHNNY: Money? (*Shaking his head*) No.

JOHNNY'S FATHER (*From inside the house*): Johnny?

JOHNNY (*Jumping to his feet*): Pa?

JOHNNY'S FATHER: Did you call?

JOHNNY: Yeah. How are you?

JOHNNY'S FATHER: Fine, Johnny. How are you?

JOHNNY: Fine, Pa.

JOHNNY'S FATHER: Is that all you woke me up for?

JOHNNY (*To his* GRANDMOTHER): He's fine. (*Louder to his* FATHER) The old lady wanted to know.

JOHNNY'S FATHER (*In Armenian, to the old lady*): Good light, Ma. (*To* JOHNNY, *in English*) What do you mean, old? She's not so old.

JOHNNY: I don't mean old. You know what I mean.

(JOHNNY'S FATHER *comes out on the porch, buttoning his shirt, nods to the old lady, looks out of the corner of his eye at the sun, exactly the same way* JOHNNY *did, smiling the same way, stretches all over, faces the sun, leaps down the steps and turns one somersault, not so good. The somersault leaves him flat on his back*)

JOHNNY: You ought to get a little more exercise, Pa. You're always sitting down.

JOHNNY'S FATHER (*On his back*): Johnny, your father is a great poet. I may not be able to turn a somersault as well as you, but if you want to know what kind of an athlete I am, just read the poetry I wrote yesterday.

JOHNNY: Is it really good, Pa?

JOHNNY'S FATHER: Good?

(*He leaps to his feet, like an acrobat*)

It's great. I'm going to send it to *The Atlantic Monthly*, too.

JOHNNY: Oh, I forgot, Pa. There's a paper on the porch.

JOHNNY'S FATHER (*Going up to the porch*): You mean a morning paper, Johnny?

JOHNNY: Yeah.

JOHNNY'S FATHER: Well, that's a pleasant surprise. Where in the world did you get it?

JOHNNY: Henry gave it to me.

JOHNNY'S FATHER: Henry? Who's Henry?

JOHNNY: He's a boy who hasn't got a mother or a *father*, either. He sure can whistle, too.

JOHNNY'S FATHER (*Picking up the paper, opening it*): That was certainly nice of him.

(*He loses himself in the headlines*)

JOHNNY'S GRANDMOTHER (*To both of them, to herself, and to the world*): Where's that man?

JOHNNY'S FATHER (*Deep in the news*): Hmmm?

JOHNNY: Who?

JOHNNY'S GRANDMOTHER: You know. That old man who blew the horn.

(*She pantomimes the blowing of a horn*)

JOHNNY: Oh. Mr. MacGregor? They took him back to the Old People's Home.

JOHNNY'S FATHER (*Reading the paper*): Austria. Germany. France. England. Russia. Zeppelins. Submarines. Tanks. Machine guns. Bombs. (*Shaking his head*) They've gone crazy again.

JOHNNY'S GRANDMOTHER (*To* JOHNNY, *reproachfully*): Why don't you speak Armenian, boy?

JOHNNY: I can't talk Armenian.

JOHNNY'S FATHER (*To* JOHNNY): What's the matter?

JOHNNY: She wants to know about Mr. MacGregor.

JOHNNY'S GRANDMOTHER (*To* JOHNNY'S FATHER): Where is he?

JOHNNY'S FATHER (*In Armenian*): He's back in the Old People's Home.

JOHNNY'S GRANDMOTHER (*Shaking her head sadly*): Ahkh, ahkh, the poor old prisoner.

JOHNNY: Is it like a prison, Pa?

JOHNNY'S FATHER: I don't know for sure, Johnny.

JOHNNY'S GRANDMOTHER (*Furiously, the way her son and grandson speak when they are irritated*): Why doesn't he come back and stay here where he belongs?

(*She goes into the house*)

JOHNNY: That's right, Pa. Why doesn't Mr. MacGregor come back and stay here? Does he have to stay in that place?

JOHNNY'S FATHER: If you're an old, old man, Johnny, and haven't got any people, and no money, I guess you do.

JOHNNY: I sure get lonesome for him sometimes. Don't you, Pa?

JOHNNY'S FATHER: To tell you the truth, Johnny, I do.

JOHNNY: I'm always remembering him, especially the music. And the way he drinks water.

JOHNNY'S FATHER: He's a great man.

JOHNNY: Is his heart really in the highlands like he said, Pa?

JOHNNY'S FATHER: Not exactly.

JOHNNY: Is he really five thousand miles from home, too?

JOHNNY'S FATHER: At least that many.

JOHNNY: Do you think he'll ever get home again some day?

JOHNNY'S FATHER: He's an old man, Johnny. He will.

JOHNNY: You mean he'll take a train and a boat and get back where the highlands are?

JOHNNY'S FATHER: Not that, Johnny. It's a little different from that. He'll *die*.

JOHNNY: Is that the only way a man gets home?

JOHNNY'S FATHER: That's the only way.

> (*All this time, of course,* JOHNNY'S FATHER *has been turning the pages of the morning paper, and* JOHNNY *has been going through various kinds of acrobatics, walking on the porch railing, leaping down, turning somersaults, standing on his head, and so forth. Some of his questions have been asked while he has been standing on his head.*

> *A sharp whistle is heard in the distance.*)

JOHNNY (*Eagerly*): It's Mr. Wiley, the mailman, Pa.

> (JOHNNY'S FATHER *jumps to his feet, dropping the paper*)

JOHNNY: Do you think maybe we'll get a letter from New York with a check in it maybe?

JOHNNY'S FATHER: I don't know, Johnny.

> (MR. WILEY, *riding a bicycle, arrives. He is almost knocked off the bicycle by* JOHNNY *and* JOHNNY'S FATHER)

MR. WILEY (*Getting off the bicycle as if it were a horse*): Good morning, Mr. Alexander.

JOHNNY'S FATHER: Good morning, Mr. Wiley.

JOHNNY: Any mail for us, Mr. Wiley?

MR. WILEY (*Bringing a packet of letters from his bag, loosening the strap, and looking them over*): Well, now, let me see, Johnny. I think I've got something here for your father.

JOHNNY: Is it from New York?

MR. WILEY (*Holding a flat envelope*): Yes, it is, Johnny. Well, Mr. Alexander, it looks like Winter's coming again. The geese were flying this morning.

JOHNNY'S FATHER (*Excited, tense, yet eager to be casual*): Yes, I know. (*To himself*) I know. I know.

JOHNNY: If *I* ever get a letter from New York I'm going to save it up.

MR. WILEY (*He wants to talk*): How are things, Mr. Alexander?

JOHNNY'S FATHER: I've been lucky in my work, thank you, Mr. Wiley.

JOHNNY: My father was in New York once. Weren't you, Pa?

JOHNNY'S FATHER: Yes, I was, Johnny. How is your family, Mr. Wiley?

MR. WILEY: All fine, except the littlest one, Joe. He's always crying. That's one thing I can't stand either, a baby crying all the time. I don't know what it does to me, but it makes me lose all faith in everything. When Joe cries I say to myself, Aw, what's the use?

JOHNNY: I guess I'll reach New York some day before I die.

JOHNNY'S FATHER: It's nothing, Mr. Wiley. He'll stop crying after a while.

MR. WILEY: Well, I hope so, and the sooner the better.

(*He goes off with the envelope*)

Good-by, Mr. Alexander. Good-by, Johnny.

JOHNNY'S FATHER: Mr. Wiley.

(MR. WILEY *hands over the envelope. They say good-by, and* MR. WILEY *rides off.* JOHNNY'S FATHER *holds the envelope before him, obviously eager to open it, yet fearful to do so*)

JOHNNY (*Impatient*): All right, Pa. Go ahead; open it. What are you waiting for?

JOHNNY'S FATHER (*Angry, roaring*): Johnny, I'm scared. I can't understand how I, *your* father, can be so scared.

JOHNNY: You don't sound scared, Pa. Who's it from?

JOHNNY'S FATHER: It's from *The Atlantic Monthly* all right. You remember them poems I wrote after Mr. MacGregor was here?

JOHNNY: Maybe they've bought the poems.

JOHNNY'S FATHER: Bought them, my eye. They don't buy *poetry*, Johnny. They *scare* you to death. (*Reading his name and address with great solemnity, awful fearfulness and terrible rage*) Ben Alexander, 2226 San Benito Avenue, Fresno, California.

JOHNNY: It's for you all right, Pa. Why don't you open it?

JOHNNY'S FATHER (*Roaring*): I'm scared, I tell you. I'm scared and ashamed. *Those poems were great.* How can it be that I'm scared?

JOHNNY (*Also defiant*): Don't be scared, Pa.

JOHNNY'S FATHER (*Angry*): Why do they clamor for all

things but the best? Why do they destroy themselves running after things of death, and thrust aside all things of life? I can't understand it. There's no hope for *anybody*.

JOHNNY: Sure there is, Pa. (*Furiously*): Who the hell is *The Atlantic Monthly*?

JOHNNY'S FATHER (*Angry*): Johnny, go away. Go away. Please go away.

JOHNNY (*Angry, too*): All right, Pa.

> (JOHNNY *goes around the house, reappears, looks at his father a moment, and then knows he must stay out of the way*)

> (*It is obvious that* JOHNNY'S FATHER *knows* The Atlantic Monthly *has sent back the poems. It is equally obvious that he can't believe the poems have come back. It is obvious too that the poems are great, because the man is. He paces about like a tiger. He seems to be speaking to the world, even though his lips are set. At last he tears the envelope open, in a fury. The envelope falls. He unfolds the manuscript of poems. A slip of white, heavy paper falls to the floor of the porch. He stands, very tall, and very proud, and reads the poems to himself, turning the pages swiftly*)

JOHNNY'S FATHER (*Furiously*): Ah, you crazy, miserable fools.

> (*He sits on the steps of the porch and buries his face in his hands. The manuscript of poems is on the steps.*
>
> *After several minutes he kicks the poems off the steps of the porch onto the ground and takes up the morning paper again, looking at the headlines*)

> (*Quietly, with deep fury, his voice mounting in intensity*)

Go ahead, kill *everybody*. Declare War on one another. Take the people by the thousands and mangle them. Their poor hearts and their poor spirits and their poor bodies. Give them ugliness. Pollute their dreams. Horrify them. Distort them with hatred for one another. Befoul

the legend of the living, you maniacs whose greatness is
measured by the number you destroy.

(JOHNNY *appears at the side of the house, unseen*)
(*He stands in a trance, listening to his father*)

(*The sky begins to darken*)

You frauds of the world. You wretched and ungodly.

(*He stands and points a finger, as if across the*
world)

Go ahead. *Fire* your feeble guns. You won't kill *anything.*
(*Quietly, smiling*) There will always be poets in the
world.

(*Lightning flashes silently*)

The house. The sky is dark, as at the beginning of
a storm. An occasional deep and faraway roar of
thunder is heard, and a flash of lightning is seen.
JOHNNY'S FATHER *is on the steps of the porch, smil-*
ing: a foolish, tragic, desolate, lonely smile. Every-
thing is the same; the manuscript of poems is on
the ground; the envelope is on the porch. The news-
paper too. It is several hours later.

JOHNNY'S FATHER (*Shaking his head foolishly, unable to*
accept the truth): Johnny. (*Pause. A little louder*)
Johnny. (*Pause, softer this time*) Johnny. (*Roaring*)
Johnny.

(*The boy comes around the house shyly and stands*
before his father)

(*His father looks up, fire in his eye, defiant, bitter,*
stubborn, powerful)

JOHNNY'S FATHER (*Tenderly, but with tremendous power*):
Have you had your breakfast?
JOHNNY (*Shyly*): I'm not hungry, Pa.
JOHNNY'S FATHER: You go on inside now and eat.
JOHNNY: I'm not hungry.
JOHNNY'S FATHER: You do what I tell you.
JOHNNY: I won't eat unless you do.
JOHNNY'S FATHER: You do what I *tell* you.
JOHNNY: I won't eat unless you do.
JOHNNY'S FATHER: I'm not hungry.

JOHNNY: I'll go down to Mr. Kosak's and see if I can get something.

JOHNNY'S FATHER (*Humiliated. Taking the boy's arm*): No, Johnny.

(*He pauses, obviously trying to find words with which to explain about themselves and the grocer*)

Johnny? I though we'd be getting some money. I didn't think it would be this way. Now, go on inside and eat.

JOHNNY (*Going up the stairs*): You got to eat, too.

(*He goes into the house*)

(*There is a silent flash of lightning*)

(*A* MAN *in a business suit, and a young* HUSBAND *and* WIFE *with a* BABY *in the mother's arms, come up*)

THE REAL ESTATE MAN: This is the house. The rent's six dollars a month. It's not exactly fancy, but it'll keep out the rain and cold.

(JOHNNY'S FATHER *has been staring at the people, his vision frozen*)

THE REAL ESTATE MAN (*Coming up to* JOHNNY'S FATHER, *extending his hand, while the others stand back in a group*): Remember me? I put up the "For Rent" sign.

JOHNNY'S FATHER (*Rising*): I remember. How do you do.

THE REAL ESTATE MAN (*Embarrassed*): Well. Mr. Corey, the owner of the house, is out of town, and these people are looking for a house. *Right away.*

JOHNNY'S FATHER: Of course. I can leave any time. Have they furniture?

THE REAL ESTATE MAN (*Turning to the poor family*): Have you furniture?

THE HUSBAND: No.

JOHNNY'S FATHER (*To the family*): You can have my furniture. There isn't much of it, but it'll do. There's a pretty good stove.

THE WIFE (*With the dignity of the poor*): We wouldn't want to take *your* furniture.

JOHNNY'S FATHER: That's all right. I haven't paid rent for three months. I'll leave the furniture for the rent.

(THE REAL ESTATE MAN *tries to speak*)

JOHNNY'S FATHER: It's all right. I'm sorry I haven't the $18. The furniture's worth about that much. You can let these people have it till Mr. Corey gets back. (*To the family*) Do you want to go through the house?

THE HUSBAND: It looks all right.

THE REAL ESTATE MAN (*Going*): Then that's settled. (*To the people*) The rent's six dollars a month. We pay the water.

JOHNNY'S FATHER (*To the people*): You can move in any time.

THE HUSBAND: Thank you very much. We'll be back this afternoon or tomorrow.

> (*They are going as* JOHNNY *comes out with a plate containing two slices of bread and a small bunch of grapes*)

JOHNNY: Who were those people?

JOHNNY'S FATHER: Just some people walking by.

JOHNNY: What were you talking about?

JOHNNY'S FATHER: Just talking, Johnny.

JOHNNY (*Shouting; very angry*): Don't feel bad, Pa.

JOHNNY'S FATHER (*Turning and looking at the boy with love, amazement, admiration, and delight, laughing suddenly*): I don't feel bad, Johnny. Let the world be the world, and God love everyone.

JOHNNY (*Bantering*): All right then. Let's eat.

> (*He puts the plate on the top step and they sit down together and begin to eat.*
>
> *They eat in silence, looking at one another, the boy looking at his father out of the corner of his eye as he had looked at the sun; the father looking at the boy the same way. The boy begins to smile. The father begins to smile too*)

JOHNNY: Do you like grapes, Pa?

JOHNNY'S FATHER: Of course I like grapes.

JOHNNY: Pa?

JOHNNY'S FATHER: Yes?

JOHNNY: Is it really like a prison?

JOHNNY'S FATHER: Sometimes I'm *sure* it is. Sometimes I *know* it never can be.

JOHNNY: What, Pa?

JOHNNY'S FATHER: I guess it's fifty-fifty, Johnny. You know. It's both.

JOHNNY: I mean, do you think he gets homesick sometimes?

JOHNNY'S FATHER: I'm sure he does.

JOHNNY: I wish he'd come back.

JOHNNY'S FATHER: I'd like to see him again.

JOHNNY: I remember him all the time.

JOHNNY'S FATHER: I do too. I'll always remember him.

JOHNNY: So will I. Did he *have* to go back, Pa?

JOHNNY'S FATHER: I guess he did.

JOHNNY: He seemed like a nice young man.

JOHNNY'S FATHER: You mean the young man who came and got him?

JOHNNY: Yeah, you know. That young man who talked so sharp, like he was speaking in front of an audience.

JOHNNY'S FATHER: He was all right.

(*There is one more grape on the plate*)

JOHNNY: Go ahead, Pa. Take it.

JOHNNY'S FATHER (*Blithely*): No, that's yours, Johnny. I counted.

JOHNNY: All right, Pa.

(*He takes the last grape and eats it*)

Is it stealing, Pa?

JOHNNY'S FATHER (*Comically*): Well, some say it is and some say it isn't. (*Dramatically*) I say it isn't. (*Shouting*) You took them off the vines, didn't you?

JOHNNY: I took them off the vines all right, Pa.

JOHNNY'S FATHER (*Comically*): Then it couldn't very well be stealing.

JOHNNY: When would it be stealing?

JOHNNY'S FATHER (*Tossing it off like nothing*): The way I see it, Johnny, stealing is where there's unnecessary damage or cruelty to an innocent one, so that there may be undeserved profit or power to one who is not innocent.

JOHNNY: Oh. (*Pause*) Well, if it isn't stealing, Pa, I guess I'll go get some more.

(*He gets up*)

They'll be all gone pretty soon. (*Goes off*)

JOHNNY'S FATHER (*When the boy is gone, laughing*): My son John. My God, how fortunate I have been. How grateful I am.

(He picks up the manuscript of poems, puts it in his coat pocket, and walks down the street)

The inside of Mr. Kosak's Grocery Store. Again MR. KOSAK *is sleeping on his folded arms. The store looks more poverty-stricken than before. The family apparently has been eating the stock.* JOHNNY'S FATHER *comes into the store quietly, almost shyly.* MR. KOSAK *lifts his head, blinks his eyes, stands.*

JOHNNY'S FATHER (*Almost guiltily*): I'm Johnny's father.

(The two men stand staring at one another a moment, each of them delighted, embarrassed, impressed, pleased, and angry about the same things in the world: greed, deceit, unkindliness, disproportion. They each begin to smile, then shake hands warmly)

MR. KOSAK: I recognize you. Johnny has told me about you. It is an honor.

JOHNNY'S FATHER: You are a kind man.

MR. KOSAK: I do not know.

JOHNNY'S FATHER (*Slowly*): I have come to say good-by. To apologize. To thank you.

MR. KOSAK (*Swiftly*): You're not going away?

JOHNNY'S FATHER: I'm sorry, yes.

MR. KOSAK: We shall all miss Johnny.

JOHNNY'S FATHER: I have no money. I am in debt to you.

MR. KOSAK: It is nothing.

JOHNNY'S FATHER: I may not see you again.

(He brings the manuscript of poems from his pocket)

(*Powerfully*) I am a poet. *These* are some of my poems. (*Swiftly*) I am not offering them to you in place of the money I owe you. Money is another thing. (*Pleading*) Will you keep them for your kindness?

MR. KOSAK (*Sincerely*): I cannot take your poems. (*Pause*)

JOHNNY'S FATHER: I hope you have been prospering.

MR. KOSAK: The people have no money. I do not know how I am going to put in new stock.

JOHNNY'S FATHER: I'm sorry.

MR. KOSAK: In the Winter it is worse. The packing-houses are closed. There are no jobs. I would give them something if I could, but this Winter I have no money for new

stock. I may have to close the store. There is hardly
enough for my family.

JOHNNY'S FATHER (*Touched and angry*): These poems. Let
me tell you they are the finest I have ever written. I want
to leave them with you.

(*Mr. Kosak's daughter* ESTHER, *a beautiful girl of
seven, comes into the store, from the back*)

MR. KOSAK: This is my daughter Esther. Esther, this is
Johnny's father.

JOHNNY'S FATHER: Johnny's told me about you.

ESTHER (*Really pleased, but shy*): How do you do.

MR. KOSAK: They're going away.

ESTHER (*Shocked*): Oh.

JOHNNY'S FATHER: Johnny will miss you.

(*The girl's lips tremble, tears come to her eyes. She
turns and runs out of the store*)

MR. KOSAK: Everything is like that.

JOHNNY'S FATHER: They are children.

MR. KOSAK: Yes, but it's that way from the beginning and
it never changes. Only women never learn to believe it.

JOHNNY'S FATHER: Won't you give *her* these poems?

MR. KOSAK: Please. It's nothing. She will cry for a while, but
it is nothing.

JOHNNY'S FATHER: Here. (*Giving* MR. KOSAK *the poems*)
You will be doing me a kindness by keeping them.
(*Loudly, to God and the world*) Don't you see, poetry
must be *read* to be poetry. It may be that one reader is
all that I deserve. If this is so, I want that reader to be
you.

MR. KOSAK: Thank you. I am unworthy.

JOHNNY'S FATHER (*Smiling*): Good-by.

MR. KOSAK: Good-by.

(JOHNNY'S FATHER *goes out of the store. The grocer
takes his glasses out of his pocket, puts them on,
unfolds the manuscript, and standing in the middle
of the store, begins to read, softly, to himself, moving his lips. The expression of his face begins to
change. Rain begins to fall. His daughter* ESTHER
comes back into the store)

MR. KOSAK (*Reading from one of the poems, in a quiet
voice*): Deep in the bowels of the earth, and far dis-

persed into the green waters of the sea, and held tight
within the hardness of rock, I thee remember, love, remember me.

>   (*The* GIRL *begins to sob aloud, and the* FATHER
>   *turns and goes to her*)

>   *The living room of the house. Some time later.*
>   JOHNNY'S FATHER *is at his table, looking over a
>   stack of manuscripts. It is still raining. Every once
>   in a while he gets up and goes to the window.*

JOHNNY'S FATHER: What the hell's happened to him?

>   (*He goes back to his manuscripts and looks over
>   some poems, grows irritated with them, throws
>   them down, and goes to the window again. Then
>   begins to walk back and forth, waiting.*

>   *At last* JOHNNY *tears up the front porch stairs, busts
>   into the house, closes the door quickly, and bolts it.
>   He is breathless and scared. You know he is one
>   who has been pursued. He has four medium-sized
>   bunches of purple-red Emperors; a half dozen black
>   figs; and two pomegranates.*)

JOHNNY (*Excited and breathless*): Where shall I hide them,
Pa?

JOHNNY'S FATHER: What's the matter, Johnny?

JOHNNY: You said it wasn't stealing, Pa.

JOHNNY'S FATHER (*With furious irritation*): Well, it isn't.

JOHNNY: What about the farmer's dog, then?

JOHNNY'S FATHER: What are you talking about? What
farmer's dog?

JOHNNY: The farmer's dog that chased me all the way here.

JOHNNY'S FATHER (*Roaring*): Dog? Do you mean to tell me
a dog chased you? What kind of a dog?

JOHNNY: I didn't get a chance to take a good look, but I
guess it's a great big one.

JOHNNY'S FATHER (*Very angry at this awful humiliation*):
Did the God damn thing try to bite you or anything,
Johnny?

JOHNNY: I don't think so, Pa, but I thought it was going to
any minute.

JOHNNY'S FATHER: Did it growl at you?

JOHNNY: It wasn't exactly a growl.

JOHNNY'S FATHER: What happened?

JOHNNY: I just ran all the way, with the dog right behind me.

JOHNNY'S FATHER: Where is it now?

JOHNNY: It's *outside*, I think, Pa. Are you sure it isn't stealing?

JOHNNY'S FATHER (*Very angry, eating three or four grapes*): Of course it isn't stealing. I'll take care of the dog. No man or beast can scare your father, Johnny. Always remember that.

(*He goes cautiously to the window and peeks out*)

JOHNNY: Is it out there, Pa?

JOHNNY'S FATHER: There's a little dog out there, Johnny. It's asleep, I think.

JOHNNY (*Jumping bitterly*): *I knew it*. It's the farmer's dog, waiting for me.

JOHNNY'S FATHER: It's not a very big dog, Johnny.

JOHNNY: Yeah, but if it's stealing—if it's the *farmer's* dog—what about that?

JOHNNY'S FATHER: Why, that little bitty dog doesn't belong to anybody, Johnny. That little dog is looking for a friend, I bet.

JOHNNY: It chased me all the way. Are you sure, Pa?

JOHNNY'S FATHER: Sure I'm sure, Johnny. I'm no poet for nothing. I understand things.

(*The dog begins to growl and bark.* JOHNNY'S FATHER *jumps back from the window, frightened.* JOHNNY *grows tense and speechless*)

JOHNNY (*Whispering*): What is it, Pa?

JOHNNY'S FATHER: Somebody's coming, I think.

JOHNNY: You see, Pa? *It is stealing*. It's the farmer.

(*He runs to the table and gathers the fruit into his arms. His* GRANDMOTHER *comes running into the room*)

JOHNNY'S GRANDMOTHER (*In Armenian*): What's all the hullabaloo, in the rain?

JOHNNY'S FATHER: Shhhh.

(JOHNNY *takes the fruit out of the living room; returns, scared to death. The dog is still growling and barking.* JOHNNY'S FATHER *is even more scared than* JOHNNY)

JOHNNY (*Sore, and now defiant*): God damn it, Pa. Now
look at the mess we're in.

JOHNNY'S FATHER: I wish I had a cigarette.

JOHNNY (*Now worrying about his father; to his grandmother, in Armenian*): Are there cigarettes?

> (JOHNNY'S GRANDMOTHER *runs into the next room*)

> (*The dog stops growling*)

JOHNNY: You see, Pa? It's the farmer. Where shall I hide?
Don't open the door.

JOHNNY'S FATHER: *Open the door?* Help me with this table.

> (*They push the table up against the door, and tip-
toe back to the center of the room.* JOHNNY'S GRAND-
MOTHER *runs back with one cigarette and one match
which she hands to* JOHNNY'S FATHER, *who lights
the cigarette, inhales deeply, and straightens up*)

JOHNNY'S FATHER (*Dramatically*): *I* am the one who took
the fruit, understand, Johnny?

JOHNNY: Don't open the door, Pa.

> (JOHNNY'S FATHER *picks up a small stool, takes it
quietly to the table up against the door, places it on
the table, to make it heavier*)

> (JOHNNY *picks up a chair and puts it on the table.
The* OLD LADY *puts a vase on the table.* JOHNNY'S
FATHER *adds three books to the barricade. In fact,
as the knocks continue, the family little by little
puts all the household goods up against the door*)

JOHNNY'S FATHER: Don't be afraid, Johnny.

JOHNNY: He can't get in, can he, Pa?

JOHNNY'S FATHER: I don't think so.

> (*The* GRANDMOTHER, *the* FATHER *and the* SON *stand
together in the bare room, defying the world.*

> *There is a long pause, full of a mingling of awful
fear and furious defiance.*

> *After half a minute the silence is broken.*

> *It is a solo on the bugle: "My Heart's in the High-
lands."*

> *The sun comes out*)

JOHNNY (*Shouting*): It's Mr. MacGregor.

JOHNNY'S FATHER (*Running to the window, lifting it, and shouting out to* MAC GREGOR): Welcome, Mr. Mac-Gregor. Johnny, rearrange the furniture.

> (JOHNNY'S FATHER *returns to the barricade and helps* JOHNNY *and his* GRANDMOTHER *rearrange the furniture. At last everything is out of the way.* JOHNNY'S FATHER *swings open the door.* JASPER MAC GREGOR, *still playing the solo, preceded by the dog, which is a very small street dog, comes in. The dog runs around playfully, all excited.* MAC GREGOR'S *eyes are full of grief and joy.* JOHNNY *begins making trips to the kitchen, returning with the fruit, on a plate, and a pitcher of water.* MAC GREGOR *finishes the solo. There is a moment when everybody stands stock-still, including the dog.* JOHNNY *offers* MAC-GREGOR *the pitcher of water*)

MAC GREGOR (*Weary*): Not this time, Johnny.

JOHNNY'S FATHER: Welcome, my friend.

MAC GREGOR: I've run away. They're after me now, but I won't go back. They stole my bugle. They tried to keep me in bed. They said I was sick. I'm not sick; I'm old. I know my days on earth are numbered. I want them to be with you. Don't let them take me back.

JOHNNY'S FATHER: I won't.

> (*He draws out a chair for the old man*)

Please sit down.

> (*They all sit down.* MAC GREGOR *looks around at everybody*)

MAC GREGOR: It's good to see you again.

JOHNNY: Is your heart still in the highlands?

MAC GREGOR (*Nodding*): In the highlands, son.

JOHNNY'S FATHER (*Angry*): *Johnny.*

JOHNNY (*Sore, too*): What?

JOHNNY'S FATHER: Shut up.

JOHNNY: Why?

JOHNNY'S FATHER: *Why?* What do you get so dumb for every once in a while? Can't you see Mr. MacGregor is weary?

JOHNNY (*To* MAC GREGOR): Are you?

MAC GREGOR (*Nods*): But where's *your* mother, son?

JOHNNY: She's dead.

MAC GREGOR (*Almost to himself*): Not dead, Johnny.

(*He shakes his head*)

In the highlands.

JOHNNY'S GRANDMOTHER (*To his father*): What's he saying?

JOHNNY'S FATHER (*Shaking his head*): Nothing. (*To* MAC-GREGOR) Won't you eat?

MAC GREGOR (*Looking at the plate*): One grape. No more.

(*He plucks a grape off a bunch, puts it in his mouth. Suddenly turns, startled*)

Are they coming?

JOHNNY'S FATHER: Don't be afraid, my friend. Lie down and rest.

(JOHNNY'S FATHER *takes the* OLD MAN *to the couch. The* OLD MAN *stretches out, face up.* JOHNNY'S FATHER *returns to the table. Nobody is eating. The* OLD MAN *jumps up suddenly. It's nothing again. He gets up and returns to the table*)

MAC GREGOR: You won't let them take me back, will you?

JOHNNY'S FATHER: No.

(*He breaks open a pomegranate and hands* MAC-GREGOR *half*)

Try to eat something.

MAC GREGOR: Thank you, my friend.

(*He eats some of the pomegranate*)

(*There is a knock on the door,* MAC GREGOR *leaps to his feet, furiously*)

MAC GREGOR (*Roaring*): You'll not take me back. I warn you. I'll fall down and die. I belong here, with these people.

JOHNNY'S FATHER (*Scared*): Shall we open the door?

JOHNNY (*Also scared*): Shall we?

MAC GREGOR (*Powerful*): Of course we'll open the door.

(*He goes to the door, opens it. It is* RUFE APLEY, *the carpenter, who is a little shaken up by* MAC-GREGOR'S *fury*)

RUFE APLEY: Hello, Mr. MacGregor.

JOHNNY: Who is it?

RUFE APLEY: It's Rufe Apley.

MAC GREGOR: How do you do, Rufe.

JOHNNY'S FATHER (*At the door*): Come in, Rufe.

> (RUFE *comes in. He has a loaf of bread, a sausage and two eggs in his hands*)

RUFE: I was sitting home doing nothing when I heard that song again. I was sure it was Mr. MacGregor.

MAC GREGOR: I'm delighted you remembered.

RUFE: Nobody could ever forget that song, Mr. MacGregor. I brought these few things.

MAC GREGOR (*Taking them and putting them on the table*): Thank you, my friend, thank you.

> (*There is another knock at the door. It is* SAM WALLACE; *he is a lineman, in full regalia: overalls, tools hanging all over him, tape, straps around his calves, spikes, everything. He has cheese and tomatoes and radishes with him*)

WALLACE: I *knew* it was Mr. MacGregor. I said to myself, I'll go over with a few little things to eat.

MAC GREGOR: This is indeed a pleasant surprise.

RUFE (*Obviously trying hard to say something*): Ah, Mr. MacGregor?

MAC GREGOR: Yes, my friend? Speak up. I'm a plain man, no different in any way from yourself.

RUFE: My wife's sister and her family are outside. I know they'd like to hear you play again. There are some other people.

MAC GREGOR (*Flattered*): Of course I'll play. I'm over eighty and not long for this world. Before I go I'd like to become a part of you who shall live after I am dead. Are there children out there too?

RUFE: Seven. My wife's sister's kids.

> (*Three or four more neighbors come in, bringing food.* MAC GREGOR *takes up his bugle. Everybody follows him out of the room to the porch, except* JOHNNY'S FATHER. MAC GREGOR *begins to play the solo again. This time he's too old and weak to really play, but he finishes the solo as well as he is able to.*
>
> JOHNNY'S FATHER *paces about the room, smiling, frowning, loving the place. The door to the kitchen*

opens quietly and ESTHER KOSAK *stands in the doorway.* JOHNNY'S FATHER *turns and sees her. She is
no longer crying. She has something clutched in
her fist)*

JOHNNY'S FATHER (*Quietly*): Hello, Esther.
ESTHER: Where's Johnny?
JOHNNY'S FATHER: I'll go get him.

(*He goes out on the porch*)

(*The* GIRL *stands alone in terrible sadness and loneliness. After a moment* JOHNNY *comes rushing in,
all excited, but calms down quickly when he begins
to feel the mood of the girl*)

JOHNNY: Hello, Esther.
ESTHER: Hello, Johnny.
JOHNNY: What's the matter?
ESTHER: My father read me the poems.
JOHNNY: What?
ESTHER (*Holding out her hand*): Here. This is all I've got.

(JOHNNY *takes a handful of coins*)

I've been saving up for Christmas.

(*She begins to cry, turns, and runs out of the
house*)

JOHNNY (*Deeply touched and furious, sensing something
profound and beautiful and terrible*): Holy Moses.

(*His face takes on boyhood's tragic expression of
grief, and he begins to cry. He throws the coins
against the wall and falls down, sobbing*)

Who the hell wants that stuff?

(JOHNNY'S FATHER *comes back*)

JOHNNY'S FATHER: Johnny. (*Going closer*) Johnny?
JOHNNY (*Sobbing and angry*): She brought me money.
JOHNNY'S FATHER: It's no use crying, Johnny.
JOHNNY (*Jumping up*): Who's crying?

(*He cries harder than ever*)

JOHNNY'S FATHER: Go wash your face. It's nothing.
JOHNNY (*Going*): Something's wrong somewhere.

(MAC GREGOR *finishes the solo, the people are silent with awe and the knowledge that something is wrong.* MAC GREGOR'S *voice is heard for a moment in a speech*)

MAC GREGOR (*Wearily*): The years, my friends. I have walked to the end of them. I'm sorry I can no longer play for you. Thank you. Thank you.

(JOHNNY'S FATHER *walks back and forth in the room. He sits down at the table and looks at the food.* MAC GREGOR *and* JOHNNY'S GRANDMOTHER *return and sit at the table. The dog lies down in a corner*)

MAC GREGOR (*He lifts the water pitcher, drinks a little*):

They wouldn't let me play.
    (*He drinks a little more*)
They *stole* my bugle.
    (*He drinks a little more*)
They said I was sick.
    (*He drinks a little more*)

I'm as strong as a bull. If they come to take me back, I shall pretend that I am dying. I shall play the death scene from "King Lear." I shall play *all* the death scenes.

(JOHNNY *returns solemnly. They are all at the table. Nobody can eat but the* OLD LADY. *There is a long silence. The* OLD LADY *stops eating*)

JOHNNY'S GRANDMOTHER: What's the matter? Why this terrible gloom?

(MAC GREGOR *rises*)

MAC GREGOR (*Reciting, remembering lines from Shakespeare, and inventing a few of his own*):
Blow, winds, and crack your cheeks!
Rage! blow!
You cataracts and hurricanes, spout
Till you have drenched our steeples,
    drowned the cocks!
You sulphurous and thought-executing fires,
Singe my white head!
Humble thy belly-full, spit fire, spout rain!
I never gave you kingdom, call'd you children.

Here I stand, your slave,
A poor infirm, weak and despised old man.

To be or not to be . . .

> (*Tragically*)

To be— To be—
What? A fool? A man mocked by destiny?
Turned away from home and fire and love?
I am a man more sinned against than sinning.
Arms! Arms! Sword! Fire!
Corruption in the place! The little dogs and all,
Tray, Blanche, Sweetheart. See? They bark at me.
O, that way madness lies—no more of that—
Let me shun that. My wits begin to turn.

> (JOHNNY *goes to him, and kneels*)

Come on, my boy, how dost my boy? Art cold?
Let me alone! Wilt break my heart?
And my poor fool is hang'd.
No, no, no life!
Why should a dog, a horse, a rat have life
And thou no life at all?
Thou'lt come no more,
Never, never, never, never!
Pray you undo this button—thank you, sir—

> (*Holds the bugle before him*)

Do you see this? Look on her. Look.
Look there, look there!!

> (*While* MAC GREGOR *is acting* JOHNNY *returns to the coins on the floor and picks them up one by one and looks at them.*
>
> *The room is in absolute silence. A horse and wagon in the street is heard; then steps on the front porch; then a knock at the door.* JOHNNY'S FATHER *goes to the door. It is* PHILIP CARMICHAEL *and two guards from the Old People's Home. The guards stand at attention at the door*)

CARMICHAEL: We heard him playing. He's very sick. We've come to take him back.

JOHNNY'S FATHER: Please come in. (*He enters*) (*To* MAC-GREGOR) Mr. MacGregor. (*There is no answer*)

JOHNNY'S FATHER (*Louder*): Mr. MacGregor. (*Goes closer*) Mr. MacGregor. Mr. Mac—

> (CARMICHAEL *hurries over to* MAC GREGOR *and examines him*)

CARMICHAEL: He's dead.

JOHNNY: No, he isn't. He was acting.

JOHNNY'S FATHER: By God, he *was* the greatest Shakespearean actor of our day.

CARMICHAEL: I'm sorry this had to happen here.

JOHNNY'S FATHER: Why not? Why not here? This is where he wanted it to be.

JOHNNY: He *was* acting, Pa. He isn't dead.

> (*He goes to* MAC GREGOR)

Are you, Mr. MacGregor?

> (*There is no answer, of course*)

CARMICHAEL: We'll take him back.

JOHNNY'S FATHER: Here's his bugle. Keep it with him.

> (JOHNNY'S FATHER *lifts* MAC GREGOR *and carries him out. The guards carry him up the street.*
>
> *The light of the afternoon sun increases to the same intensity as at the beginning of the play.*
>
> *The horse and wagon goes off. There is a moment of strange silence, and the faint far-away sound of the bugle solo. A knock at the door.* JOHNNY'S FATHER *opens the door. It's the young* HUSBAND *and* WIFE. *The* BABY *is crying. They come in*)

THE WIFE: The kid is tired and sleepy.

JOHNNY'S FATHER: The house is ready. (*To* JOHNNY) Get your stuff. (*To the* OLD LADY, *in Armenian*) We're going.

> (*He gets a straw suitcase from under the couch and throws his poems, books, envelopes, one loaf of bread, and a few of the other items of food into it. The* OLD LADY *puts a shawl around her head and shoulders.* JOHNNY *leaves all his junk; takes only the handful of coins. The* BABY *stops crying. The dog follows* JOHNNY *around. The music increases in intensity*)

THE HUSBAND: Thank you very much.
THE WIFE: Have you some place to go?
JOHNNY'S FATHER: Yes, we have. Good-by.
THE HUSBAND AND WIFE: Good-by.

(*They go out of the house to the street*)

JOHNNY: Where the hell do we think we're going, Pa?
JOHNNY'S FATHER: Never mind, Johnny. You just follow *me*.
JOHNNY: I'm not mentioning any names, Pa, but something's wrong somewhere.

(*The music grows louder. They walk up the street*)

The Time of Your Life

To George Jean Nathan

Note

"The Time of Your Life" was produced by Eddie Dowling in conjunction with The Theatre Guild, and directed by Mr. Dowling and myself. It was first performed in New Haven at the Shubert Theatre, Saturday evening, October 7, 1939. From New Haven it moved to the Plymouth Theatre in Boston for a run of two weeks. It opened in New York at the Booth Theatre on Wednesday, October 25.

This is the cast which opened the play:

The Newsboy	ROSS BAGDASARIAN
The Drunkard	JOHN FARRELL
Willie	WILL LEE
Joe	EDDIE DOWLING
Nick	CHARLES DE SHEIM
Tom	EDWARD ANDREWS
Kitty Duval	JULIE HAYDON
Dudley	CURT CONWAY
Harry	GENE KELLY
Wesley	REGINALD BEANE
Lorene	NENE VIBBER
Blick	GROVER BURGESS
Arab	HOUSELEY STEVENS, SR.
Mary L.	CELESTE HOLME
Krupp	WILLIAM BENDIX
McCarthy	TOM TULLY
Kit Carson	LEN DOYLE
Nick's Ma	MICHELETTE BURANI
Sailor	RANDOLPH WADE
Elsie	CATHIE BAILEY
A Killer	EVELYN GELLER
Her Side Kick	MARY CHEFFEY
A Society Lady	EVA LEONARD BOYNE
A Society Gentleman	AINSWORTH ARNOLD
First Cop	RANDOLPH WADE
Second Cop	JOHN FARRELL

I wish to express my sincere gratitude to each member of the cast.

Preface

Statistics

The first draft was written in six days, in New York, beginning Monday, May 8, 1939, and ending Saturday, May 13. The first title was "The Light Fantastic." There were to have been six acts, one for each day of work. It turned out that the number of acts was five instead of six. Five or six, however, the idea was to write the play in six days. In the number of days of any worker's week. Writers are workers.

George Jean Nathan read the play, liked it and wrote about it in *Newsweek*. Eddie Dowling bought the play.

The writing of the play was, in great part, the consequence of the encouragement of George Jean Nathan and John Mason Brown who voted for "My Heart's in the Highlands," my first play, as the play of the 1938–1939 season; which, in turn, landed me as a guest at the Drama Critics' Circle Dinner at The Algonquin; which, in another turn, enabled me to meet all the critics who are members of the circle, as well as Mr. Dowling, who sat across the table from me, and along about ten o'clock at night said, "Any play you write, I'll buy sight unseen." This is the kind of American talk I respect. I asked Mr. Dowling if he was on the level and he assured me that he was. I asked him why, and he told me he believed in my future as a playwright. I felt fine and pretty sure I would have a good play for him very soon, so I began to brag about myself to John Anderson and Tallulah Bankhead and any other critic or actress or playwright who happened to be near by and unable to get away swiftly.

I didn't begin to write the play the next morning because at the time I was living a social life. I began not living a social life the next day, and by Monday, May 8th, I was ready to be a writer again. I began to write.

The idea was also to find out why a writer can't write in New York. What's to stop him? The answer is, of course, nothing. A writer can write anywhere, under any circumstance or complication of circumstances, and nothing's to stop him. He can write well, and he can do it as swiftly as the work involved needs to be done swiftly. In the case of this play it needed to be done very swiftly. The weather was muggy. My room at The Great Northern Hotel had no view, little ventilation, and as soon as possible I wanted to go to Ireland for a long-delayed visit. I also needed money urgently and knew I couldn't earn any unless I had a play to offer Mr. Dowling.

The play was written on a rented Royal Portable Typewriter, which I later bought for $30 from Miss Sophe Rabson, manager of Rabson's, which was across the street from The Great Northern on 56th Street, but is now in a new building, and where Miss Rabson graciously allowed me to listen to any phonograph record I cared to listen to, without any obligation; and where a young clerk named Bill was always ready to listen to me on the theme of human nature and so on; and where Miss Rabson's brothers, numbering, I believe, seven, were always pleased to let me watch their television sets and inquire two or three times a day about the cost of new and used Capeharts.

The cigarettes smoked were Chesterfields. The cigars were panatelas. I have forgotten the name of the brand, but they were ten cents straight. The food was Automat food, mainly chicken pie, and occasionally a late supper at the Golden Horn, after which I would sleep an hour or so. The liquor was Scotch.

The play was written night and day. The work did me good. The social life makes me feel ridiculous after a while. Six days of hard work is all I need to restore me to the pride and dignity of the worker, however.

This work was the first substantial work I had ever done in New York. It was also the longest work I had ever done, anywhere. I felt very good about it. Even if it was a bad play (and I had no reason to believe that it was not a good play), there was nothing lost, nothing to lose, and if the worst came to the worst I was simply broke and would have to borrow money somewhere and go back to San Francisco, instead of visiting Dublin.

Nathan, as I've said, liked the play and Dowling drew up a contract with me and advanced me an enormous sum of money. The title by that time was "The Time of Your Life. I studied the play every now and then and made certain changes in it. I considered other titles, inasmuch as I wasn't sure people wouldn't imagine the play wasn't some fluffy drawing-room comedy. Mr. Nathan's "Sunset Sonata" didn't seem quite right. Certain things were lifted out of the play. New things were put into it. I went to Dublin.

The play has been revised four or five times, and is still likely to be revised. Even now, there are certain changes I would like to make in my first play, "My Heart's in the Highlands." Everything is there of course, as everything is in a child of three, or a man of thirty, or a man of sixty, but there is always room for refinement.

The World of a Play

Like "My Heart's in the Highlands," "The Time of Your Life" will very likely take an important place in the development of the new American theater. I know why, but I am going to leave the full details to the critics, as I believe in the right of every profession to function. In one dimension I shall probably always understand the play better than anybody else, but in another I shall certainly never understand it as fully as critics, professional or amateur. Every performance of a play varies, if ever so little. Every audience beholding a play varies, if ever so little. Every individual in every audience varies, if ever so little. A play is a world, with its own inhabitants and its own laws and its own values. Although the real world is always essentially the same, it is actually never the same from one hour to another, never exactly the same, so that the same thing today as yesterday, is a different thing, nevertheless. One world furnishes itself to us every morning, and we furnish ourselves to a new world every morning. The world never changes and is always changing, and we in turn never change and are always changing. The world of a play is slightly more secure because considerably less complex, since a play consists of isolation, whereas the world has nothing to be isolated from. The writer of a play himself varies, if ever so little. The parts in a play vary, greatly or less greatly. The people taken from the world and placed in a play vary, greatly superficially, only very little deeply. The players in a play, as themselves, vary considerably.

Unlike the poem, essay, story, or novel, a play is not fully created in itself, as a play. It is not an affair, finally, between one man and one man: the writer and the reader. It becomes fully created only through the deliberate and cultivated functioning of a considerable number of people rehearsed to behave harmoniously and on schedule, so that a desired meaning and message will be conveyed to each individual beholding the play, a meaning which more or less should be the same to all the individuals in the audience.

"The Time of Your Life" is a play of our time. The people in the play are people you are likely to see any day in almost any part of America, certainly at least in certain kinds of American places. Most of the critics said they didn't understand my first play. After a while a few of them turned around and said they did, but on the whole the critics appeared not to like the play because they didn't know why they liked it. I predict that fewer critics will need to imagine that they cannot understand this play. I know a few critics won't like it at all, and that many critics will not like all of it.

I don't want this state of affairs to change.

WILLIAM SAROYAN

San Francisco, December 1939

IN THE TIME of your life, live—so that in that good time there shall be no ugliness or death for yourself or for any life your life touches. Seek goodness everywhere, and when it is found, bring it out of its hiding-place and let it be free and unashamed. Place in matter and in flesh the least of the values, for these are the things that hold death and must pass away. Discover in all things that which shines and is beyond corruption. Encourage virtue in whatever heart it may have been driven into secrecy and sorrow by the shame and terror of the world. Ignore the obvious, for it is unworthy of the clear eye and the kindly heart. Be the inferior of no man, nor of any man be the superior. Remember that every man is a variation of yourself. No man's guilt is not yours, nor is any man's innocence a thing apart. Despise evil and ungodliness, but not men of ungodliness or evil. These, understand. Have no shame in being kindly and gentle, but if the time comes in the time of your life to kill, kill and have no regret. In the time of your life, live—so that in that wondrous time you shall not add to the misery and sorrow of the world, but shall smile to the infinite delight and mystery of it.

THE PEOPLE

JOE, *a young loafer with money and a good heart*

TOM, *his admirer, disciple, errand boy, stooge and friend*

KITTY DUVAL, *a young woman with memories*

NICK, *owner of Nick's Pacific Street Saloon, Restaurant, and Entertainment Palace*

ARAB, *an Eastern philosopher and harmonica-player*

KIT CARSON, *an old Indian-fighter*

MC CARTHY, *an intelligent and well-read longshoreman*

KRUPP, *his boyhood friend, a waterfront cop who hates his job but doesn't know what else to do instead*

HARRY, *a natural-born hoofer who wants to make people laugh but can't*

WESLEY, *a colored boy who plays a mean and melancholy boogie-woogie piano*

DUDLEY, *a young man in love*

ELSIE, *a nurse, the girl he loves*

LORENE, *an unattractive woman*

MARY L., *an unhappy woman of quality and great beauty*

WILLIE, *a marble-game maniac*

BLICK, *a heel*

MA, *Nick's mother*

A KILLER

HER SIDE KICK

A COP

ANOTHER COP

A SAILOR

A SOCIETY GENTLEMAN

A SOCIETY LADY

THE DRUNKARD

THE NEWSBOY

ANNA, *Nick's daughter*

THE PLACE

Nick's Pacific Street Saloon, Restaurant, and Entertainment Palace at the foot of Embarcadero, in San Fran-

cisco. A suggestion of room 21 at The New York Hotel, upstairs, around the corner.

THE TIME

Afternoon and night of a day in October, 1939.

Act One

Nick's is an American place: a San Francisco waterfront honky-tonk.

At a table, JOE: *always calm, always quiet, always thinking, always eager, always bored, always superior. His expensive clothes are casually and youthfully worn and give him an almost boyish appearance. He is thinking.*

Behind the bar, NICK: *a big red-headed young Italian-American with an enormous naked woman tattooed in red on the inside of his right arm. He is studying The Racing Form.*

The ARAB, *at his place at the end of the bar. He is a lean old man with a rather ferocious old-country mustache, with the ends twisted up. Between the thumb and forefinger of his left hand is the Mohammedan tattoo indicating that he has been to Mecca. He is sipping a glass of beer.*

It is about eleven-thirty in the morning. SAM *is sweeping out. We see only his back. He disappears into the kitchen. The* SAILOR *at the bar finishes his drink and leaves, moving thoughtfully, as though he were trying very hard to discover how to live.*

The NEWSBOY *comes in.*

NEWSBOY (*Cheerfully*): Good-morning, everybody.
(*No answer. To* NICK) Paper, Mister?

> NICK *shakes his head, no. The* NEWSBOY *goes to* JOE.

Paper, Mister?

> JOE *shakes his head, no. The* NEWSBOY *walks away, counting papers.*

JOE (*Noticing him*): How many you got?
NEWSBOY: Five.

> JOE *gives him a quarter, takes all the papers, glances*

at the headlines with irritation, throws them away.
The NEWSBOY *watches carefully, then goes.*

ARAB (*Picks up paper, looks at headlines, shakes head as
if rejecting everything else a man might say about the
world*): No foundation. All the way down the line.

The DRUNK *comes in. Walks to the telephone, looks
for a nickel in the chute, sits down at* JOE'S *table.*
NICK *takes the* DRUNK *out. The* DRUNK *returns.*

DRUNK (*Champion of the Bill of Rights*): This is a free
country, ain't it?

WILLIE, *the marble-game maniac, explodes through
the swinging doors and lifts the forefinger of his
right hand comically, indicating one beer. He is a
very young man, not more than twenty. He is
wearing heavy shoes, a pair of old and dirty cordu-
roys, a light green turtle-neck jersey with a large
letter "F" on the chest, an oversize two-button
tweed coat, and a green hat, with the brim up.*
NICK *sets out a glass of beer for him, he drinks it,
straightens up vigorously, saying Aaah, makes a
solemn face, gives* NICK *a one-finger salute of adieu,
and begins to leave, refreshed and restored in spirit.
He walks by the marble game, halts suddenly, turns,
studies the contraption, gestures as if to say, Oh, no.
Turns to go, stops, returns to the machine, studies
it, takes a handful of small coins out of his pants
pocket, lifts a nickel, indicates with a gesture, One
game, no more. Puts the nickel in the slot, pushes
in the slide, making an interesting noise.*

NICK: You can't beat that machine.
WILLIE: Oh, yeah?

*The marbles fall, roll, and take their place. He
pushes down the lever, placing one marble in position. Takes a very deep breath, walks in a small
circle, excited at the beginning of great drama.
Stands straight and pious before the contest. Himself vs. the machine. Willie vs. Destiny. His skill
and daring vs. the cunning and trickery of the
novelty industry of America, and the whole challenging world. He is the last of the American*

pioneers, with nothing more to fight but the ma-
chine, with no other reward than lights going on
and off, and six nickels for one. Before him is the
last champion, the machine. He is the last chal-
lenger, the young man with nothing to do in the
world. WILLIE *grips the knob delicately, studies the*
situation carefully, draws the knob back, holds it a
moment, and then releases it. The first marble rolls
out among the hazards, and the contest is on. At the
very beginning of the play "The Missouri Waltz" is
coming from the phonograph. The music ends here.
This is the signal for the beginning of the play.
JOE *suddenly comes out of his reverie. He whistles*
the way people do who are calling a cab that's
about a block away, only he does it quietly. WILLIE
turns around, but JOE *gestures for him to return to*
his work. NICK *looks up from The Racing Form.*

JOE (*Calling*): Tom. (*To himself*) Where the hell is he,
every time I need him?

(*He looks around calmly: the nickel-in-the-slot*
phonograph in the corner; the open public tele-
phone; the stage; the marble-game; the bar; and so
on. He calls again, this time very loud)

Hey, Tom.

NICK (*With morning irritation*): What do you want?

JOE (*Without thinking*): I want the boy to get me a watermelon, that's what *I* want. What do *you* want? Money, or
love, or fame, or what? You won't get them studying The
Racing Form.

NICK: I like to keep abreast of the times.

TOM *comes hurrying in. He is a great big man of*
about thirty or so who appears to be much younger
because of the childlike expression of his face: hand-
some, dumb, innocent, troubled, and a little bewil-
dered by everything. He is obviously adult in years,
but it seems as if by all rights he should still be a
boy. He is defensive as clumsy, self-conscious, over-
grown boys are. He is wearing a flashy cheap suit.
JOE *leans back and studies him with casual disap-*
proval. TOM *slackens his pace and becomes clumsy*
and embarrassed, waiting for the bawling-out he's
pretty sure he's going to get.

JOE (*Objectively, severely, but a little amused*): Who saved
  your life?

TOM (*Sincerely*): You did, Joe. Thanks.

JOE (*Interested*): How'd I do it?

TOM (*Confused*): What?

JOE (*Even more interested*): *How'd I do it?*

TOM: Joe, you know how you did it.

JOE (*Softly*): I want you to answer me. How'd I save your
  life? I've forgotten.

TOM (*Remembering, with a big sorrowful smile*): You
  made me eat all that chicken soup three years ago when
  I was sick and hungry.

JOE (*Fascinated*): *Chicken soup?*

TOM (*Eagerly*): Yeah.

JOE: Three years? Is it that long?

TOM (*Delighted to have the information*): Yeah, sure.
  1937. 1938. 1939. This is 1939, Joe.

JOE (*Amused*): Never mind what year it is. Tell me the
  whole story.

TOM: You took me to the doctor. You gave me money for
  food and clothes, and paid my room rent. Aw, Joe, you
  know all the different things you did.

> JOE *nods, turning away from* TOM *after each question.*

JOE: You in good health now?

TOM: Yeah, Joe.

JOE: You got clothes?

TOM: Yeah, Joe.

JOE: You eat three times a day. Sometimes four?

TOM: Yeah, Joe. Sometimes five.

JOE: You got a place to sleep?

TOM: Yeah, Joe.

> JOE *nods. Pauses. Studies* TOM *carefully.*

JOE: Then, where the hell have you been?

TOM (*Humbly*): Joe, I was out in the street listening to the
  boys. They're talking about the trouble down here on the
  waterfront.

JOE (*Sharply*): I want you to be around when I need you.

TOM (*Pleased that the bawling-out is over*): I won't do it
  again. Joe, one guy out there says there's got to be a
  revolution before anything will ever be all right.

JOE (*Impatient*): I know all about it. Now, here. Take this money. Go up to the Emporium. You know where the Emporium is?

TOM: Yeah, sure, Joe.

JOE: All right. Take the elevator and go up to the fourth floor. Walk around to the back, to the toy department. Buy me a couple of dollars' worth of toys and bring them here.

TOM (*Amazed*): Toys? What *kind* of toys, Joe?

JOE: Any kind of toys. Little ones that I can put on this table.

TOM: What do you want toys for, Joe?

JOE (*Mildly angry*): What?

TOM: All right, all right. You don't have to get sore at *everything*. What'll people think, a big guy like me buying toys?

JOE: *What people?*

TOM: Aw, Joe, you're always making me do crazy things for you, and *I'm* the guy that gets embarrassed. You just sit in this place and make me do all the dirty work.

JOE (*Looking away*): Do what I tell you.

TOM: O.K., but I wish I knew *why*.

> *He makes to go.*

JOE: Wait a minute. Here's a nickel. Put it in the phonograph. Number seven. I want to hear that waltz again.

TOM: Boy, I'm glad *I* don't have to stay and listen to it. Joe, what do you hear in that song anyway? We listen to that song ten times a day. Why can't we hear number six, or two, or nine? There are a lot of other numbers.

JOE (*Emphatically*): Put the nickel in the phonograph. (*Pause*) Sit down and wait till the music's over. Then go get me some toys.

TOM: O.K. O.K.

JOE (*Loudly*): Never mind being a martyr about it either. The cause isn't worth it.

> TOM *puts the nickel into the machine, with a ritual of impatient and efficient movement which plainly shows his lack of sympathy or enthusiasm. His manner also reveals, however, that his lack of sympathy is spurious and exaggerated. Actually, he is fascinated by the music, but is so confused by it that he pretends he dislikes it.*
>
> *The music begins. It is another variation of "The*

Missouri Waltz," *played dreamily and softly, with
perfect orchestral form, and with a theme of weeping in the horns repeated a number of times.*

At first TOM *listens with something close to irritation, since he can't understand what is so attractive
in the music to* JOE, *and what is so painful and confusing in it to himself. Very soon, however, he is
carried away by the melancholy story of grief and
nostalgia of the song.*

*He stands, troubled by the poetry and confusion in
himself.*

JOE, *on the other hand, listens as if he were not
listening, indifferent and unmoved. What he's interested in is* TOM. *He turns and glances at* TOM.

KITTY DUVAL, *who lives in a room in The New
York Hotel, around the corner, comes beyond the
swinging doors quietly, and walks slowly to the
bar, her reality and rhythm a perfect accompaniment to the sorrowful American music, which is her
music, as it is Tom's. Which the world drove out of
her, putting in its place brokenness and all manner
of spiritually crippled forms. She seems to understand this, and is angry. Angry with herself, full of
hate for the poor world, and full of pity and contempt for its tragic, unbelievable, confounded
people. She is a small powerful girl, with that kind
of delicate and· rugged beauty which no circumstance of evil or ugly reality can destroy. This
beauty is that element of the immortal which is in
the seed of good and common people, and which is
kept alive in some of the female of our kind, no
matter how accidentally or pointlessly they may
have entered the world.* KITTY DUVAL *is somebody.
There is an angry purity, and a fierce pride, in her.*

*In her stance, and way of walking, there is grace
and arrogance.* JOE *recognizes her as a great person
immediately. She goes to the bar.*

KITTY: Beer.

NICK *places a glass of beer before her mechanically.*

*She swallows half the drink, and listens to the music
again.*

TOM *turns and sees her. He becomes dead to every-*
thing in the world but her. He stands like a lump,
fascinated and undone by his almost religious ado-
ration for her. JOE *notices* TOM.

JOE (*Gently*): Tom.

TOM *begins to move toward the bar, where* KITTY *is*
standing.

(*Loudly*) Tom.

TOM *halts, then turns, and* JOE *motions to him to*
come over to the table. TOM *goes over.*

(*Quietly*) Have you got everything straight?

TOM (*Out of the world*): What?

JOE: What do you mean, what? I just gave you some
instructions.

TOM (*Pathetically*): What do you want, Joe?

JOE: I want you to come to your senses.

He stands up quietly and knocks Tom's hat off.
TOM *picks up his hat quickly.*

TOM: I got it, Joe. I got it. The Emporium. Fourth floor. In
the back. The toy department. Two dollars' worth of
toys. That you can put on a table.

KITTY (*To herself*): Who the hell is he to push a big man
like that around?

JOE: I'll expect you back in a half hour. Don't get sidetracked anywhere. Just do what I tell you.

TOM (*Pleading*): Joe? Can't I bet four bits on a horse race?
There's a long shot—Precious Time—that's going to win
by ten lengths. I got to have money.

JOE *points to the street.* TOM *goes out.* NICK *is comb-*
ing his hair, looking in the mirror.

NICK: I thought you wanted him to get you a watermelon.

JOE: I forgot.

(*He watches* KITTY *a moment. To* KITTY, *clearly,*
slowly, with great compassion)

What's the dream?

KITTY (*Moving to* JOE, *coming to*): What?

JOE (*Holding the dream for her*): What's the dream, *now*?

KITTY (*Coming still closer*): What dream?

JOE: What dream! The dream you're dreaming.

NICK: Suppose he did bring you a watermelon? What the hell would you do with it?

JOE (*Irritated*): I'd put it on this table. I'd look at it. Then I'd eat it. What do you *think* I'd do with it, sell it for a profit?

NICK: How should I know what *you'd* do with *anything?* What I'd like to know is, where do you get your money from? What work do you do?

JOE (*Looking at* KITTY): Bring us a bottle of champagne.

KITTY: Champagne?

JOE (*Simply*): Would you rather have something else?

KITTY: What's the big idea?

JOE: I thought you might like some champagne. I myself am very fond of it.

KITTY: Yeah, but what's the big idea? You can't push *me* around.

JOE (*Gently but severely*): It's not in my nature to be unkind to another human being. I have only contempt for wit. Otherwise I might say something obvious, therefore cruel, and perhaps untrue.

KITTY: You be careful what you think about me.

JOE (*Slowly, not looking at her*): I have only the noblest thoughts for both your person, and your spirit.

NICK (*Having listened carefully and not being able to make it out*): What are you talking about?

KITTY: You shut up. You—

JOE: He owns this place. He's an important man. All kinds of people come to him looking for work. Comedians. Singers. Dancers.

KITTY: I don't care. He can't call me names.

NICK: All right, sister. I know how it is with a two-dollar whore in the morning.

KITTY (*Furiously*): Don't you dare call me names. I used to be in burlesque.

NICK: If you were ever in burlesque, I used to be Charlie Chaplin.

KITTY (*Angry and a little pathetic*): I *was* in burlesque. I played the burlesque circuit from coast to coast. I've had flowers sent to me by European royalty. I've had dinner with young men of wealth and social position.

NICK: You're dreaming.

KITTY (*To* JOE): *I was in burlesque.* Kitty Duval. That was my name. Life-size photographs of me in costume in front of burlesque theaters all over the country.

JOE (*Gently, coaxingly*): I believe you. Have some champagne.

NICK (*Going to table, with champagne bottle and glasses*): There he goes again.

JOE: Miss Duval?

KITTY (*Sincerely, going over*): That's not my *real* name. That's my *stage* name.

JOE: I'll call you by your stage name.

NICK (*Pouring*): All right, sister, make up your mind. Are you going to have champagne with him, or not?

JOE: Pour the lady some wine.

NICK: O.K., Professor. Why you come to this joint instead of one of the high-class dumps uptown is more than I can understand. Why don't you have champagne at the St. Francis? Why don't you drink with a lady?

KITTY (*Furiously*): Don't you call me names—you dentist.

JOE: Dentist?

NICK (*Amazed, loudly*): What kind of cussing is that? (*Pause. Looking at* KITTY, *then at* JOE, *bewildered*) This guy doesn't belong here. The only reason I've got champagne is because *he* keeps ordering it all the time. (*To* KITTY) Don't think you're the only one he drinks champagne with. He drinks with *all* of them. (*Pause*) He's crazy. Or something.

JOE (*Confidentially*): Nick, I think you're going to be all right in a couple of centuries.

NICK: I'm sorry, I don't understand your English.

> JOE *lifts his glass.*

> KITTY *slowly lifts hers, not quite sure of what's going on.*

JOE (*Sincerely*): To the spirit, Kitty Duval.

KITTY (*Beginning to understand, and very grateful, looking at him*): Thank you.

> *They drink.*

JOE (*Calling*): Nick.

NICK: Yeah?

JOE: Would you mind putting a nickel in the machine again? Number—

NICK: Seven. I know. I know. I don't mind at all, Your Highness, although, personally, I'm not a lover of music. (*Going to the machine*) As a matter of fact I think Tchaikowsky was a dope.

JOE: Tchaikowsky? Where'd you ever hear of Tchaikowsky?

NICK: He was a dope.

JOE: Yeah. Why?

NICK: They talked about him on the radio one Sunday morning. He was a sucker. He let a woman drive him crazy.

JOE: I see.

NICK: I stood behind that bar listening to the God damn stuff and cried like a baby. *None but the lonely heart!* He was a dope.

JOE: What made you cry?

NICK: What?

JOE (*Sternly*): What made you cry, Nick?

NICK (*Angry with himself*): I don't know.

JOE: I've been underestimating you, Nick. Play number seven.

NICK: They get everybody worked up. They give everybody stuff they shouldn't have.

> NICK *puts the nickel into the machine and the Waltz begins again. He listens to the music. Then studies The Racing Form.*

KITTY (*To herself, dreaming*): I like champagne, and everything that goes with it. Big houses with big porches, and big rooms with big windows, and big lawns, and big trees, and flowers growing everywhere, and big shepherd dogs sleeping in the shade.

NICK: I'm going next door to Frankie's to make a bet. I'll be right back.

JOE: Make one for me.

NICK (*Going to* JOE): Who do you like?

JOE (*Giving him money*): Precious Time.

NICK: *Ten dollars?* Across the board?

JOE: No. On the nose.

NICK: O.K.

> (*He goes*)

> DUDLEY R. BOSTWICK, *as he calls himself, breaks through the swinging doors, and practically flings himself upon the open telephone beside the phonograph.*

> DUDLEY *is a young man of about twenty-four or twenty-five, ordinary and yet extraordinary. He is*

smallish, as the saying is, neatly dressed in bargain clothes, over-worked and irritated by the routine and dullness and monotony of his life, apparently nobody and nothing, but in reality a great personality. The swindled young man. Educated, but without the least real understanding. A brave, dumb, salmon-spirit struggling for life in weary, stupefied flesh, dueling ferociously with a banal mind which has been only irritated by what it has been taught. He is a great personality because, against all these handicaps, what he wants is simple and basic: a woman. This urgent and violent need, common yet miraculous enough in itself, considering the unhappy environment of the animal, is the force which elevates him from nothingness to greatness. A ridiculous greatness, but in the nature of things beautiful to behold. All that he has been taught, and everything he believes, is phony, and yet he himself is real, almost super-real, because of this indestructible force in himself. His face is ridiculous. His personal rhythm is tense and jittery. His speech is shrill and violent. His gestures are wild. His ego is disjointed and epileptic. And yet deeply he possesses the same wholeness of spirit, and directness of energy, that is in all species of animals. There is little innate or cultivated spirit in him, but there is no absence of innocent animal force. He is a young man who has been taught that he has a chance, as a person, and believes it. As a matter of fact, he hasn't a chance in the world, and should have been told by somebody, or should not have had his natural and valuable ignorance spoiled by education, ruining an otherwise perfectly good and charming member of the human race.

At the telephone he immediately begins to dial furiously, hesitates, changes his mind, stops dialing, hangs up furiously, and suddenly begins again.

Not more than half a minute after the firecracker arrival of DUDLEY R. BOSTWICK, *occurs the polka-and-waltz arrival of* HARRY.

HARRY *is another story.*

He comes in timidly, turning about uncertainly,

awkward, out of place everywhere, embarrassed and encumbered by the contemporary costume, sick at heart, but determined to fit in somewhere. His arrival constitutes a dance.

His clothes don't fit. The pants are a little too large. The coat, which doesn't match, is also a little too large, and loose.

He is a dumb young fellow, but he has ideas. A philosophy, in fact. His philosophy is simple and beautiful. The world is sorrowful. The world needs laughter. HARRY *is funny. The world needs* HARRY. HARRY *will make the world laugh.*

He has probably had a year or two of high school. He has also listened to the boys at the pool room.

He's looking for Nick. He goes to the ARAB, *and says, Are you Nick? The* ARAB *shakes his head. He stands at the bar, waiting. He waits very busily.*

HARRY (*As* NICK *returns*): You Nick?

NICK (*Very loudly*): I am Nick.

HARRY (*Acting*): Can you use a great comedian?

NICK (*Behind the bar*): Who, for instance?

HARRY (*Almost angry*): Me.

NICK: You? What's funny about you?

> DUDLEY *at the telephone, is dialing. Because of some defect in the apparatus the dialing is very loud.*

DUDLEY: Hello. Sunset 7349? May I speak to Miss Elsie Mandelspiegel? (*Pause*)

HARRY (*With spirit and noise, dancing*): I dance and do gags and stuff.

NICK: In costume? Or are you wearing your costume?

DUDLEY: All I need is a cigar.

KITTY (*Continuing the dream of grace*): I'd walk out of the house, and stand on the porch, and look at the trees, and smell the flowers, and run across the lawn, and lie down under a tree, and read a book. (*Pause*) A book of poems, maybe.

DUDLEY (*Very, very clearly*): Elsie Mandelspiegel. (*Impatiently*) She has a room on the fourth floor. She's a nurse at the Southern Pacific Hospital. Elsie Mandelspiegel. She works at night. Elsie. Yes.

He begins waiting again.

WESLEY, *a colored boy, comes to the bar and stands near* HARRY, *waiting.*

NICK: Beer?

WESLEY: No, sir. I'd like to talk to you.

NICK (*To* HARRY): All right. Get funny.

HARRY (*Getting funny, an altogether different person, an actor with great energy, both in power of voice, and in force and speed of physical gesture*): Now, I'm standing on the corner of Third and Market. I'm looking around. I'm figuring it out. There it is. Right in front of me. The whole city. The whole world. People going by. They're going somewhere. I don't know where, but they're going. I ain't going *anywhere*. Where the hell can you go? I'm figuring it out. All right, I'm a citizen. A fat guy bumps his stomach into the face of an old lady. They were in a hurry. Fat and old. *They bumped.* Boom. I don't know. It may mean war. *War.* Germany. England. Russia. I don't know for sure. (*Loudly, dramatically, he salutes, about faces, presents arms, aims, and fires*) WAAAAAR.

> *He blows a call to arms.* NICK *gets sick of this, indicates with a gesture that* HARRY *should hold it, and goes to* WESLEY.

NICK: What's on your mind?

WESLEY (*Confused*): Well—

NICK: Come on. Speak up. Are you hungry, or what?

WESLEY: Honest to God, I ain't hungry. All I want is a job. I don't want no charity.

NICK: Well, what can you do, and how good are you?

WESLEY: I can run errands, clean up, wash dishes, anything.

DUDLEY (*On the telephone, very eagerly*): Elsie? Elsie, this is Dudley. Elsie, I'll jump in the bay if you don't marry me. Life isn't worth living without you. I can't sleep. I can't think of anything but you. All the time. Day and night and night and day. Elsie, I love you. I love you. What? (*Burning up*) Is this Sunset 7-3-4-9? (*Pause*) 7943? (*Calmly, while* WILLIE *begins making a small racket*) Well, what's *your* name? *Lorene?* Lorene Smith? I thought you were Elsie Mandelspiegel. What? Dudley. Yeah. Dudley R. Bostwick. Yeah. R. It stands for Raoul, but I never spell it out. I'm pleased to meet you, too. What? There's a lot of noise around here. (WILLIE *stops hitting the marble-game.*) Where am I? At Nick's, on Pacific Street. I work at the S. P. I told them I was sick and they gave me the afternoon off. Wait a minute. I'll ask them. I'd like to meet *you*, too. Sure. I'll ask them. (*Turns around to* NICK) What's this address?

NICK: Number 3 Pacific Street, you cad.

DUDLEY: Cad? You don't know how I've been suffering on account of Elsie. I take things too ceremoniously. I've got to be more lackadaisical. (*Into telephone*) Hello, Elenore? I mean, Lorene. It's number 3 Pacific Street. Yeah. Sure. I'll wait for you. How'll you know me? You'll *know* me. I'll recognize *you*. Good-by, now. (*He hangs up*)

HARRY (*Continuing his monologue, with gestures, movements, and so on*): I'm standing there. I didn't do anything to anybody. Why should *I* be a soldier? (*Sincerely, insanely*) BOOOOOOOOOM. WAR! O.K. War. *I* retreat. *I* hate war. I move to Sacramento.

NICK (*Shouting*): All right, Comedian. Lay off a minute.

HARRY (*Broken-hearted, going to* WILLIE): Nobody's got a sense of humor any more. The world's dying for comedy like never before, but nobody knows how to *laugh*.

NICK (*To* WESLEY): Do you belong to the union?

WESLEY: What union?

NICK: For the love of Mike, where've you been? Don't you know you can't come into a place and ask for a job and get one and go to work, just like that. You've got to belong to one of the unions.

WESLEY: I didn't know. I got to have a job. Real soon.

NICK: Well, you've got to belong to a union.

WESLEY: I don't want any favors. All I want is a chance to earn a living.

NICK: Go on into the kitchen and tell Sam to give you some lunch.

WESLEY: Honest, I ain't hungry.

DUDLEY (*Shouting*):What I've gone through for Elsie.

HARRY: I've got all kinds of funny ideas in my head to help make the world happy again.

NICK (*Holding* WESLEY): No, he isn't hungry.

> WESLEY *almost faints from hunger.* NICK *catches him just in time. The* ARAB *and* NICK *go off with* WESLEY *into the kitchen.*

HARRY (*To* WILLIE): See if you think this is funny. It's my own idea. I created this dance myself. It comes after the monologue.

> HARRY *begins to dance.* WILLIE *watches a moment, and then goes back to the game. It's a goofy dance, which* HARRY *does with great sorrow, but much energy.*

DUDLEY: Elsie. Aw, gee, Elsie. What the hell do I want to see Lorene Smith for? Some girl I don't know.

> JOE *and* KITTY *have been drinking in silence. There is no sound now except the soft shoe shuffling of* HARRY, *the Comedian.*

JOE: What's the dream now, Kitty Duval?

KITTY (*Dreaming the words and pictures*): I dream of home. Christ, I always dream of home. I've no *home*. I've no place. But I always dream of all of us together again. We had a farm in Ohio. There was nothing good about it. It was always sad. There was always trouble. But I always dream about it as if I could go back and Papa would be there and Mamma and Louie and my little brother Stephen and my sister Mary. I'm Polish. Duval! My name isn't Duval, it's Koranovsky. Katerina Koranovsky. We lost everything. The house, the farm, the trees, the horses, the cows, the chickens. Papa died. He was old. He was thirteen years older than Mamma. We moved to Chicago. We tried to work. We tried to stay together. Louie got in trouble. The fellows he was with killed him for something. I don't know what. Stephen ran away from home. Seventeen years old. I don't know where he is. Then Mamma died. (*Pause*) What's the dream? I dream of home.

> NICK *comes out of the kitchen with* WESLEY.

NICK: Here. Sit down here and rest. That'll hold you for a *while*. Why didn't you tell me you were hungry? You all right now?

WESLEY (*Sitting down in the chair at the piano*): Yes, I am. Thank you. I didn't know I was *that* hungry.

NICK: Fine. (*To* HARRY *who is dancing*) Hey. What the hell do you think you're doing?

HARRY (*Stopping*): That's my own idea. I'm a natural-born dancer and comedian.

WESLEY *begins slowly, one note, one chord at a time, to play the piano.*

NICK: You're no good. Why don't you try some other kind of work? Why don't you get a job in a store, selling something? What do you want to be a comedian for?

HARRY: I've got something for the world and they haven't got sense enough to let me give it to them. Nobody knows me.

DUDLEY: Elsie. Now I'm waiting for some dame I've never seen before. Lorene Smith. Never saw her in my life. Just happened to get the wrong number. She turns on the personality, and I'm a cooked Indian. Give me a beer, please.

HARRY: Nick, you've got to see my act. It's the greatest thing of its kind in America. All I want is a chance. No salary to begin. Let me try it out tonight. If I don't wow 'em, O.K., I'll go home. If vaudeville wasn't dead, a guy like me would have a chance.

NICK: You're not funny. You're a sad young punk. What the hell do you want to try to be funny for? You'll break everybody's heart. What's there for you to be funny about? You've been poor all your life, haven't you?

HARRY: I've been poor all right, but don't forget that some things count more than some other things.

NICK: What counts more, for instance, than what else, for instance?

HARRY: Talent, for instance, counts more than money, for instance, that's what, and I've got talent. I get new ideas night and day. Everything comes natural to me. I've got style, but it'll take me a little time to round it out. That's all.

By now WESLEY *is playing something of his own which is very good and out of the world. He plays about half a minute, after which* HARRY *begins to dance.*

NICK (*Watching*): I run the lousiest dive in Frisco, and a guy arrives and makes me stock up with champagne. The whores come in and holler at me that they're ladies. Talent comes in and begs me for a chance to show itself. Even society people come here once in a while. I don't know what for. Maybe it's liquor. Maybe it's the location. Maybe it's my personality. Maybe it's the crazy person-

ality of the joint. The old honky-tonk. (*Pause*) Maybe
they can't feel at home anywhere else.

> *By now* WESLEY *is really playing, and* HARRY *is
> going through a new routine.* DUDLEY *grows sadder
> and sadder.*

KITTY: Please dance with me.

JOE (*Loudly*): I never learned to dance.

KITTY: Anybody can dance. Just hold me in your arms.

JOE: I'm very fond of you. I'm *sorry*. I *can't* dance. I wish
to God I could.

KITTY: Oh, please.

JOE: Forgive me. I'd like to very much.

> KITTY *dances alone.* TOM *comes in with a package.
> He sees* KITTY *and goes ga-ga again. He comes out
> of the trance and puts the bundle on the table in
> front of* JOE.

JOE (*Taking the package*): What'd you get?

TOM: Two dollars' worth of toys. That's what you sent me
for. The girl asked me what I wanted with toys. I didn't
know what to tell her. (*He stares at* KITTY, *then back at*
JOE?) Joe? I've got to have some money. After all you've
done for me, I'll do anything in the world for you, but,
Joe, you got to give me some money once in a while.

JOE: What do you want it for?

> TOM *turns and stares at* KITTY *dancing.*

JOE (*Noticing*): Sure. Here. Here's five. (*Shouting*) Can
you dance?

TOM (*Proudly*): I got second prize at the Palomar in Sacramento five years ago.

JOE (*Loudly, opening package*): O.K., dance with her.

TOM: You mean *her?*

JOE (*Loudly*): I mean Kitty Duval, the burlesque queen.
I mean the queen of the world burlesque. Dance with
her. She wants to dance.

TOM (*Worshiping the name Kitty Duval, helplessly*): Joe,
can I tell you something?

JOE (*He brings out a toy and winds it*): You don't have to.
I know. You love her. You *really* love her. I'm not blind.
I know. But take care of yourself. Don't get sick that way
again.

NICK (*Looking at and listening to* WESLEY *with amaze-*

ment): Comes in here and wants to be a dish-washer. Faints from hunger. And then sits down and plays better than Heifetz.

JOE: Heifetz plays the violin.

NICK: All right, don't get careful. He's good, ain't he?

TOM (*To* KITTY): Kitty.

JOE (*He lets the toy go, loudly*): Don't *talk*. Just *dance*.

> TOM *and* KITTY *dance.* NICK *is at the bar, watching everything.* HARRY *is dancing.* DUDLEY *is grieving into his beer.* LORENE SMITH, *about thirty-seven, very overbearing and funny-looking, comes to the bar.*

NICK: What'll it be, lady?

LORENE (*Looking about and scaring all the young men*): I'm looking for the young man I talked to on the telephone. Dudley R. Bostwick.

DUDLEY (*Jumping, running to her, stopping, shocked*): Dudley R. (*Slowly*) Bostwick? Oh, yeah. He left here ten minutes ago. You mean Dudley Bostwick, that poor man on crutches?

LORENE: Crutches?

DUDLEY: Yeah. Dudley Bostwick. That's what he *said* his name was. He said to tell you not to wait.

LORENE: Well. (*She begins to go, turns around*) Are you sure *you're* not Dudley Bostwick?

DUDLEY: Who—me? (*Grandly*) My name is Roger Tenefrancia. I'm a French-Canadian. I never saw the poor fellow before.

LORENE: It seems to me your voice is like the voice I heard over the telephone.

DUDLEY: A coincidence. An accident. A quirk of fate. One of those things. Dismiss the thought. That poor cripple hobbled out of here ten minutes ago.

LORENE: He said he was going to commit suicide. I only wanted to be of help. (*She goes*)

DUDLEY: Be of help? What kind of help could she be, of?

> DUDLEY *runs to the telephone in the corner.*

Gee whiz, Elsie. Gee whiz. I'll never leave you again.

He turns the pages of a little address book.

Why do I always forget the number? I've tried to get her on the phone a hundred times this week and I still forget the number. She won't come to the phone, but I keep trying anyway. She's out. She's not in. She's working. I get the wrong number. Everything goes haywire. I can't sleep. (*Defiantly*) She'll come to the phone one of these days. If there's anything to true love at all, she'll come to the phone. Sunset 7349.

He dials the number, as JOE *goes on studying the toys. They are one big mechanical toy, whistles, and a music box.* JOE *blows into the whistles, quickly, by way of getting casually acquainted with them.*

TOM *and* KITTY *stop dancing.* TOM *stares at her.*

DUDLEY: Hello. Is this Sunset 7349? May I speak to Elsie? Yes. (*Emphatically, and bitterly*) No, this is *not* Dudley Bostwick. This is Roger Tenefrancia of Montreal, Canada. I'm a childhood friend of Miss Mandelspiegel. We went to kindergarten together. (*Hand over phone*) God damn it. (*Into phone*) Yes. I'll wait, thank you.

TOM: I love you.

KITTY: You want to go to my room? (TOM *can't answer*) Have you got two dollars?

TOM (*Shaking his head with confusion*): I've got *five* dollars, but I *love* you.

KITTY (*Looking at him*): You want to spend *all* that money?
        TOM *embraces her. They go.* JOE *watches. Goes back to the toy.*

JOE: Where's that longshoreman, McCarthy?

NICK: He'll be around.

JOE: What do you think he'll have to say today?

NICK: Plenty, as usual. I'm going next door to see who won that third race at Laurel.

JOE: Precious Time won it.

NICK: That's what you think. (*He goes*)

JOE (*To himself*): A horse named McCarthy is running in the sixth race today.

DUDLEY: (*On the phone*): Hello. Hello, Elsie? Elsie? (*His voice weakens; also his limbs*) My God. She's come to the phone. Elsie, I'm at Nick's on Pacific Street. You've got to come here and talk to me. Hello. Hello, Elsie? (*Amazed*) Did she hang up? Or was I disconnected?

He hangs up and goes to bar.

WESLEY *is still playing the piano.* HARRY *is still danc-*

ing. JOE *has wound up the big mechanical toy and is watching it work.*

NICK *returns.*

NICK (*Watching the toy*): Say. That's some gadget.

JOE: How much did I win?

NICK: How do you know you *won?*

JOE: Don't be silly. He said Precious Time was going to win by ten lengths, didn't he? He's in love, isn't he?

NICK: O.K. I don't know why, but Precious Time won. You got eighty for ten. How do you do it?

JOE (*Roaring*): Faith. Faith. How'd he win?

NICK: By a nose. Look him up in The Racing Form. The slowest, the cheapest, the worst horse in the race, and the worst jockey. What's the matter with my luck?

JOE: How much did you lose?

NICK: Fifty cents.

JOE: You should never gamble.

NICK: Why not?

JOE: You always bet fifty cents. You've got no more faith than a flea, that's why.

HARRY (*Shouting*): How do you like this, Nick?

He is really busy now, all legs and arms.

NICK (*Turning and watching*): Not bad. Hang around. You can wait table. (*To* WESLEY) Hey. Wesley. Can you play that again tonight?

WESLEY (*Turning, but still playing the piano*): I don't know for sure, Mr. Nick. I can play *something.*

NICK: Good. *You* hang around, too.

He goes behind the bar.

The atmosphere is now one of warm, natural, American ease; every man innocent and good; each doing what he believes he should do, or what he must do. There is deep American naïveté and faith in the behavior of each person. No one is competing with anyone else. No one hates anyone else. Every man is living, and letting live. Each man is following his destiny as he feels it should be followed; or is abandoning it as he feels it must, by now, be abandoned; or is forgetting it for the moment as he feels he should forget it. Although everyone is dead serious, there is unmistakable smiling and humor in the scene; a sense of the human body and spirit emerging from the world-imposed state of stress and fretfulness, fear and awkwardness, to the more natural state of casualness and grace. Each person belongs to the environment, in his own person, as himself: WESLEY *is playing better than ever.* HARRY *is hoofing better than ever.* NICK *is behind the bar shining glasses.* JOE *is smiling at the toy and studying it.* DUDLEY, *although still troubled, is at least calm now and full of melancholy poise.* WILLIE, *at the marble-game, is happy. The* ARAB *is deep in his memories, where he wants to be.*

Into this scene and atmosphere comes BLICK.

BLICK *is the sort of human being you dislike at sight. He is no different from anybody else physically. His face is an ordinary face. There is nothing obviously wrong with him, and yet you know that it is impossible, even by the most generous expansion of understanding, to accept him as a human being. He is the strong man without strength—strong only among the weak—the weakling who uses force on the weaker.*

BLICK *enters casually, as if he were a customer, and immediately* HARRY *begins slowing down.*

BLICK (*Oily, and with mock-friendliness*): Hello, Nick.

NICK (*Stopping his work and leaning across the bar*): What do you want to come here for? You're too big a man for a little honky-tonk.

BLICK (*Flattered*): Now, Nick.

NICK: Important people never come here. *Here.* Have a drink. (*Whiskey bottle*)

BLICK: Thanks, I don't drink.

NICK (*Drinking the drink himself*): Well, why don't you?

BLICK: I have responsibilities.

NICK: You're head of the lousy Vice Squad. There's no vice here.

BLICK (*Sharply*): Street-walkers are working out of this place.

NICK (*Angry*): What do you want?

BLICK (*Loudly*): I just want you to know that it's got to stop.

The music stops. The mechanical toy runs down.

There is absolute silence, and a strange fearfulness and disharmony in the atmosphere now. HARRY *doesn't know what to do with his hands or feet.* WESLEY's *arms hang at his sides.* JOE *quietly pushes the toy to one side of the table eager to study what is happening.* WILLIE *stops playing the marble-game, turns around and begins to wait.* DUDLEY *straightens up very, very vigorously, as if to say: "Nothing can scare me. I know love is the only thing." The* ARAB *is the same as ever, but watchful.* NICK *is arrogantly aloof. There is a moment of this silence and tension, as though* BLICK *were waiting for everybody to acknowledge his presence. He is obviously flattered by the acknowledgment of Harry, Dudley, Wesley, and Willie, but a little irritated by Nick's aloofness and unfriendliness.*

NICK: Don't look at me. I can't tell a street-walker from a lady. You married?

BLICK: You're not asking *me* questions. *I'm* telling *you.*

NICK (*Interrupting*): You're a man of about forty-five or so. You *ought* to know better.

BLICK (*Angry*): Street-walkers are working out of this place.

NICK (*Beginning to shout*): Now, don't start any trouble with me. People come here to drink and loaf around. I don't care who they are.

BLICK: Well, I do.

NICK: The only way to find out if a lady is a street-walker is to walk the streets with her, go to bed, and make sure. You wouldn't want to do that. You'd *like* to, of course.

BLICK: Any more of it, and I'll have your joint closed.

NICK (*Very casually, without ill-will*): Listen. I've got no use for you, or anybody like you. You're out to change the world from something bad to something worse. Something like yourself.

BLICK (*Furious pause, and contempt*): I'll be back tonight.

He begins to go.

NICK (*Very angry but very calm*): Do yourself a big favor and don't come back tonight. Send somebody else. I don't like your personality.

BLICK (*Casually, but with contempt*): Don't break any laws. I don't like yours, either.

He looks the place over, and goes.

There is a moment of silence. Then WILLIE *turns and puts a new nickel in the slot and starts a new game.* WESLEY *turns to the piano and rather falteringly begins to play. His heart really isn't in it.* HARRY *walks about, unable to dance.* DUDLEY *lapses into his customary melancholy, at a table.* NICK *whistles a little: suddenly stops.* JOE *winds the toy.*

JOE (*Comically*): Nick. You going to kill that man?

NICK: I'm disgusted.

JOE: Yeah? Why?

NICK: Why should I get worked up over a guy like that? Why should I hate *him?* He's nothing. He's nobody. He's a mouse. But every time he comes into this place I get burned up. He doesn't want to drink. He doesn't want to sit down. He doesn't want to take things easy. Tell me one thing?

JOE: Do my best.

NICK: What's a punk like *that* want to go out and try to change the world for?

JOE (*Amazed*): Does *he* want to change the world, too?

NICK (*Irritated*): You know what I mean. What's he want to bother people for? He's *sick.*

JOE (*Almost to himself, reflecting on the fact that Blick too wants to change the world*): I guess he wants to change the world at that.

NICK: So I go to work and hate him.

JOE: It's not him, Nick. It's everything.

NICK: Yeah, *I know.* But I've still got no use for him. He's no good. You know what I mean? He hurts little people. (*Confused*) One of the girls tried to commit suicide on account of him. (*Furiously*) I'll break his head if he hurts anybody around here. This is *my* joint. (*Afterthought*) Or anybody's *feelings,* either.

JOE: He may not be so bad, deep down underneath.

NICK: I know all about him. He's no good.

During this talk WESLEY *has really begun to play the piano, the toy is rattling again, and little by little* HARRY *has begun to dance.* NICK *has come around the bar, and now, very much like a child —forgetting all his anger—is watching the toy work.*

He begins to smile at everything: turns and listens to WESLEY: *watches* HARRY: *nods at the* ARAB: *shakes his head at* DUDLEY: *and gestures amiably about* WILLIE. *It's his joint all right.*

It's a good, low-down, honky-tonk American place that lets people alone.

NICK: I've got a good joint. There's nothing wrong here. Hey. Comedian. Stick to the dancing tonight. I think you're O.K. Wesley? Do some more of that tonight. That's fine!

HARRY: Thanks, Nick. Gosh, I'm on my way at last. (*On telephone*) Hello, Ma? Is that you, Ma? Harry. I got the job.

He hangs up and walks around, smiling.

NICK (*Watching the toy all this time*): Say, that really is something. What is that, anyway?

MARY L. *comes in.*

JOE (*Holding it toward* NICK, *and* MARY L.): Nick, this is a toy. A contraption devised by the cunning of man to drive boredom, or grief, or anger out of children. A noble gadget. A gadget, I might say, infinitely nobler than any other I can think of at the moment.

Everybody gathers around Joe's table to look at the toy. The toy stops working. JOE *winds the music box. Lifts a whistle: blows it, making a very strange, funny and sorrowful sound.*

Delightful. Tragic, but delightful.

WESLEY *plays the music-box theme on the piano.*

MARY L. *takes a table.*

NICK: Joe. That girl, Kitty. What's she mean, calling me a dentist? I wouldn't hurt anybody, let alone a tooth.

NICK *goes to Mary L.'s table.* HARRY *imitates the toy. Dances. The piano music comes up, the light dims slowly, while the piano solo continues.*

CURTAIN

Act Two

An hour later. All the people who were at Nick's when the curtain came down are still there. JOE *at his table, quietly shuffling and turning a deck of cards, and at the same time watching the face of the woman, and looking at the initials on her handbag, as though they were the symbols of the lost glory of the world. The* WOMAN, *in turn, very casually regards* JOE *occasionally. Or rather senses him; has sensed him in fact the whole hour. She is mildly tight on beer, and* JOE *himself is tight, but as always completely under control; simply sharper. The others are about, at tables, and so on.*

JOE: Is it Madge—Laubowitz?

MARY: Is what *what?*

JOE: Is the name Mabel Lepescu?

MARY: What name?

JOE: The name the initials M. L. stand for. The initials on your bag.

MARY: No.

JOE (*After a long pause, thinking deeply what the name might be, turning a card, looking into the beautiful face of the woman*): Margie Longworthy?

MARY (*All this is very natural and sincere, no comedy on the part of the people involved: they are both solemn, being drunk*): No.

JOE (*His voice higher-pitched, as though he were growing a little alarmed*): Midge Laurie?

(MARY *shakes her head*)

My initials are J. T.

MARY (*Pause*): John?

JOE: No. (*Pause*) Martha Lancaster?

MARY: No. (*Slight pause*) Joseph?

JOE: Well, not exactly. That's my first name, but everybody calls me Joe. The last name is the tough one. I'll help you a little. I'm Irish. (*Pause*) Is it just plain Mary?

MARY: Yes, it is. I'm Irish, too. At least on my father's side. English on my mother's side.

JOE: I'm Irish on both sides. Mary's one of my favorite names. I guess that's why I didn't think of it. I met a girl in Mexico City named Mary once. She was an American from Philadelphia. She got married there. In Mexico City, I mean. While I was *there*. We were in love, too. At least *I* was. You never know about anyone else. They were engaged, you see, and her mother was with her, so they went through with it. Must have been six or seven years ago. She's probably got three or four children by this time.

MARY: Are you still in love with her?

JOE: Well—no. To tell you the truth, I'm not sure. I guess I am. I didn't even know she was engaged until a couple of days before they got married. I thought *I* was going to marry her. I kept thinking all the time about the kind of kids we would be likely to have. My favorite was the third one. The first two were fine. Handsome and fine and intelligent, but that third one was different. Dumb and goofy-looking. I liked *him* a lot. When she told me she was going to be married, I didn't feel so bad about the first two, it was that dumb one.

MARY (*After a pause of some few seconds*): What do you do?

JOE: Do? To tell you the truth, nothing.

MARY: Do you always drink a great deal?

JOE (*Scientifically*): Not *always*. Only when I'm awake. I sleep seven or eight hours every night, you know.

MARY: How nice. I mean to drink when you're awake.

JOE (*Thoughtfully*): It's a privilege.

MARY: Do you really *like* to drink?

JOE (*Positively*): As much as I like to *breathe*.

MARY (*Beautifully*): Why?

JOE (*Dramatically*): Why do I like to drink? (*Pause*) Because I don't like to be gypped. Because I don't like to be dead most of the time and just a little alive every once in a long while. (*Pause*) If I don't drink, I become fascinated by unimportant things—like everybody else. I get busy. Do things. All kinds of little stupid things, for all kinds of little stupid reasons. Proud, selfish, *ordinary* things. I've done them. Now I don't do anything. *I live all the time.* Then I go to sleep.

(*Pause*)

MARY: Do you sleep well?

JOE (*Taking it for granted*): Of course.

MARY (*Quietly, almost with tenderness*): What are your plans?

JOE (*Loudly, but also tenderly*): Plans? I haven't *got* any. I just get up.

MARY (*Beginning to understand everything*): Oh, yes. Yes, of course.

DUDLEY *puts a nickel in the phonograph.*

JOE (*Thoughtfully*): Why do I drink? (*Pause, while he thinks about it. The thinking appears to be profound and complex, and has the effect of giving his face a very comical and naive expression*) That question calls for a pretty complicated answer. (*He smiles abstractly*)

MARY: Oh, I didn't mean—

JOE (*Swiftly, gallantly*): No. No. I *insist.* I *know* why. It's just a matter of finding words. Little ones.

MARY: It really doesn't matter.

JOE (*Seriously*): Oh, yes, it does. (*Clinically*) Now, why do I drink? (*Scientifically*) No. Why does *anybody* drink? (*Working it out*) Every day has twenty-four hours.

MARY (*Sadly, but brightly*): Yes, that's true.

JOE: Twenty-four hours. Out of the twenty-four hours at *least* twenty-three and a half are—my God, I don't know why—dull, dead, boring, empty, and murderous. Minutes on the clock, *not time of living.* It doesn't make any difference who you are or what you do, twenty-three and a half hours of the twenty-four are spent *waiting.*

MARY: Waiting?

JOE (*Gesturing, loudly*): And the more you wait, the less there is to wait *for.*

MARY (*Attentively, beautifully his student*): Oh?

JOE (*Continuing*): That goes on for days and days, and weeks and months and years, and years, and the first thing you know *all* the years are dead. All the minutes are dead. You yourself are dead. There's nothing to wait for any more. Nothing except *minutes* on the *clock.* No time of life. Nothing but minutes, and idiocy. Beautiful, bright, intelligent idiocy. (*Pause*) Does that answer your question?

MARY (*Earnestly*): I'm afraid it does. Thank you. You shouldn't have gone to all the trouble.

JOE: No trouble at all. (*Pause*) You have children?

MARY: Yes. Two. A son and a daughter.

JOE (*Delighted*): How swell. Do they look like you?

MARY: Yes.

JOE: Then why are you sad?

MARY: I was always sad. It's just that after I was married I was allowed to drink.

JOE (*Eagerly*): Who are you waiting for?

MARY: No one.

JOE (*Smiling*): I'm not waiting for anybody, either.

MARY: My husband, of course.

JOE: Oh, sure.

MARY: He's a lawyer.

JOE (*Standing, leaning on the table*): He's a great guy. I like him. I'm very fond of him.

MARY (*Listening*): You have responsibilities?

JOE (*Loudly*): One, and *thousands*. As a matter of fact, I feel responsible to everybody. At least to everybody I meet. I've been trying for three years to find out if it's possible to live what I think is a civilized life. I mean a life that can't hurt any other life.

MARY: You're famous?

JOE: Very. Utterly unknown, but very famous. Would you like to dance?

MARY: All right.

JOE (*Loudly*): I'm *sorry*. I don't dance. I didn't think you'd like to.

MARY: To tell you the truth, I don't like to dance at all.

JOE (*Proudly. Commentator*): I can hardly walk.

MARY: You mean you're tight?

JOE (*Smiling*): No. I mean *all* the time.

MARY (*Looking at him closely*): Were you ever in Paris?

JOE: In 1929, and again in 1934.

MARY: What month of 1934?

JOE: Most of April, all of May, and a little of June.

MARY: I was there in November and December that year.

JOE: We were there almost at the same time. You were married?

MARY: Engaged.

(*They are silent a moment, looking at one another. Quietly and with great charm*)

Are you *really* in love with me?

JOE: Yes.

MARY: Is it the champagne?

JOE: Yes. Partly, at least. (*He sits down*)

MARY: If you don't see me again, will you be very unhappy?

JOE: Very.

MARY (*Getting up*): I'm so pleased.

> JOE *is deeply grieved that she is going. In fact, he is almost panic-stricken about it, getting up in a way that is full of furious sorrow and regret.*

I must go now. Please don't get up.

> JOE *is up, staring at her with amazement.*

Good-by.

JOE (*Simply*): Good-by.

> *The* WOMAN *stands looking at him for a moment, then turns and goes.* JOE *stands staring after her for a long time. Just as he is slowly sitting down again, the* NEWSBOY *enters, and goes to Joe's table.*

NEWSBOY: Paper, Mister?

JOE: How many you got this time?

NEWSBOY: Eleven.

> JOE *buys them all, looks at the lousy headlines, throws them away.*

> *The* NEWSBOY *looks at* JOE, *amazed. He walks over to* NICK *at the bar.*

NEWSBOY (*Troubled*): Hey, Mister, do you own this place?

NICK (*Casually but emphatically*): I own this place.

NEWSBOY: Can you use a great lyric tenor?

NICK (*Almost to himself*): Great lyric tenor? (*Loudly*) Who?

NEWSBOY (*Loud and the least bit angry*): Me. I'm getting too big to sell papers. I don't want to holler headlines all the time. I want to *sing*. You can use a great lyric tenor, can't you?

NICK: What's lyric about you?

NEWSBOY (*Voice high-pitched, confused*): My voice.

NICK: Oh. (*Slight pause, giving in*) All right, then—sing!

> *The* NEWSBOY *breaks into swift and beautiful song: "When Irish Eyes Are Smiling."* NICK *and* JOE *listen*

> *carefully:* NICK *with wonder,* JOE *with amazement and delight.*

NEWSBOY (*Singing*):
When Irish eyes are smiling,
Sure 'tis like a morn in Spring.
In the lilt of Irish laughter,
You can hear the angels sing.
When Irish hearts are happy,
All the world seems bright and gay.
But when Irish eyes are smiling—

NICK (*Loudly, swiftly*): Are you Irish?

NEWSBOY (*Speaking swiftly, loudly, a little impatient with the irrelevant question*): No. I'm Greek. (*He finishes the song, singing louder than ever*) Sure they steal your heart away.

> *He turns to* NICK *dramatically, like a vaudeville singer begging his audience for applause.* NICK *studies the boy eagerly.* JOE *gets to his feet and leans toward the* BOY *and* NICK.

NICK: Not bad. Let me hear you again about a year from now.

NEWSBOY (*Thrilled*): Honest?

NICK: Yeah. Along about November 7th, 1940.

NEWSBOY (*Happier than ever before in his life, running over to* JOE): Did you hear it too, Mister?

JOE: Yes, and it's great. What part of Greece?

NEWSBOY: Salonica. Gosh, Mister. Thanks.

JOE: Don't wait a year. Come back with some papers a little later. You're a great singer.

NEWSBOY (*Thrilled and excited*): Aw, thanks, Mister. So long. (*Running, to* NICK) Thanks, Mister.

> *He runs out.* JOE *and* NICK *look at the swinging doors.* JOE *sits down.* NICK *laughs.*

NICK: Joe, people are so wonderful. Look at that kid.

JOE: Of course they're wonderful. Every one of them is wonderful.

> MC CARTHY *and* KRUPP *come in, talking.*

> MC CARTHY *is a big man in work clothes, which make him seem very young. He is wearing black jeans, and a blue workman's shirt. No tie. No hat. He has broad shoulders, a lean intelligent face, thick*

*black hair. In his right back pocket is the longshore-
man's hook. His arms are long and hairy. His sleeves
are rolled up to just below his elbows. He is a casual
man, easy-going in movement, sharp in perception,
swift in appreciation of charm or innocence or comedy, and gentle in spirit. His speech is clear and full
of warmth. His voice is powerful, but modulated.
He enjoys the world, in spite of the mess it is, and
he is fond of people, in spite of the mess they are.*

KRUPP *is not quite as tall or broad-shouldered as*
MC CARTHY. *He is physically encumbered by his
uniform, club, pistol, belt, and cap. And he is
plainly not at home in the role of policeman. His
movement is stiff and unintentionally pompous. He
is a naive man, essentially good. His understanding
is less than McCarthy's, but he is honest and he
doesn't try to bluff.*

KRUPP: You don't understand what I mean. Hi-ya, Joe.

JOE: Hello, Krupp.

MC CARTHY: Hi-ya, Joe.

JOE: Hello, McCarthy.

KRUPP: Two beers, Nick. (*To* MC CARTHY) All I do is carry
out orders, carry out orders. I don't know what the idea
is behind the order. Who it's for, or who it's against, or
why. All I do is carry it out.

NICK *gives them beer.*

MC CARTHY: You don't read enough.

KRUPP: I do read. I read *The Examiner* every morning.
The Call-Bulletin every night.

MC CARTHY: And carry out orders. What are the orders
now?

KRUPP: To keep the peace down here on the waterfront.

MC CARTHY: Keep it for who? (*To* JOE) Right?

JOE (*Sorrowfully*): Right.

KRUPP: How do I know for who? The peace. Just keep it.

MC CARTHY: It's got to be kept for somebody. Who would
you suspect it's kept for?

KRUPP: For citizens!

MC CARTHY: I'm a citizen!

KRUPP: All right, I'm keeping it for you.

MC CARTHY: By hitting me over the head with a club? (*To*
JOE) Right?

JOE (*Melancholy, with remembrance*): I don't know.

KRUPP: Mac, you know I never hit you over the head with a club.

MC CARTHY: But you will if you're on duty at the time and happen to stand on the opposite side of myself, on duty.

KRUPP: We went to Mission High together. We were always good friends. The only time we ever fought was that time over Alma Haggerty. Did you marry Alma Haggerty? (*To* JOE) Right?

JOE: Everything's right.

MC CARTHY: No. Did you? (*To* JOE) Joe, are you with me or against me?

JOE: I'm with everybody. One at a time.

KRUPP: No. And that's just what I mean.

MC CARTHY: You mean neither one of us is going to marry the thing we're fighting for?

KRUPP: *I don't even know what it is.*

MC CARTHY: You don't read enough, I tell you.

KRUPP: Mac, you don't know what you're fighting for, either.

MC CARTHY: It's so simple, it's fantastic.

KRUPP: All right, what are you fighting for?

MC CARTHY: For the rights of the inferior. Right?

JOE: Something like that.

KRUPP: The who?

MC CARTHY: The inferior. The world full of Mahoneys who haven't got what it takes to make monkeys out of everybody else, near by. The men who were created equal. Remember?

KRUPP: Mac, you're not inferior.

MC CARTHY: I'm a longshoreman. And an idealist. I'm a man with too much brawn to be an intellectual, exclusively. I married a small, sensitive, cultured woman so that my kids would be sissies instead of suckers. A strong man with any sensibility has no choice in this world but to be a heel, or a *worker*. I haven't the heart to be a heel, so I'm a worker. I've got a son in high school who's already thinking of being a writer.

KRUPP: I wanted to be a writer once.

JOE: Wonderful.

> He puts down the paper, looks at KRUPP and
> MC CARTHY.

MC CARTHY: They *all* wanted to be writers. Every maniac

in the world that ever brought about the murder of people through war started out in an attic or a basement writing poetry. It stank. So they got even by becoming important heels. And it's still going on.

KRUPP: Is it really, Joe?

JOE: Look at today's paper.

MC CARTHY: Right now on Telegraph Hill is some punk who is trying to be Shakespeare. Ten years from now he'll be a senator. Or a communist.

KRUPP: Somebody ought to do something about it.

MC CARTHY (*Mischievously, with laughter in his voice*): The thing to do is to have more magazines. Hundreds of them. *Thousands*. Print everything they write, so they'll believe they're immortal. That way keep them from going haywire.

KRUPP: Mac, you ought to be a writer yourself.

MC CARTHY: I hate the tribe. They're mischief-makers. Right?

JOE (*Swiftly*): Everything's right. Right and wrong.

KRUPP: Then why do you read?

MC CARTHY (*Laughing*): It's relaxing. It's soothing. (*Pause*) The lousiest people born into the world are writers. Language is all right. It's the people who use language that are lousy.

> The ARAB *has moved a little closer, and is listening carefully.*

(*To the* ARAB) What do you think, Brother?

ARAB (*After making many faces, thinking very deeply*): No foundation. All the way down the line. What. What-not. Nothing. I go walk and look at sky. (*He goes*)

KRUPP: What? What-not? (*To* JOE) What's that mean?

JOE (*Slowly, thinking, remembering*): What? What-not? That means this side, that side. Inhale, exhale. What: birth. What-not: death. The inevitable, the astounding, the magnificent seed of growth and decay in all things. Beginning, and end. That man, in his own way, is a prophet. He is one who, with the help of *beer*, is able to reach that state of deep understanding in which what and what-not, the reasonable and the unreasonable, are *one*.

MC CARTHY: Right.

KRUPP: If you can understand that kind of talk, how can you be a longshoreman?

MC CARTHY: I come from a long line of McCarthys who never married or slept with anything but the most powerful and quarrelsome flesh.

He drinks beer.

KRUPP: I could listen to you two guys for hours, but I'll be damned if I know what the hell you're talking about.

MC CARTHY: The consequence is that all the McCarthys are too great and too strong to be heroes. Only the weak and unsure perform the heroic. They've *got* to. The more heroes you have, the worse the history of the world becomes. Right?

JOE: Go outside and look at it.

KRUPP: You sure can philos—philosoph— Boy, you can talk.

MC CARTHY: I wouldn't talk this way to anyone but a man in uniform, and a man who couldn't understand a word of what I was saying. The party I'm speaking of, my friend, is *YOU*.

The phone rings.

HARRY gets up from his table suddenly and begins a new dance.

KRUPP (*Noticing him, with great authority*): Here. Here. What do you think you're doing?

HARRY (*Stopping*): I just got an idea for a new dance. I'm trying it out. Nick. Nick, the phone's ringing.

KRUPP (*To* MC CARTHY): Has he got a right to do that?

MC CARTHY: The living have danced from the beginning of time. I might even say, the dance and the life have moved along together, until now we have— (*To* HARRY) Go into your dance, son, and show us what we have.

HARRY: I haven't got it worked out *completely* yet, but it starts out like this.

He dances.

NICK (*On phone*): Nick's Pacific Street Restaurant, Saloon, and Entertainment Palace. Good afternoon. Nick speaking. (*Listens*) Who? (*Turns around*) Is there a Dudley Bostwick in the joint?

DUDLEY jumps to his feet and goes to phone.

DUDLEY (*On phone*): Hello. Elsie? (*Listens*) You're coming down? (*Elated. To the saloon*) She's coming down. (*Pause*) No. I won't drink. Aw, gosh, Elsie.

He hangs up, looks about him strangely, as if he were just born, walks around touching things, putting chairs in place, and so on.

MC CARTHY (*To* HARRY): Splendid. Splendid.

HARRY: Then I go into this little routine. (*He demonstrates*)

KRUPP: Is that good, Mac?

MC CARTHY: It's awful, but it's honest and ambitious, like everything else in this great country.

HARRY: Then I work along into this. (*He demonstrates*) And *this* is where I *really* get going. (*He finishes the dance*)

MC CARTHY: Excellent. A most satisfying demonstration of the present state of the American body and soul. Son, you're a genius.

HARRY (*Delighted, shaking hands with* MC CARTHY): I go on in front of an audience for the first time in my life tonight.

MC CARTHY: They'll be delighted. Where'd you learn to dance?

HARRY: Never took a lesson in my life. I'm a natural-born dancer. And *comedian*, too.

MC CARTHY (*Astounded*): You can make people *laugh?*

HARRY (*Dumbly*): I can be funny, but they won't laugh.

MC CARTHY: That's odd. Why not?

HARRY: I don't know. They just won't laugh.

MC CARTHY: Would you care to be funny now?

HARRY: I'd like to try out a new monologue I've been thinking about.

MC CARTHY: Please do. I promise you if it's funny I shall *roar* with laughter.

HARRY: This is it. (*Goes into the act, with much energy*) I'm up at Sharkey's on Turk Street. It's a quarter to nine, daylight saving. Wednesday, the eleventh. What I've got is a headache and a 1918 nickel. What I *want* is a cup of coffee. If I buy a cup of coffee with the nickel, I've got to walk home. I've got an eight-ball problem. George the Greek is shooting a game of snooker with Pedro the Filipino. *I'm in rags.* They're wearing thirty-five dollar suits, made to order. I haven't got a cigarette. They're smoking Bobby Burns panatelas. I'm thinking it over, like I always do. George the Greek is in a tough spot. If I buy a cup of coffee, I'll want another cup. What happens? My *ear* aches! My ear. George the Greek takes the cue. Chalks it.

Studies the table. Touches the cue-ball delicately. Tick. What happens? He makes the three-ball! What do I do? I get confused. *I go out and buy a morning paper.* What the hell do I want with a morning paper? What I *want* is a cup of coffee, and a good used car. I go out and buy a morning paper. Thursday, the twelfth. Maybe the headline's about *me.* I take a quick look. *No. The head-line is not about me.* It's about Hitler. Seven thousand miles away. I'm here. Who the hell is Hitler? Who's behind the eight-ball? I turn around. *Everybody's behind the eight-ball!*

> *Pause.* KRUPP *moves toward* HARRY *as if to make an important arrest.* HARRY *moves to the swinging doors.* MC CARTHY *stops* KRUPP.

MC CARTHY (*To* HARRY): It's the funniest thing I've ever heard. Or *seen,* for that matter.

HARRY (*Coming back to* MC CARTHY): Then, why don't you laugh?

MC CARTHY: I don't know, *yet.*

HARRY: I'm always getting funny ideas that nobody will laugh at.

MC CARTHY (*Thoughtfully*): It may be that you've stumbled headlong into a new kind of comedy.

HARRY: Well, what good is it if doesn't make anybody laugh?

MC CARTHY: There are *kinds* of laughter, son. I must say, in all truth, that I *am* laughing, although not *out loud.*

HARRY: I want to *hear* people laugh. *Out loud.* That's why I keep thinking of funny things to say.

MC CARTHY: Well. They may catch on in time. Let's go, Krupp. So long, Joe.

> MC CARTHY *and* KRUPP *go.*

JOE: So long. (*After a moment's pause*) Hey, Nick.

NICK: Yeah.

JOE: Bet McCarthy in the last race.

NICK: You're crazy. That horse is a double-crossing, no-good—

JOE: Bet everything you've got on McCarthy.

NICK: I'm not betting a nickel on him. *You* bet everything you've got on McCarthy.

JOE: I don't need money.

NICK: What makes you think McCarthy's going to win?

JOE: McCarthy's name's McCarthy, isn't it?

NICK: Yeah. So what?

JOE: The *horse* named McCarthy is going to win, *that's all.* Today.

NICK: Why?

JOE: You do what I tell you, and everything will be all right.

NICK: McCarthy likes to talk, that's all. (*Pause*) Where's Tom?

JOE: He'll be around. He'll be miserable, but he'll be around. Five or ten minutes more.

NICK: You don't believe that Kitty, do you? About being in burlesque?

JOE (*Very clearly*): I believe dreams sooner than statistics.

NICK (*Remembering*): She sure is somebody. Called me a dentist.

> TOM, *turning about, confused, troubled, comes in, and hurries to Joe's table.*

JOE: What's the matter?

TOM: Here's your five, Joe. I'm in trouble again.

JOE: If it's not organic, it'll cure itself. If it is organic, science will cure it. What is it, organic or non-organic?

TOM: Joe, I don't know— (*He seems to be completely broken-down*)

JOE: What's eating you? I want you to go on an errand for me.

TOM: It's Kitty.

JOE: What about her?

TOM: She's up in her room, crying.

JOE: Crying?

TOM: Yeah, she's been crying for over an hour. I been talking to her all this time, but she won't stop.

JOE: What's she crying about?

TOM: I don't know. I couldn't understand anything. She kept crying and telling me about a big house and collie dogs all around and flowers and one of her brother's dead and the other one lost somewhere. Joe, I can't stand Kitty crying.

JOE: You want to marry the girl?

TOM (*Nodding*): Yeah.

JOE (*Curious and sincere*): Why?

TOM: I don't know why, exactly, Joe. (*Pause*) Joe, I don't like to think of Kitty out in the streets. I guess I love her, that's all.

JOE: She's a nice girl.

TOM: She's like an angel. She's not like those other street-walkers.

JOE (*Swiftly*): Here. Take all this money and run next door to Frankie's and bet it on the nose of McCarthy.

TOM (*Swiftly*): All this money, Joe? McCarthy?

JOE: Yeah. Hurry.

TOM (*Going*): Ah, Joe. If McCarthy wins we'll be rich.

JOE: Get going, will you?

> TOM *runs out and nearly knocks over the* ARAB *coming back in.* NICK *fills him a beer without a word.*

ARAB: No foundation, anywhere. Whole world. No foundation. All the way down the line.

NICK (*Angry*): McCarthy! Just because you got a little lucky this morning, you have to go to work and throw away eighty bucks.

JOE: He wants to marry her.

NICK: Suppose she doesn't want to marry *him?*

JOE (*Amazed*): Oh, yeah. (*Thinking*) Now, why wouldn't she want to marry a nice guy like Tom?

NICK: She's been in burlesque. She's had flowers sent to her by European royalty. She's dined with young men of quality and social position. She's above Tom.

> TOM *comes running in.*

TOM (*Disgusted*): They were running when I got there. Frankie wouldn't take the bet. McCarthy didn't get a call till the stretch. I thought we were going to save all this money. Then McCarthy won by *two* lengths.

JOE: What'd he pay, fifteen to one?

TOM: Better, but Frankie wouldn't take the bet.

NICK (*Throwing a dish towel across the room*): Well, for the love of Mike.

JOE: Give me the money.

TOM (*Giving back the money*): We would have had about a thousand five hundred dollars.

JOE (*Bored, casually, inventing*): Go up to Schwabacher-Frey and get me the biggest Rand-McNally map of the nations of Europe they've got. On your way back stop at one of the pawn shops on Third Street, and buy me a good revolver and some cartridges.

TOM: She's up in her room crying, Joe.

JOE: Go get me those things.

NICK: What are you going to do, study the map, and then go out and shoot somebody?

JOE: I want to read the names of some European towns and rivers and valleys and mountains.

NICK: What do you want with the revolver?

JOE: I want to study it. I'm interested in things. Here's twenty dollars, Tom. Now go get them things.

TOM: A big map of Europe. And a revolver.

JOE: Get a good one. Tell the man you don't know anything about firearms and you're trusting him not to fool you. Don't pay more than ten dollars.

TOM: Joe, you got something on your mind. Don't go fool with a revolver.

JOE: Be sure it's a good one.

TOM: Joe.

JOE (*Irritated*): What, Tom?

TOM: Joe, what do you send me out for crazy things for all the time?

JOE (*Angry*): They're not crazy, Tom. Now, get going.

TOM: What about Kitty, Joe?

JOE: Let her cry. It'll do her good.

TOM: If she comes in here while I'm gone, talk to her, will you, Joe? Tell her about me.

JOE: O.K. Get going. Don't load that gun. Just buy it and bring it here.

TOM (*Going*): You won't catch me loading any gun.

JOE: Wait a minute. Take these toys away.

TOM: Where'll I take them?

JOE: Give them to some kid. (*Pause*) No. Take them up to Kitty. Toys stopped me from crying once. That's the reason I had you buy them. I wanted to see if I could find out *why* they stopped me from crying. I remember they seemed awfully stupid at the time.

TOM: Shall I, Joe? Take them up to Kitty? Do you think they'd stop *her* from crying?

JOE: They might. You get curious about the way they work and you forget whatever it is you're remembering that's making you cry. That's what they're for.

TOM: Yeah. Sure. The girl at the store asked me what I wanted with toys. I'll take them up to Kitty. (*Tragically*) She's like a little girl. (*He goes*)

WESLEY: Mr. Nick, can I play the piano again?

NICK: Sure. Practice all you like—until I tell you to stop.

WESLEY: You going to pay me for playing the piano?

NICK: Sure. I'll give you enough to get by on.

WESLEY (*Amazed and delighted*): Get money for playing the piano?

> *He goes to the piano and begins to play quietly.* HARRY *goes up on the little stage and listens to the music. After a while he begins a soft shoe dance.*

NICK: What were you crying about?

JOE: My mother.

NICK: What about her?

JOE: She was dead. I stopped crying when they gave me the toys.

> NICK'S MOTHER, *a little old woman of sixty or so, dressed plainly in black, her face shining, comes in briskly, chattering loudly in Italian, gesturing.* NICK *is delighted to see her.*

NICK'S MOTHER (*In Italian*): Everything all right, Nickie?

NICK (*In Italian*): Sure, Mamma.

> (NICK'S MOTHER *leaves as gaily and as noisily as she came, after half a minute of loud Italian family talk.*)

JOE: Who was that?

NICK (*To* JOE, *proudly and a little sadly*): My mother. (*Still looking at the swinging doors*)

JOE: What'd she say?

NICK: Nothing. Just wanted to see me. (*Pause*) What do you want with that gun?

JOE: I study things, Nick.

> *An old man who looks as if he might have been Kit Carson at one time walks in importantly, moves about, and finally stands at Joe's table.*

KIT CARSON: Murphy's the name. Just an old trapper. Mind if I sit down?

JOE: Be delighted. What'll you drink?

KIT CARSON (*Sitting down*): Beer. Same as I've been drinking. And thanks.

JOE (*To* NICK): Glass of beer, Nick.

> NICK *brings the beer to the table,* KIT CARSON *swallows it in one swig, wipes his big white mustache with the back of his right hand.*

KIT CARSON (*Moving in*): I don't suppose you ever fell in love with a midget weighing thirty-nine pounds?

JOE (*Studying the man*): Can't say I have, but have another beer.

KIT CARSON (*Intimately*): Thanks, thanks. Down in Gallup, twenty years ago. Fellow by the name of Rufus Jenkins came to town with six white horses and two black ones. Said he wanted a man to break the horses for him because his left leg was wood and he couldn't do it. Had a meeting at Parker's Mercantile Store and finally came to blows, me and Henry Walpal. Bashed his head with a brass cuspidor and ran away to Mexico, but he didn't die.

Couldn't speak a word. Took up with a cattle-breeder named Diego, educated in California. Spoke the language better than you and me. Said, Your job, Murph, is to feed them prize bulls. I said, Fine, what'll I feed them? He said, Hay, lettuce, salt, beer, and aspirin.

Came to blows two days later over an accordion he claimed I stole. I had *borrowed* it. During the fight I busted it over his head; ruined one of the finest accordions I ever saw. Grabbed a horse and rode back across the border. Texas. Got to talking with a fellow who looked honest. Turned out to be a Ranger who was looking for me.

JOE: Yeah. You were saying, a thirty-nine-pound midget.

KIT CARSON: Will I ever forget that lady? Will I ever get over that amazon of small proportions?

JOE: Will you?

KIT CARSON: If I live to be sixty.

JOE: Sixty? You look more than sixty now.

KIT CARSON: That's trouble showing in my face. Trouble and complications. I was fifty-eight three months ago.

JOE: That accounts for it, then. Go ahead, tell me more.

KIT CARSON: Told the Texas Ranger my name was Rothstein, mining engineer from Pennsylvania, looking for something worth while. Mentioned two places in Houston. Nearly lost an eye early one morning, going down the stairs. Ran into a six-footer with an iron-claw where his right hand was supposed to be. Said, You broke up my home. Told him I was a stranger in Houston. The girls gathered at the top of the stairs to see a fight. Seven of them. Six feet and an iron claw. That's bad on the nerves. Kicked him in the mouth when he swung for my head with the claw. Would have lost an eye except for quick thinking. He rolled into the gutter and pulled a gun. Fired seven times. I was back upstairs. Left the place an hour later, dressed in silk and feathers, with a hat swung around over my face. Saw him standing on the corner, waiting. Said, Care for a wiggle? Said he didn't. I went on down the street and left town. I don't suppose you ever had to put a dress on to save your skin, did you?

JOE: No, and I never fell in love with a midget weighing thirty-nine pounds. Have another beer?

KIT CARSON: Thanks. (*Swallows glass of beer*) Ever try to herd cattle on a bicycle?

JOE: No. I never got around to that.

KIT CARSON: Left Houston with sixty cents in my pocket, gift of a girl named Lucinda. Walked fourteen miles in fourteen hours. Big house with barb-wire all around, and big dogs. One thing I never could get around. Walked past the gate, anyway, from hunger and thirst. Dogs jumped up and came for me. Walked right into them, growing older every second. Went up to the door and knocked. Big negress opened the door, closed it quick. Said, On your way, white trash.

Knocked again. Said, On your way. Again. On your way. Again. This time the old man himself opened the door, ninety, if he was a day. Sawed-off shotgun, too.

Said, I ain't looking for trouble, Father. I'm hungry and thirsty, name's Cavanaugh.

Took me in and made mint juleps for the two of us.

Said, Living here alone, Father?

Said, Drink and ask no questions. Maybe I am and maybe I ain't. You saw the lady. Draw your own conclusions.

I'd heard of that, but didn't wink out of tact. If I told you that old Southern gentleman was my grandfather, you wouldn't believe me, would you?

JOE: I might.

KIT CARSON: Well, it so happens he wasn't. Would have been romantic if he had been, though.

JOE: Where did you herd cattle on a bicycle?

KIT CARSON: Toledo, Ohio, 1918.

JOE: Toledo, Ohio? They don't herd cattle in Toledo.

KIT CARSON: They don't anymore. They did in 1918. One fellow did, leastaways. Bookkeeper named Sam Gold. Straight from the East Side, New York. Sombrero, lariats, Bull Durham, two head of cattle and two bicycles. Called his place The Gold Bar Ranch, two acres, just outside the city limits.

That was the year of the War, you'll remember.

JOE: Yeah, I remember, but how about herding them two cows on a bicycle? How'd you do it?

KIT CARSON: Easiest thing in the world. Rode no hands. Had to, otherwise couldn't lasso the cows. Worked for Sam Gold till the cows ran away. Bicycles scared them. They went into Toledo. Never saw hide nor hair of them again. Advertised in every paper, but never got them back. Broke his heart. Sold both bikes and returned to New York.

Took four aces from a deck of red cards and walked to town. Poker. Fellow in the game named Chuck Collins, liked to gamble. Told him with a smile I didn't suppose he'd care to bet a hundred dollars I wouldn't hold four aces the next hand. Called it. My cards were red on the blank side. The other cards were blue. Plumb forgot all about it. Showed him four aces. Ace of spades, ace of clubs, ace of diamonds, ace of hearts. I'll remember them four cards if I live to be sixty. Would have been killed on the spot except for the hurricane that year.

JOE: Hurricane?

KIT CARSON: You haven't forgotten the Toledo hurricane of 1918, have you?

JOE: No. There was no hurricane in Toledo in 1918, or any other year.

KIT CARSON: For the love of God, then what do you suppose that commotion was? And how come I came to in Chicago, dream-walking down State Street?

JOE: I guess they scared you.

KIT CARSON: No, that wasn't it. You go back to the papers of November 1918, and I think you'll find there was a hurricane in Toledo. I remember sitting on the roof of a two-story house, floating northwest.

JOE (*Seriously*): Northwest?

KIT CARSON: Now, son, don't tell me you don't believe me, either?

JOE (*Pause. Very seriously, energetically and sharply*): Of course I believe you. Living is an art. It's not book-keeping. It takes a lot of rehearsing for a man to get to be himself.

KIT CARSON (*Thoughtfully, smiling, and amazed*): You're the first man I've ever met who believes me.

JOE (*Seriously*): Have another beer.

> TOM *comes in with the Rand-McNally book, the revolver, and the box of cartridges.* KIT *goes to bar.*

JOE (*To* TOM): Did you give her the toys?

TOM: Yeah, I gave them to her.

JOE: Did she stop crying?

TOM: No. She started crying harder than ever.

JOE: That's funny. I wonder why.

TOM: Joe, if I was a minute earlier, Frankie would have taken the bet and now we'd have about a thousand five hundred dollars. How much of it would you have given me, Joe?

JOE: If she'd marry you—*all* of it.

TOM: Would you, Joe?

JOE (*Opening packages, examining book first, and revolver next*): Sure. In this realm there's only one subject, and you're it. It's my duty to see that my subject is happy.

TOM: Joe, do you think we'll ever have eighty dollars for a race sometime again when there's a fifteen-to-one shot that we like, weather good, track fast, they get off to a good start, our horse doesn't get a call till the stretch, we think we're going to lose all that money, and then it wins, by a nose?

JOE: I didn't quite get that.

TOM: You know what I mean.

JOE: You mean the impossible. No, Tom, we won't. We were just a little late, that's all.

TOM: We might, Joe.

JOE: It's not likely.

TOM: Then how am I ever going to make enough money to marry her?

JOE: I don't know, Tom. Maybe you aren't.

TOM: Joe, I got to marry Kitty. (*Shaking his head*) You ought to see the crazy room she lives in.

JOE: What kind of a room is it?

TOM: It's little. It crowds you in. It's bad, Joe. Kitty don't belong in a place like that.

JOE: You want to take her away from there?

TOM: Yeah. I want her to live in a house where there's room enough to live. Kitty ought to have a garden, or something.

JOE: You want to take care of her?

TOM: Yeah, sure, Joe. I ought to take care of somebody good that makes me feel like *I'm* somebody.

JOE: That means you'll have to get a job. What can you do?

TOM: I finished high school, but I don't know what I can do.

JOE: Sometimes when you think about it, what do you think you'd like to do?

TOM: Just sit around like you, Joe, and have somebody run errands for me and drink champagne and take things easy and never be broke and never worry about money.

JOE: That's a noble ambition.

NICK (*To* JOE): How do you do it?

JOE: I really don't know, but I think you've got to have the full co-operation of the Good Lord.

NICK: I can't understand the way you talk.

TOM: Joe, shall I go back and see if I can get her to stop crying?

JOE: Give me a hand and I'll go with you.

TOM (*Amazed*): What! You're going to get up already?

JOE: She's crying, isn't she?

TOM: She's crying. Worse than ever now.

JOE: I thought the toys would stop her.

TOM: I've seen you sit in one place from four in the morning till two the next morning.

JOE: At my best, Tom, I don't travel by foot. That's all. Come on. Give me a hand. I'll find some way to stop her from crying.

TOM (*Helping* JOE): Joe, I never did tell you. You're a different kind of a guy.

JOE (*Swiftly, a little angry*): Don't be silly. I don't understand things. I'm trying to understand them.

> JOE *is a little drunk. They go out together. The lights go down slowly, while* WESLEY *plays the piano, and come up slowly on:*

Act Three

*A cheap bed in Nick's to indicate room 21 of The
New York Hotel, upstairs, around the corner from
Nick's. The bed can be at the center of Nick's, or
up on the little stage. Everything in Nick's is the
same, except that all the people are silent, im-
mobile and in darkness, except* WESLEY *who is playing the piano softly and sadly.* KITTY DUVAL, *in a
dress she has carried around with her from the early
days in Ohio, is seated on the bed, tying a ribbon in
her hair. She looks at herself in a hand mirror. She
is deeply grieved at the change she sees in herself.
She takes off the ribbon, angry and hurt. She lifts a
book from the bed and tries to read. She begins to
sob again. She picks up an old picture of herself
and looks at it. Sobs harder than ever, falling on the
bed and burying her face. There is a knock, as if at
the door.*

KITTY (*Sobbing*): Who is it?
TOM'S VOICE: Kitty, it's me. Tom. Me and Joe.

JOE, followed by TOM, *comes to the bed quietly.*
JOE *is holding a rather large toy carousel.* JOE
studies KITTY *a moment.*

*He sets the toy carousel on the floor, at the foot of
Kitty's bed.*

TOM (*Standing over* KITTY *and bending down close to her*):
Don't cry any more, Kitty.
KITTY (*Not looking, sobbing*): I don't like this life.

*JOE starts the carousel which makes a strange, sor-
rowful, tinkling music. The music begins slowly,
becomes swift, gradually slows down, and ends.*
JOE *himself is interested in the toy, watches and
listens to it carefully.*

TOM (*Eagerly*): Kitty. Joe got up from his chair at Nick's

just to get you a toy and come here. This one makes music. We rode all over town in a cab to get it. Listen.

> KITTY *sits up slowly, listening, while* TOM *watches her. Everything happens slowly and somberly.* KITTY *notices the photograph of herself when she was a little girl. Lifts it, and looks at it again.*

TOM (*Looking*): Who's that little girl, Kitty?

KITTY: That's me. When I was seven. (KITTY *hands the photo to* TOM)

TOM (*Looking, smiling*): Gee, you're pretty, Kitty.

> JOE *reaches up for the photograph, which* TOM *hands to him.* TOM *returns to* KITTY *whom he finds as pretty now as she was at seven.* JOE *studies the photograph.* KITTY *looks up at* TOM. *There is no doubt that they really love one another.* JOE *looks up at them.*

KITTY: Tom?

TOM (*Eagerly*): Yeah, Kitty.

KITTY: Tom, when you were a little boy what did you want to be?

TOM (*A little bewildered, but eager to please her*): What, Kitty?

KITTY: Do you remember when you were a little boy?

TOM (*Thoughtfully*): Yeah, I remember sometimes, Kitty.

KITTY: What did you want to be?

TOM (*Looks at* JOE. JOE *holds Tom's eyes a moment. Then* TOM *is able to speak*): Sometimes I wanted to be a locomotive engineer. Sometimes I wanted to be a policeman.

KITTY: I wanted to be a great actress. (*She looks up into Tom's face*) Tom, didn't you ever want to be a doctor?

TOM (*Looks at* JOE. JOE *holds Tom's eyes again, encouraging Tom by his serious expression to go on talking*): Yeah, now I remember. Sure, Kitty. I wanted to be a doctor—*once.*

KITTY (*Smiling sadly*): I'm so glad. Because I wanted to be an actress and have a young doctor come to the theater and see me and fall in love with me and send me flowers.

> (JOE *pantomimes to* TOM, *demanding that he go on talking*)

TOM: I would do that, Kitty.

KITTY: I wouldn't know who it was, and then one day I'd
see him in the street and fall in love with him. I wouldn't
know *he* was the one who was in love with me. I'd think
about him all the time. I'd dream about him. I'd dream
of being near him the rest of my life. I'd dream of having
children that looked like him. I wouldn't be an actress all
the time. Only until I found him and fell in love with
him. After that we'd take a train and go to beautiful cities
and see the wonderful people everywhere and give
money to the poor and whenever people were sick he'd
go to them and make them well again.

> TOM *looks at* JOE, *bewildered, confused, and full of
> sorrow.* KITTY *is deep in memory, almost in a trance.*

JOE (*Gently*): Talk to her, Tom. Be the wonderful young
doctor she dreamed about and never found. Go ahead.
Correct the errors of the world.
TOM: Joe. (*Pathetically*) I don't know what to say.

> There is rowdy singing in the hall. A loud young
> VOICE *sings: "Sailing, sailing, over the bounding
> main."*

VOICE: Kitty. Oh, Kitty!

> KITTY *stirs, shocked, coming out of the trance.*

Where the hell are you? Oh, Kitty.

> TOM *jumps up, furiously.*

WOMAN'S VOICE (*In the hall*): Who you looking for, Sailor
Boy?
VOICE: The most beautiful lay in the world.
WOMAN'S VOICE: Don't go any further.
VOICE (*With impersonal contempt*): You? No. Not you.
Kitty. You stink.
WOMAN'S VOICE (*Rasping, angry*): Don't you dare talk to
me that way. You pickpocket.
VOICE (*Still impersonal, but louder*): Oh, I see. Want to
get tough, hey? Close the door. Go hide.
WOMAN'S VOICE: You pickpocket. All of you.

> The door slams.

VOICE (*Roaring with laughter which is very sad*): Oh—
Kitty. Room 21. Where the hell is that room?
TOM (*To* JOE): Joe, I'll kill him.

KITTY (*Fully herself again, terribly frightened*): Who is it?

> *She looks long and steadily at* TOM *and* JOE. TOM *is standing, excited and angry.* JOE *is completely at ease, his expression full of pity.* KITTY *buries her face in the bed.*

JOE (*Gently*): Tom. Just take him away.

VOICE: Here it is. Number 21. Three naturals. Heaven. My blue heaven. The west, a nest, and you. Just Molly and me. (*Tragically*) Ah, to hell with everything.

> *A young* SAILOR, *a good-looking boy of no more than twenty or so, who is only drunk and lonely, comes to the bed, singing sadly.*

SAILOR: Hi-ya, Kitty. (*Pause*) Oh. Visitors. Sorry. A thousand apologies. (*To* KITTY) I'll come back later.

TOM (*Taking him by the shoulders, furiously*): If you do, I'll kill you.

> JOE *holds* TOM. TOM *pushes the frightened boy away.*

JOE (*Somberly*): Tom. You stay here with Kitty. I'm going down to Union Square to hire an automobile. I'll be back in a few minutes. We'll ride out to the ocean and watch the sun go down. Then we'll ride down the Great Highway to Half Moon Bay. We'll have supper down there, and you and Kitty can dance.

TOM (*Stupefied, unable to express his amazement and gratitude*): Joe, you mean you're going to go on an errand for *me?* You mean you're not going to send me?

JOE: That's right.

> *He gestures toward* KITTY, *indicating that* TOM *shall talk to her, protect the innocence in her which is in so much danger when* TOM *isn't near, which* TOM *loves so deeply.* JOE *leaves.* TOM *studies* KITTY, *his face becoming child-like and somber. He sets the carousel into motion, listens, watching* KITTY, *who lifts herself slowly, looking only at* TOM. TOM *lifts the turning carousel and moves it slowly toward* KITTY, *as though the toy were his heart. The piano music comes up loudly and the lights go down, while* HARRY *is heard dancing swiftly.*

BLACKOUT

Act Four

A little later

WESLEY, *the colored boy, is at the piano.*

HARRY *is on the little stage, dancing.*

NICK *is behind the bar.*

The ARAB *is in his place.*

KIT CARSON *is asleep on his folded arms.*

The DRUNKARD *comes in. Goes to the telephone for the nickel that might be in the return-chute.* NICK *comes to take him out. He gestures for* NICK *to hold on a minute. Then produces a half dollar.* NICK *goes behind the bar to serve the* DRUNKARD *whiskey.*

THE DRUNKARD: To the old, God bless them. (*Another*) To the new, God love them. (*Another*) To—children and small animals, like little dogs that don't bite. (*Another. Loudly*) To reforestation. (*Searches for money. Finds some*) To—President Taft.

He goes out

The telephone rings.

KIT CARSON (*Jumping up, fighting*): Come on, *all* of you, if you're looking for trouble. I never asked for quarter and I always gave it.

NICK (*Reproachfully*): Hey, Kit Carson.

DUDLEY (*On the phone*): Hello. Who? Nick? Yes. He's here. (*To* NICK) It's for you. I think it's important.

NICK (*Going to the phone*): Important! *What's* important?

DUDLEY: He sounded like big-shot.

NICK: Big *what*? (*To* WESLEY *and* HARRY): Hey, you. Quiet. I want to hear this important stuff.

WESLEY *stops playing the piano.* HARRY *stops dancing.* KIT CARSON *comes close to* NICK

KIT CARSON: If there's anything I can do, name it I'll do it for you. I'm fifty-eight years old; been through three wars; married four times; the father of countless children whose *names* I don't even know. I've got no money. I live from hand to mouth. But if there's anything I can do, name it. I'll do it.

NICK (*Patiently*): Listen, Pop. For a moment, please sit down and go back to sleep—*for me.*

KIT CARSON: I can do that, too.

> *He sits down, folds his arms, and puts his head into them. But not for long. As* NICK *begins to talk, he listens carefully, gets to his feet, and then begins to express in pantomime the moods of each of Nick's remarks.*

NICK (*On phone*): Yeah? (*Pause*) Who? Oh, I see. (*Listens*) Why don't you leave them alone? (*Listens*) The church-people? Well, to hell with the church-people. I'm a Catholic myself. (*Listens*) All right. I'll send them away. I'll tell them to lay low for a couple of days. Yeah, I know how it is.

> *Nick's daughter* ANNA *comes in shyly, looking at her father, and stands unnoticed by the piano.*

What? (*Very angry*) Listen. I don't like that Blick. He was here this morning, and I told him not to come back. I'll keep the girls out of here. You keep Blick out of here. (*Listens*) I know his brother-in-law is important, but I don't want him to come down here. He looks for trouble everywhere, and he always finds it. I don't break any laws. I've got a dive in the lousiest part of town. Five years nobody's been robbed, murdered, or gypped. I leave people alone. Your swanky joints uptown make trouble for you every night. (NICK *gestures to* WESLEY— *keeps listening on the phone—puts his hand over the mouthpiece. To* WESLEY *and* HARRY.) Start playing again. My ears have got a headache. Go into your dance, son. (WESLEY *begins to play again.* HARRY *begins to dance.* NICK, *into mouthpiece.*) Yeah. I'll keep them out. Just see that Blick doesn't come around and start something. (*Pause*) O.K. (*He hangs up*)

KIT CARSON: Trouble coming?

NICK: That lousy Vice Squad again. It's that gorilla Blick.

KIT CARSON: Anybody at all. You can count on me. What kind of a gorilla is this gorilla Blick?

NICK: Very dignified. Toenails on his fingers.

ANNA (*To* KIT CARSON, *with great, warm, beautiful pride, pointing at* NICK): That's my father.

KIT CARSON (*Leaping with amazement at the beautiful voice, the wondrous face, the magnificent event*): Well, bless your heart, child. Bless your lovely heart. I had a little daughter point me out in a crowd once.

NICK (*Surprised*): Anna. What the hell are you doing here? Get back home where you belong and help Grandma cook me some supper.

> ANNA *smiles at her father, understanding him, knowing that his words are words of love. She turns and goes, looking at him all the way out, as much as to say that she would cook for him the rest of her life.* NICK *stares at the swinging doors.* KIT CARSON *moves toward them, two or three steps.* ANNA *pushes open one of the doors and peeks in, to look at her father again. She waves to him. Turns and runs.* NICK *is very sad. He doesn't know what to do. He gets a glass and a bottle. Pours himself a drink. Swallows some. It isn't enough, so he pours more and swallows the whole drink.*

(*To himself*) My beautiful, beautiful baby. Anna, she is you again. (*He brings out a handkerchief, touches his eyes, and blows his nose.* KIT CARSON *moves close to* NICK, *watching Nick's face.* NICK *looks at him. Loudly, almost making* KIT *jump*) You're broke, aren't you?

KIT CARSON: Always. Always.

NICK: All right. Go into the kitchen and give Sam a hand. Eat some food and when you come back you can have a couple of beers.

KIT CARSON (*Studying* NICK): Anything at all. I know a good man when I see one. (*He goes*)

> ELSIE MANDELSPIEGEL *comes into Nick's. She is a beautiful, dark girl, with a sorrowful, wise, dreaming face, almost on the verge of tears, and full of pity. There is an aura of dream about her. She moves softly and gently, as if everything around her were unreal and pathetic.* DUDLEY *doesn't notice her for a moment or two. When he does finally see her, he is so amazed, he can barely move or speak. Her*

presence has the effect of changing him completely.
He gets up from his chair, as if in a trance, and
walks toward her, smiling sadly.

ELSIE (*Looking at him*): Hello, Dudley.

DUDLEY (*Broken-hearted*): Elsie.

ELSIE: I'm sorry. (*Explaining*) So many people are sick.
Last night a little boy died. I love you, but—

> *She gestures, trying to indicate how hopeless love is.*
> *They sit down.*

DUDLEY (*Staring at her, stunned and quieted*): Elsie.
You'll never know how glad I am to see you. Just to see
you. (*Pathetically*) I was afraid I'd never see you again.
It was driving me crazy. I didn't want to live. Honest.

> (*He shakes his head mournfully, with dumb and*
> *beautiful affection.* TWO STREETWALKERS *come in,*
> *and pause near* DUDLEY, *at the bar*)

I know. You told me before, but I can't help it, Elsie.
I love you.

ELSIE (*Quietly, somberly, gently, with great compassion*):
I know you love me, and I love you, but don't you see
love is impossible in this world?

DUDLEY: Maybe it isn't, Elsie.

ELSIE: Love is for birds. They have wings to fly away on
when it's time for flying. For tigers in the jungle because
they don't know their end. We know *our* end. Every
night I watch over poor, dying men. I hear them breathing, crying, talking in their sleep. Crying for air and
water and love, for mother and field and sunlight. We
can never know love or greatness. We *should* know both.

DUDLEY (*Deeply moved by her words*): Elsie, I love you.

ELSIE: You want to live. *I* want to live, too, but where?
Where can we escape our poor world?

DUDLEY: Elsie, we'll find a place.

ELSIE (*Smiling at him*): All right. We'll try again. We'll go
together to a room in a cheap hotel, and dream that the
world is beautiful, and that living is full of love and
greatness. But in the morning, can we forget debts, and
duties, and the cost of ridiculous things?

DUDLEY (*With blind faith*): Sure, we can, Elsie.

ELSIE: All right, Dudley. Of course. Come on. The time for

the new pathetic war has come. Let's hurry, before they dress you, stand you in line, hand you a gun, and have you kill and be killed.

> ELSIE *looks at him gently, and takes his hand.* DUD-LEY *embraces her shyly, as if he might hurt her. They go, as if they were a couple of young animals. There is a moment of silence. One of the* STREET-WALKERS *bursts out laughing.*

KILLER: Nick, what the hell kind of a joint are you running?

NICK: Well, it's not out of the world. It's on a street in a city, and people come and go. They bring whatever they've got with them and they say what they must say.

THE OTHER STREETWALKER: It's floozies like her that raise hell with our racket.

NICK (*Remembering*): Oh, yeah. Finnegan telephoned.

KILLER: That mouse in elephant's body?

THE OTHER STREETWALKER: What the hell does *he* want?

NICK: Spend your time at the movies for the next couple of days.

KILLER: They're all lousy. (*Mocking*) All about love.

NICK: Lousy or not lousy, for a couple of days the flat-foots are going to be romancing you, so stay out of here, and lay low.

KILLER: I always was a pushover for a man in uniform, with a badge, a club and a gun.

> KRUPP *comes into the place. The girls put down their drinks.*

NICK: O.K., get going.

> The GIRLS *begin to leave and meet* KRUPP.

THE OTHER STREETWALKER: We was just going.

KILLER: We was formerly models at Magnin's.

> *They go.*

KRUPP (*At the bar*): The strike isn't enough, so they've got to put us on the tails of the girls, too. I don't know. I wish to God I was back in the Sunset holding the hands of kids going home from school, where I belong. I don't like trouble. Give me a beer.

> NICK *gives him a beer. He drinks some.*

Right now, McCarthy, my best friend, is with sixty strikers who want to stop the finks who are going to try to unload the *Mary Luckenbach* tonight. Why the hell McCarthy ever became a longshoreman instead of a professor of some kind is something I'll never know.

NICK: Cowboys and Indians, cops and robbers, longshoremen and finks.

KRUPP: They're all guys who are trying to be happy; trying to make a living; support a family; bring up children; enjoy sleep. Go to a movie; take a drive on Sunday. They're all good guys, so out of nowhere, comes trouble. All they want is a chance to get out of debt and relax in front of a radio while Amos and Andy go through their act. What the hell do they always want to make trouble for? I been thinking everything over, Nick, and you know what I think?

NICK: No. What?

KRUPP: I think we're all crazy. It came to me while I was on my way to Pier 27. All of a sudden it hit me like a ton of bricks. A thing like that never happened to me before. Here we are in this wonderful world, full of all the wonderful things—here we are—all of us, and look at us. Just look at us. We're crazy. We're nuts. We've got everything, but we always feel lousy and dissatisfied just the same.

NICK: Of course we're crazy. Even so, we've got to go on living together. (*He waves at the people in his joint*)

KRUPP: There's no hope. I don't suppose it's right for an officer of the law to feel the way I feel, but, by God, right or not right, that's how I feel. Why are we all so lousy? This is a good world. It's wonderful to get up in the morning and go out for a little walk and smell the trees and see the streets and the kids going to school and the clouds in the sky. It's wonderful just to be able to move around and whistle a song if you feel like it, or maybe try to sing one. This is a nice world. So why do they make all the trouble?

NICK: I don't know. Why?

KRUPP: We're crazy, that's why. We're no good any more. All the corruption everywhere. The poor kids selling themselves. A couple of years ago they were in grammar school. Everybody trying to get a lot of money in a hurry. Everybody betting the horses. Nobody going quietly for a little walk to the ocean. Nobody taking things easy and not wanting to make some kind of a killing. Nick, I'm going to quit being a cop. Let somebody else keep law and order. The stuff I hear about at headquarters. I'm thirty-seven years old, and I still can't get used to it. The only trouble is, the wife'll raise hell.

NICK: Ah, the wife.

KRUPP: She's a wonderful woman, Nick. We've got two of the swellest boys in the world. Twelve and seven years old.

The ARAB *gets up and moves closer to listen.*

NICK: I didn't know that.

KRUPP: Sure. But what'll I do? I've wanted to quit for seven years. I wanted to quit the day they began putting me through the school. I didn't quit. What'll I do if I quit? Where's money going to be coming in from?

NICK: That's one of the reasons we're all crazy. We don't know where it's going to be coming in from, except from wherever it happens to be coming in from at the time, which we don't usually like.

KRUPP: Every once in a while I catch myself being mean, hating people just because they're down and out, broke and hungry, sick or drunk. And then when I'm with the stuffed shirts at headquarters, all of a sudden I'm nice to them, trying to make an impression. On who? People I don't like. And I feel disgusted. (*With finality*) I'm going to quit. That's all. Quit. Out. I'm going to give them back the uniform and the gadgets that go with it. I don't want any part of it. This is a good world. What do they want to make all the trouble for all the time?

ARAB (*Quietly, gently, with great understanding*): No foundation. All the way down the line.

KRUPP: What?

ARAB: No foundation. No foundation.

KRUPP: I'll say there's no foundation.

ARAB: All the way down the line.

KRUPP (*To* NICK): Is that all he ever says?

NICK: That's all he's been saying *this* week.

KRUPP: What is he, anyway?

NICK: He's an Arab, or something like that.

KRUPP: No, I mean what's he do for a living?

NICK (*To* ARAB): What do you do for a living, brother?

ARAB: Work. Work all my life. All my life, work. From small boy to old man, work. In old country, work. In new country, work. In New York. Pittsburgh. Detroit. Chicago. Imperial Valley. San Francisco. Work. No beg. Work. For what? Nothing. Three boys in old country. Twenty years, not see. Lost. Dead. Who knows? What. What-not. No foundation. All the way down the line.

KRUPP: What'd he say last week?

NICK: Didn't say anything. Played the harmonica.

ARAB: Old country song, I play.

He brings a harmonica from his back pocket.

KRUPP: Seems like a nice guy.

NICK: Nicest guy in the world.

KRUPP (*Bitterly*): But crazy. Just like all the rest of us. Stark raving mad.

> WESLEY *and* HARRY *long ago stopped playing and dancing. They sat at a table together and talked for a while; then began playing casino or rummy.*
>
> *When the* ARAB *begins his solo on the harmonica, they stop their game to listen.*

WESLEY: You hear that?

HARRY: That's *something.*

WESLEY: That's crying. That's crying.

HARRY: I want to make people laugh.

WESLEY: That's deep, deep crying. That's crying a long time ago. That's crying a thousand years ago. Some place five thousand miles away.

HARRY: Do you think you can play to that?

WESLEY: I want to *sing* to that, but I can't *sing.*

HARRY: You try and play to that. I'll try to dance.

> WESLEY *goes to the piano, and after closer listening, he begins to accompany the harmonica solo.* HARRY *goes to the little stage and after a few efforts begins to dance to the song. This keeps up quietly for some time.*
>
> KRUPP *and* NICK *have been silent, and deeply moved.*

KRUPP (*Softly*): Well, anyhow, Nick.

NICK: Hmmmmmmm?

KRUPP: What I said. Forget it.

NICK: Sure.

KRUPP: It gets me down once in a while.

NICK: No harm in talking.

KRUPP (*The* POLICEMAN *again, loudly*): Keep the girls out of here.

NICK (*Loud and friendly*): Take it easy.

The music and dancing are now at their height.

CURTAIN

Act Five

That evening. Fog-horns are heard throughout the scene. A man in evening clothes and a top hat, and his woman, also in evening clothes, are entering.

WILLIE is still at the marble game. NICK is behind the bar. JOE is at his table, looking at the book of maps of the countries of Europe. The box containing the revolver and the box containing the cartridges are on the table, beside his glass. He is at peace, his hat tilted back on his head, a calm expression on his face. TOM is leaning against the bar, dreaming of love and Kitty. The ARAB is gone. WESLEY and HARRY are gone. KIT CARSON is watching the boy at the marble game.

LADY: Oh, come on, please.

The gentleman follows miserably.

The SOCIETY MAN and WIFE take a table. NICK gives them a menu.

Outside, in the street, the Salvation Army people are playing a song. Big drum, tambourines, cornet and singing. They are singing "The Blood of the Lamb." The music and words come into the place faintly and comically. This is followed by an old sinner testifying. It is the DRUNKARD. His words are not intelligible, but his message is unmistakable. He is saved. He wants to sin no more. And so on.

DRUNKARD (*Testifying, unmistakably drunk*): Brothers and sisters. I was a sinner. I chewed tobacco and chased women. Oh, I sinned, brothers and sisters. And then I was saved. Saved by the Salvation Army, God forgive me.

JOE: Let's see now. Here's a city. Pribor. Czecho-slovakia. Little, lovely, lonely Czecho-slovakia. I wonder what

kind of a place Pribor was? (*Calling*) Pribor! *Pribor!*
(TOM *leaps*)

LADY: What's the matter with him?

MAN (*Crossing his legs, as if he ought to go to the men's
room*): Drunk.

TOM: Who you calling, Joe?

JOE: Pribor.

TOM: Who's Pribor?

JOE: He's a Czech. And a Slav. A Czecho-slovakian.

LADY: How interesting.

MAN (*Uncrosses legs*): He's drunk.

JOE: Tom, Pribor's a city in Czecho-slovakia.

TOM: Oh. (*Pause*) You sure were nice to her, Joe.

JOE: Kitty Duval? She's one of the finest people in the
world.

TOM: It sure was nice of you to hire an automobile and take
us for a drive along the ocean-front and down to Half
Moon Bay.

JOE: Those three hours were the most delightful, the most
somber, and the most beautiful I have ever known.

TOM: Why, Joe?

JOE: Why? I'm a student. (*Lifting his voice*) Tom.
(*Quietly*) I'm a student. I study all things. All. All. And
when my study reveals something of beauty in a place
or in a person where by all rights only ugliness or death
should be revealed, then I know how full of goodness
this life is. And that's a good thing to know. That's a
truth I shall always seek to verify.

LADY: Are you *sure* he's drunk?

MAN (*Crossing his legs*): He's either drunk, or just naturally crazy.

TOM: Joe?

JOE: Yeah.

TOM: You won't get sore or anything?

JOE (*Impatiently*): What is it, Tom?

TOM: Joe, where do you get all that money? You paid for
the automobile. You paid for supper and the two bottles
of champagne at the Half Moon Bay Restaurant. You
moved Kitty out of the New York Hotel around the
corner to the St. Francis Hotel on Powell Street. I saw
you pay her rent. I saw you give her money for new
clothes. Where do you get all that money, Joe? Three
years now and I've never asked.

JOE (*Looking at* TOM *sorrowfully, a little irritated, not so much with* TOM *as with the world and himself, his own superiority. He speaks clearly, slowly and solemnly*): Now don't be a fool, Tom. Listen carefully. If anybody's got any money—to hoard or to throw away—you can be sure he stole it from other people. Not from rich people who can spare it, but from poor people who can't. From their lives and from their dreams. I'm no exception. I *earned* the money I throw away. I stole it like everybody else does. I hurt people to get it. Loafing around this way, I *still* earn money. The money itself earns *more*. I *still* hurt people. I don't know who they are, or where they are. If I did, I'd feel worse than I do. I've got a Christian conscience in a world that's got no conscience at all. The world's trying to get some sort of a *social* conscience, but it's having a devil of a time trying to do *that*. I've got money. I'll always have money, as long as this world stays the way it is. I don't work. I don't make anything. (*He sips*) I drink. I worked when I was a kid. I worked *hard*. I mean hard, Tom. People are supposed to enjoy living. I got tired. (*He lifts the gun and looks at it while he talks*) I decided to get even on the world. Well, you can't enjoy living unless you work. Unless you do something. I don't do anything. I don't *want* to do anything any more. There isn't anything I can do that won't make me feel embarrassed. Because I can't do simple, good things. I haven't the patience. And I'm too smart. Money is the guiltiest thing in the world. It stinks. Now, don't ever bother me about it again.

TOM: I didn't mean to make you feel bad, Joe.

JOE (*Slowly*): Here. Take this gun out in the street and give it to some worthy hold-up man.

LADY: What's he saying?

MAN (*Uncrosses legs*): You wanted to visit a honky-tonk. Well, *this* is a honky-tonk. (*To the world*) Married twenty-eight years and she's still looking for adventure.

TOM: How should I know who's a hold-up man?

JOE: Take it away. Give it to somebody.

TOM (*Bewildered*): Do I *have* to *give* it to somebody?

JOE: Of course.

TOM: Can't I take it back and get some of our money?

JOE: Don't talk like a business man. Look around and find somebody who appears to be in need of a gun and give it to him. It's a good gun, isn't it?

TOM: The man said it was, but how can I tell who needs a gun?

JOE: Tom, you've seen good people who needed guns, haven't you?

TOM: I don't remember. Joe, I might give it to the wrong kind of guy. He might do something crazy.

JOE: All right. I'll find somebody myself. (TOM *rises*) Here's some money. Go get me this week's *Life, Liberty, Time,* and six or seven packages of chewing gum.

TOM (*Swiftly, in order to remember each item*): *Life, Liberty, Time,* and six or seven packages of chewing gum?

JOE: That's right.

TOM: All that chewing gum? What kind?

JOE: Any kind. Mix 'em up. All kinds.

TOM: Licorice, too?

JOE: Licorice, by all means.

TOM: Juicy Fruit?

JOE: Juicy Fruit.

TOM: Tutti-frutti?

JOE: Is there such a gum?

TOM: I think so.

JOE: All right. Tutti-Frutti, too. Get *all* the kinds. Get as many kinds as they're selling.

TOM: *Life, Liberty, Time,* and all the different kinds of gum. (*He begins to go*)

JOE (*Calling after him loudly*): Get some jelly beans too. All the different colors.

TOM: All right, Joe.

JOE: And the longest panatela cigar you can find. Six of them.

TOM: Panatela. I got it.

JOE: Give a news-kid a dollar.

TOM: O.K., Joe.

JOE: Give some old man a dollar.

JOE: O.K., Joe.

JOE: Give them Salvation Army people in the street a couple of dollars and ask them to sing that song that goes—(*He sings loudly*) Let the lower lights be burning, send a gleam across the wave.

TOM (*Swiftly*): Let the lower lights be burning, send a gleam across the wave.

JOE: That's it. (*He goes on with the song, very loudly and religiously*) Some poor, dying, struggling seaman, you may rescue, you may save. (*Halts*)

TOM: O.K., Joe. I got it. *Life, Liberty, Time,* all the kinds of gum they're selling, jelly beans, six panatela cigars, a dollar for a news-kid, a dollar for an old man, two dollars for the Salvation Army. (*Going*) Let the lower lights be burning, send a gleam across the wave.

JOE: That's it.

LADY: He's absolutely insane.

MAN (*Wearily crossing legs*): You asked me to take you to a honky-tonk, instead of to the Mark Hopkins. You're *here* in a honky-tonk. I can't help it if he's crazy. Do you want to go back to where people *aren't* crazy?

LADY: No, not just yet.

MAN: Well, all right then. Don't be telling me every minute that he's crazy.

LADY: You needn't be huffy about it.

> MAN *refuses to answer, uncrosses legs.*
>
> When JOE *began to sing,* KIT CARSON *turned away from the marble game and listened. While the man and woman are arguing he comes over to Joe's table.*

KIT CARSON: Presbyterian?

JOE: I attended a Presbyterian Sunday School.

KIT CARSON: Fond of singing?

JOE: On occasion. Have a drink?

KIT CARSON: Thanks.

JOE: Get a glass and sit down.

> KIT CARSON *gets a glass from* NICK, *returns to the table, sits down,* JOE *pours him a drink, they touch glasses just as the Salvation Army people begin to fulfill the request. They sip some champagne, and at the proper moment begin to sing the song together, sipping champagne, raising hell with the tune, swinging it, and so on. The* SOCIETY LADY *joins them, and is stopped by her* HUSBAND.

Always was fond of that song. Used to sing it at the top of my voice. Never saved a seaman in my life.

KIT CARSON (*Flirting with the* SOCIETY LADY *who loves it*): I saved a seaman once. Well, he wasn't exactly a seaman. He was a darky named Wellington. Heavy-set sort of a fellow. Nice personality, but no friends to speak of. Not until I came along, at any rate. In New Orleans. In the summer of the year 1899. No. Ninety-eight. I was a lot younger of course, and had no mustache, but was regarded by many people as a man of means.

JOE: Know anything about guns?

KIT CARSON (*Flirting*): All there is to know. Didn't fight the Ojibways for nothing. Up there in the Lake Takalooca Country, in Michigan. (*Remembering*) Along about in 1881 or two. Fought 'em right up to the shore of the Lake. Made 'em swim for Canada. One fellow in particular, an Indian named Harry Daisy.

JOE (*Opening the box containing the revolver*): What sort of a gun would you say this is? Any good?

KIT CARSON (*At sight of gun, leaping*): Yep. That looks like a pretty nice hunk of shooting iron. That's a six-shooter. Shot a man with a six-shooter once. Got him through the palm of his right hand. Lifted his arm to wave to a friend. Thought it was a bird. Fellow named, I believe, Carroway. Larrimore Carroway.

JOE: Know how to work one of these things?

> He offers KIT CARSON *the revolver, which is old and enormous.*

KIT CARSON (*Laughing at the absurd question*): Know how to work it? Hand me that little gun, son, and I'll show you all about it.

> JOE hands KIT *the revolver.*

(*Importantly*) Let's see now. This is probably a new kind of six-shooter. After my time. Haven't nicked an Indian in years. I believe this here place is supposed to move out. (*He fools around and gets the barrel out for loading*) That's it. There it is.

JOE: Look all right?

KIT CARSON: It's a good gun. You've got a good gun there, son. I'll explain it to you. You see these holes? Well, that's where you put the cartridges.

JOE (*Taking some cartridges out of the box*): Here. Show me how it's done.

KIT CARSON (*A little impatiently*): Well, son, you take 'em one by one and put 'em in the holes, like this. There's one. Two. Three. Four. Five. Six. Then you get the barrel back in place. Then cock it. Then all you got to do is aim and fire.

He points the gun at the LADY *and* GENTLEMAN *who
scream and stand up, scaring* KIT CARSON *into paralysis.*

The gun is loaded, but uncocked.

JOE: It's all set?

KIT CARSON: Ready to kill.

JOE: Let me hold it.

KIT *hands* JOE *the gun. The* LADY *and* GENTLEMAN
watch, in terror.

KIT CARSON: Careful, now, son. Don't cock it. Many a man's
lost an eye fooling with a loaded gun. Fellow I used to
know named Danny Donovan lost a nose. Ruined his
whole life. Hold it firm. Squeeze the trigger. Don't snap
it. Spoils your aim.

JOE: Thanks. Let's see if I can unload it. (*He begins to
unload it*)

KIT CARSON: Of course you can.

JOE *unloads the revolver, looks at it very closely,
puts the cartridges back into the box.*

JOE (*Looking at gun*): I'm mighty grateful to you. Always
wanted to see one of those things close up. Is it really a
good one?

KIT CARSON: It's a beaut, son.

JOE (*Aims the empty gun at a bottle on the bar*): Bang!

WILLIE (*At the marble game, as the machine groans*): Oh,
Boy! (*Loudly, triumphantly*) There you are, Nick.
Thought I couldn't do it, hey? *Now*, watch.

*The machine begins to make a special kind of noise.
Lights go on and off. Some red, some green. A bell
rings loudly six times.*

One. Two. Three. Four. Five. Six.

An American flag jumps up. WILLIE *comes to attention. Salutes.*

Oh, boy, what a beautiful country.

A loud music-box version of the song "America."

JOE, KIT, *and the* LADY *get to their feet.*

(*Singing*) My country, 'tis of thee, sweet land of liberty,
of thee I sing.

Everything quiets down. The flag goes back into the machine. WILLIE *is thrilled, amazed, delighted.* EVERYBODY *has watched the performance of the defeated machine from wherever he happened to be when the performance began.*

WILLIE, *looking around at everybody, as if they had all been on the side of the machine.*

O.K. How's that? I knew I could do it. (*To* NICK) Six nickels.

NICK *hands him six nickels.* WILLIE *goes over to* JOE *and* KIT.

Took me a little while, but I finally did it. It's scientific, really. With a little skill a man can make a modest living beating the marble games. Not that that's what I want to do. I just don't like the idea of anything getting the best of me. A machine or anything else. Myself, I'm the kind of a guy who makes up his mind to do something, and then goes to work and does it. There's no other way a man can be a success at anything. (*Indicating the letter* "F" *on his sweater*) See that letter? That don't stand for some little-bitty high school somewhere. That stands for me. Faroughli. Willie Faroughli. I'm an Assyrian. We've got a civilization six or seven centuries old, I think. Somewhere along in there. Ever hear of Osman? Harold Osman? He's an Assyrian, too. He's got an orchestra down in Fresno. (*He goes to the* LADY *and* GENTLEMAN) I've never seen you before in my life, but I can tell from the clothes you wear and the company you keep (*Graciously indicating the* LADY) that you're a man who looks every problem straight in the eye, and then goes to work and *solves* it. I'm that way myself. Well. (*He smiles beautifully, takes the* GENTLEMAN's *hand furiously*) It's been wonderful talking to a nicer type of people for a change. Well. I'll be seeing you. So long. (*He turns, takes two steps, returns to the table. Very politely and seriously*) Good-by lady. You've got a good man there. Take good care of him.

WILLIE *goes, saluting* JOE *and the world.*

KIT CARSON (*To* JOE): By God, for a while there I didn't think that young Assyrian was going to do it. That fellow's got something.

TOM *comes back with the magazines and other stuff.*

JOE: Get it all?
TOM: Yeah. I had a little trouble finding the jelly beans.
JOE: Let's take a look at them.
TOM: These are the jelly beans.

> JOE *puts his hand into the cellophane bag and takes out a handful of the jelly beans, looks at them, smiles, and tosses a couple into his mouth.*

JOE: Same as ever. Have some. (*He offers the bag to* KIT)
KIT CARSON (*Flirting*): Thanks! I remember the first time I ever ate jelly beans. I was six, or at the most seven. Must have been in (*Slowly*) eighteen—seventy-seven. Seven or eight. Baltimore.
JOE: Have some, Tom.

> (TOM *takes some*)

TOM: Thanks, Joe.
JOE: Let's have some of that chewing gum.

> *He dumps all the packages of gum out of the bag onto the table.*

KIT CARSON (*Flirting*): Me and a boy named Clark. Quinton Clark. Became a Senator.
JOE: Yeah. Tutti-frutti, all right.

> *He opens a package and folds all five pieces into his mouth.*

Always wanted to see how many I could chew at one time. Tell you what, Tom. I'll bet I can chew more at one time than you can.
TOM (*Delighted*): All right.

> *They both begin to fold gum into their mouths.*

KIT CARSON: I'll referee. Now, one at a time. How many you got?
JOE: Six.
KIT CARSON: All right. Let Tom catch up with you.
JOE (*While* TOM's *catching up*): Did you give a dollar to a news-kid?
TOM: Yeah, sure.
JOE: What'd he say?
TOM: Thanks.

JOE: What sort of a kid was he?

TOM: Little, dark kid. I guess he's Italian.

JOE: Did he seem pleased?

TOM: Yeah.

JOE: That's good. Did you give a dollar to an old man?

TOM: Yeah.

JOE: Was he pleased?

TOM: Yeah.

JOE: Good. How many you got in your mouth?

TOM: Six.

JOE: All right. I got six, too.

(*Folds one more in his mouth.* TOM *folds one too*)

KIT CARSON: Seven. Seven each.

They each fold one more into their mouths, very solemnly, chewing them into the main hunk of gum.

Eight. Nine. Ten.

JOE (*Delighted*): Always wanted to do this.

He picks up one of the magazines.

Let's see what's going on in the world.

He turns the pages and keeps folding gum into his mouth and chewing.

KIT CARSON: Eleven. Twelve.

KIT *continues to count while* JOE *and* TOM *continue the contest. In spite of what they are doing, each is very serious.*

TOM: Joe, what'd you want to move Kitty into the St. Francis Hotel for?

JOE: She's a better woman than any of them tramp society dames that hang around that lobby.

TOM: Yeah, but do you think she'll feel at home up there?

JOE: Maybe not at first, but after a couple of days she'll be all right. A nice big room. A bed for sleeping in. Good clothes. Good food. She'll be all right, Tom.

TOM: I hope so. Don't you think she'll get lonely up there with nobody to talk to?

JOE (*Looking at* TOM *sharply, almost with admiration, pleased but severe*): There's nobody *anywhere* for *her* to talk to—except you.

TOM (*Amazed and delighted*): Me, Joe?

JOE (*While* TOM *and* KIT CARSON *listen carefully*, KIT *with great appreciation*): Yes, you. By the grace of God, you're the other half of that girl. Not the angry woman that swaggers into this waterfront dive and shouts because the world has kicked her around. *Anybody* can have *her*. You belong to the little kid in Ohio who once dreamed of living. Not with her carcass, for *money*, so she can have food and clothes, and pay rent. With *all* of her. I put her in that hotel, so she can have a chance to gather herself together again. She can't do that in the New York Hotel. You saw what happens there. There's nobody anywhere for her to talk to, except you. They all make her talk like a whore. After a while, she'll *believe* them. Then she won't be able to remember. She'll get lonely. Sure. People can get lonely for *misery*, even. I want her to go on being lonely for *you*, so she can come together again the way she was meant to be from the beginning. Loneliness is good for people. Right now it's the only thing for Kitty. Any more licorice?

TOM (*Dazed*): What? Licorice? (*Looking around busily*) I guess we've chewed all the licorice in. We still got Clove, Peppermint, Doublemint, Beechnut, Teaberry, and Juicy Fruit.

JOE: Licorice used to be my favorite. Don't worry about her, Tom, she'll be all right. You really want to marry her, don't you?

TOM (*Nodding*): Honest to God, Joe. (*Pathetically*) Only, I haven't got any money.

JOE: Couldn't you be a prize-fighter or something like that?

TOM: Naaaah. I couldn't hit a man if I wasn't sore at him. He'd have to do something that made me hate him.

JOE: You've got to figure out something to do that you won't mind doing very much.

TOM: I wish I could, Joe.

JOE (*Thinking deeply, suddenly*): Tom, would you be embarrassed driving a truck?

TOM (*Hit by a thunderbolt*): Joe, I never thought of that. I'd like that. Travel. Highways. Little towns. Coffee and hot cakes. Beautiful valleys and mountains and streams and trees and daybreak and sunset.

JOE: There *is* poetry in it, at that.

TOM: Joe, that's just the kind of work I *should* do. Just sit there and travel, and look, and smile, and bust out laughing. Could Kitty go with me, sometimes?

JOE: I don't know. Get me the phone book. Can you drive a truck?

TOM: Joe, you know I can drive a truck, or any kind of thing with a motor and wheels.

TOM *takes* JOE *the phone book.* JOE *turns the pages.*

JOE (*Looking*): Here! Here it is. Tuxedo 7900. Here's a nickel. Get me that number.

TOM *goes to telephone, dials the number.*

TOM: Hello.

JOE: Ask for Mr. Keith.

TOM (*Mouth and language full of gum*): I'd like to talk to Mr. Keith. (*Pause*) Mr. Keith.

JOE: Take that gum out of your mouth for a minute.

(TOM *removes the gum*)

TOM: Mr. Keith. Yeah. That's right. Hello, Mr. Keith?

JOE: Tell him to hold the line.

TOM: Hold the line, please.

JOE: Give me a hand, Tom.

TOM *helps* JOE *to the telephone.*

(*At phone, wad of gum in fingers delicately*) Keith? Joe. Yeah. Fine. Forget it. (*Pause*) Have you got a place for a good driver? (*Pause*) I don't think so. (*To* TOM) You haven't got a driver's license, have you?

TOM (*Worried*): No. But I can get one, Joe.

JOE (*At phone*): No, but he can get one easy enough. To hell with the union. He'll join later. All right, call him a Vice-President and say he drives for relaxation. Sure. What do you mean? Tonight? I don't know why not. San Diego? All right, let him start driving without a license. What the hell's the difference? Yeah. Sure. Look him over. Yeah. I'll send him right over. Right. (*He hangs up*) Thanks. (*To telephone*)

TOM: Am I going to get the job?

JOE: He wants to take a look at you.

TOM: Do I look all right, Joe?

JOE (*Looking at him carefully*): Hold up your head. Stick out your chest. How do you feel?

TOM *does these things.*

TOM: Fine.

JOE: You *look* fine, too.

> JOE *takes his wad of gum out of his mouth and wraps* Liberty *magazine around it.*

JOE: You win, Tom. Now, look. (*He bites off the tip of a very long panatela cigar, lights it, and hands one to* TOM, *and another to* KIT) Have yourselves a pleasant smoke. Here. (*He hands two more to* TOM) Give those slummers one each. (*He indicates the* SOCIETY LADY *and* GENTLEMAN)

> TOM *goes over and without a word gives a cigar each to the* MAN *and the* LADY.

> *The* MAN *is offended; he smells and tosses aside his cigar. The* WOMAN *looks at her cigar a moment, then puts the cigar in her mouth.*

MAN: What do you think you're doing?
LADY: Really, dear. I'd like to.
MAN: Oh, this is too much.
LADY: I'd *really*, really like to, dear.

> *She laughs, puts the cigar in her mouth. Turns to* KIT. *He spits out tip. She does the same.*

MAN (*Loudly*): The mother of five grown men, and she's still looking for *romance*. (*Shouts as* KIT *lights her cigar*) No. I forbid it.
JOE (*Shouting*): What's the matter with you? Why don't you leave her alone? What are you always pushing your women around for? (*Almost without a pause*) Now, look, Tom.

> *The* LADY *puts the lighted cigar in her mouth, and begins to smoke, feeling wonderful.*

Here's ten bucks.
TOM: Ten bucks?
JOE: He may want you to get into a truck and begin driving to San Diego tonight.
TOM: Joe, I got to tell Kitty.
JOE: I'll tell her.
TOM: Joe, take care of her.
JOE: She'll be all right. Stop worrying about her. She's at the St. Francis Hotel. Now, look. Take a cab to Townsend and Fourth. You'll see the big sign. Keith Motor Transport Company. He'll be waiting for you.

TOM: O.K., Joe. (*Trying hard*) Thanks, Joe.

JOE: Don't be silly. Get going.

> TOM *goes.*

> LADY *starts puffing on cigar.*

> As TOM *goes,* WESLEY *and* HARRY *come in together.*

NICK: Where the hell have you been? We've got to have some entertainment around here. Can't you see them fine people from uptown? (*He points at the* SOCIETY LADY *and* GENTLEMAN)

WESLEY: You said to come back at ten for the second show.

NICK: Did I say that?

WESLEY: Yes, sir, Mr. Nick, that's exactly what you said.

HARRY: Was the first show all right?

NICK: That wasn't a show. There was no one here to see it. How can it be a show when no one sees it? People are afraid to come down to the waterfront.

HARRY: Yeah. We were just down to Pier 27. One of the longshoremen and a cop had a fight and the cop hit him over the head with a blackjack. We saw it happen, didn't we?

WESLEY: Yes, sir, we was standing there looking when it happened.

NICK (*A little worried*): Anything else happen?

WESLEY: They was all talking.

HARRY: A man in a big car came up and said there was going to be a meeting right away and they hoped to satisfy everybody and stop the strike.

WESLEY: Right away. *Tonight.*

NICK: Well, it's about time. Them poor cops are liable to get nervous and—shoot somebody. (*To* HARRY, *suddenly*) Come back here. I want you to tend bar for a while. I'm going to take a walk over to the pier.

HARRY: Yes, sir.

NICK (*To the* SOCIETY LADY *and* GENTLEMAN): You society people made up your minds yet?

LADY: Have you champagne?

NICK (*Indicating* JOE): What do you think he's pouring out of that bottle, water or something?

LADY: Have you a chill bottle?

NICK: I've got a dozen of them chilled. He's been drinking champagne here all day and all night for a month now.

LADY: May we have a bottle?

NICK: It's six dollars.

LADY: I think we can manage.

MAN: I don't know. I *know* I don't know.

> NICK *takes off his coat and helps* HARRY *into it.*
> HARRY *takes a bottle of champagne and two glasses*
> *to the* LADY *and the* GENTLEMAN, *dancing, collects*
> *six dollars, and goes back behind the bar, dancing.*
> NICK *gets his coat and hat.*

NICK (*To* WESLEY): Rattle the keys a little, son. Rattle the keys.

WESLEY: Yes, sir, Mr. Nick.

> NICK *is on his way out. The* ARAB *enters.*

NICK: Hi-ya, *Mahmed.*

ARAB: No foundation.

NICK: All the way down the line. (*He goes*)

> WESLEY *is at the piano, playing quietly. The* ARAB
> *swallows a glass of beer, takes out his harmonica,*
> *and begins to play.* WESLEY *fits his playing to the*
> *Arab's.*
>
> KITTY DUVAL, *strangely beautiful, in new clothes,*
> *comes in. She walks shyly, as if she were embar-*
> *rassed by the fine clothes, as if she had no right to*
> *wear them. The* LADY *and* GENTLEMAN *are very im-*
> *pressed.* HARRY *looks at her with amazement.* JOE
> *is reading* Time *magazine.* KITTY *goes to his table.*
> JOE *looks up from the magazine, without the least*
> *amazement.*

JOE: Hello, Kitty.

KITTY: Hello, Joe.

JOE: It's nice seeing you again.

KITTY: I came in a cab.

JOE: You been crying again? (KITTY *can't answer. To*
HARRY) Bring a glass.

> HARRY *comes over with a glass.* JOE *pours* KITTY *a*
> *drink.*

KITTY: I've got to talk to you.

JOE: Have a drink.

KITTY: I've never been in burlesque. We were just poor.

JOE: Sit down, Kitty.

KITTY (*Sits down*): I tried other things.

JOE: Here's to you, Katerina Koranovsky. Here's to you. And Tom.

KITTY (*Sorrowfully*): Where *is* Tom?

JOE: He's getting a job tonight driving a truck. He'll be back in a couple of days.

KITTY (*Sadly*): I told him I'd marry him.

JOE: He wanted to see you and say good-by.

KITTY: He's too good for me. He's like a little boy. (*Wearily*) I'm— Too many things have happened to me.

JOE: Kitty Duval, you're one of the few truly innocent people I have ever known. He'll be back in a couple of days. Go back to the hotel and wait for him.

KITTY: That's what I mean. I can't stand being alone. I'm no good. I tried very hard. I don't know what it is. I miss— (*She gestures*)

JOE (*Gently*): Do you really want to come back here, Kitty?

KITTY: I don't know. I'm not sure. Everything *smells* different. I don't know how to feel, or what to think. (*Gesturing pathetically*) I know I don't belong there. It's what I've wanted all my life, but it's too *late*. I try to be happy about it, but all I can do is remember everything and cry.

JOE: I don't know what to tell you, Kitty. I didn't mean to hurt you.

KITTY: You haven't hurt me. You're the only person who's ever been good to me. I've never known anybody like you. I'm not sure about love any more, but I know I love you, and I know I love Tom.

JOE: I love you too, Kitty Duval.

KITTY: He'll want babies. I know he will. I know *I* will, too. Of course I will. I can't— (*She shakes her head*)

JOE: Tom's a baby himself. You'll be very happy together. He wants you to ride with him in the truck. Tom's good for you. You're good for Tom.

KITTY (*Like a child*): Do you want me to go back and wait for him?

JOE: I can't *tell* you what to do. I think it would be a good idea, though.

KITTY: I wish I could tell you how it makes me feel to be alone. It's almost worse.

JOE: It might take a whole week, Kitty. (*He looks at her sharply, at the arrival of an idea*) Didn't you speak of reading a book? A book of poems?

KITTY: I didn't know what I was saying.

JOE (*Trying to get up*): Of course you knew. I think you'll like poetry. Wait here a minute, Kitty. I'll go see if I can find some books.

KITTY: All right, Joe.

He walks out of the place, trying very hard not to wobble.

Fog-horn. Music. The NEWSBOY *comes in. Looks for* JOE. *Is broken-hearted because* JOE *is gone.*

NEWSBOY (*To* SOCIETY GENTLEMAN): Paper?

MAN (*Angry*): No.

The NEWSBOY *goes to the* ARAB.

NEWSBOY: Paper, Mister?

ARAB (*Irritated*): No foundation.

NEWSBOY: What?

ARAB (*Very angry*): No foundation.

The NEWSBOY *starts out, turns, looks at the* ARAB, *shakes head.*

NEWSBOY: No foundation? How do you figure?

BLICK *and* TWO COPS *enter.*

NEWSBOY (*To* BLICK): Paper, Mister?

(BLICK *pushes him aside. The* NEWSBOY *goes*)

BLICK (*Walking authoritatively about the place, to* HARRY): Where's Nick?

HARRY: He went for a walk.

BLICK: Who are you?

HARRY: Harry.

BLICK (*To the* ARAB *and* WESLEY): Hey, you. Shut up.

(*The* ARAB *stops playing the harmonica,* WESLEY *the piano*)

BLICK (*Studies* KITTY): What's your name, sister?

KITTY (*Looking at him*): Kitty Duval. What's it to you?

Kitty's voice is now like it was at the beginning of the play: tough, independent, bitter and hard.

BLICK (*Angry*): Don't give me any of your gutter lip. Just answer my questions.

KITTY: You go to hell, you.

BLICK (*Coming over, enraged*): Where do you live?

KITTY: The New York Hotel. Room 21.

BLICK: Where do you work?

KITTY: I'm not working just now. I'm looking for work.

BLICK: What kind of work?

(KITTY *can't answer*)

What kind of work?

(KITTY *can't answer*)

(*Furiously*) WHAT KIND OF WORK?

(KIT CARSON *comes over*)

KIT CARSON: You can't talk to a lady that way in *my* presence.

BLICK *turns and stares at* KIT. *The* COPS *begin to move from the bar.*

BLICK (*To the* COPS): It's all right, boys. I'll take care of this. (*To* KIT) What'd you say?

KIT CARSON: You got no right to hurt people. Who are *you?*

BLICK, *without a word, takes* KIT *to the street. Sounds of a blow and a groan.* BLICK *returns, breathing hard.*

BLICK (*To the* COPS): O.K., boys. You can go now. Take care of him. Put him on his feet and tell him to behave himself from now on. (*To* KITTY *again*) Now answer my question. What kind of work?

KITTY (*Quietly*): I'm a whore, you son of a bitch. You know what kind of work I do. And I know what kind you do.

MAN (*Shocked and really hurt*): Excuse me, officer, but it seems to me that your attitude—

BLICK: Shut up.

MAN (*Quietly*): —is making the poor child say things that are not true.

BLICK: Shut up, I said.

LADY: Well. (*To the* MAN) Are you going to stand for such insolence?

BLICK (*To* MAN, *who is standing*): Are you?

MAN (*Taking the* WOMAN's *arm*): I'll get a divorce. I'll start life all over again. (PUSHING *the* WOMAN) Come on. Get the hell out of here!

The MAN *hurries his* WOMAN *out of the place,* BLICK *watching them go.*

BLICK (*To* KITTY): Now. Let's begin again, and see that you tell the truth. What's your name?

KITTY: Kitty Duval.

BLICK: Where do you live?

KITTY: Until this evening I lived at the New York Hotel. Room 21. This evening I moved to the St. Francis Hotel.

BLICK: Oh. To the St. Francis Hotel. Nice place. Where do you work?

KITTY: I'm looking for work.

BLICK: What kind of work do you do?

KITTY: I'm an actress.

BLICK: I see. What movies have I seen you in?

KITTY: I've worked in burlesque.

BLICK: You're a liar.

> WESLEY *stands, worried and full of dumb resentment.*

KITTY (*Pathetically, as at the beginning of the play*): It's the truth.

BLICK: What are you doing here?

KITTY: I came to see if I could get a job here.

BLICK: Doing what?

KITTY: Singing—and—dancing.

BLICK: You can't sing or dance. What are you lying for?

KITTY: I can. I sang and danced in burlesque all over the country.

BLICK: You're a liar.

KITTY: I said lines, too.

BLICK: So you danced in burlesque?

KITTY: Yes.

BLICK: All right. Let's see what you did.

KITTY: I can't. There's no music, and I haven't got the right clothes.

BLICK: There's music. (*To* WESLEY) Put a nickel in that phonograph.

> (WESLEY *can't move*)

Come on. Put a nickel in that phonograph.

> (WESLEY *does so. To* KITTY)

All right. Get up on that stage and do a hot little burlesque number.

> KITTY *stands. Walks slowly to the stage, but is unable to move.* JOE *comes in, holding three books.*

Get going, now. Let's see you dance the way you did in burlesque, all over the country.

> KITTY *tries to do a burlesque dance. It is beautiful in a tragic way.*

BLICK: All right, start taking them off!

> KITTY *removes her hat and starts to remove her jacket.* JOE *moves closer to the stage, amazed.*

JOE (*Hurrying to* KITTY): Get down from there. (*He takes* KITTY *into his arms. She is crying*) (*To* BLICK) What the hell do you think you're doing!

WESLEY (*Like a little boy, very angry*): It's that man, Blick. He made her take off her clothes. He beat up the old man, too.

> BLICK *pushes* WESLEY *off, as* TOM *enters.* BLICK *begins beating up* WESLEY.

TOM: What's the matter, Joe? What's happened?

JOE: Is the truck out there?

TOM: Yeah, but what's happened? Kitty's crying again!

JOE: You driving to San Diego?

TOM: Yeah, Joe. But what's he doing to that poor colored boy?

JOE: Get going. Here's some money. Everything's O.K. (*To* KITTY) Dress in the truck. Take these books.

WESLEY'S VOICE: You can't hurt me. You'll get yours. You wait and see.

TOM: Joe, he's hurting that boy. I'll kill him!

JOE (*Pushing* TOM): Get out of here! Get married in San Diego. I'll see you when you get back.

> TOM *and* KITTY *go.* NICK *enters and stands at the lower end of bar.* JOE *takes the revolver out of his pocket. Looks at it.*

I've always wanted to kill somebody, but I never knew who it should be.

> *He cocks the revolver, stands real straight, holds it in front of him firmly and walks to the door. He stands a moment watching* BLICK, *aims very carefully, and pulls trigger. There is no shot.*

NICK *runs over and grabs the gun, and takes* JOE
aside.

NICK: What the hell do you think you're doing?

JOE (*Casually, but angry*): That dumb Tom. Buys a six-
shooter that won't even shoot once.

JOE *sits down, dead to the world.*

BLICK *comes out, panting for breath.*

NICK *looks at him. He speaks slowly.*

NICK: Blick! I told you to stay out of here! Now get out of
here. (*He takes* BLICK *by the collar, tightening his grip
as he speaks, and pushing him out*) If you come back
again, I'm going to take you in that room where you've
been beating up that colored boy, and I'm going to
murder you—slowly—with my hands. Beat it! (*He pushes*
BLICK *out*) (*To* HARRY) Go take care of the colored boy.

HARRY *runs out.*

WILLIE *returns and doesn't sense that anything is
changed.* WILLIE *puts another nickel into the machine, but he does so very violently. The consequence of this violence is that the flag comes up
again.* WILLIE, *amazed, stands at attention and salutes. The flag goes down. He shakes his head.*

WILLIE (*Thoughtfully*): As far as I'm concerned, this is
the *only* country in the world. If you ask me, *nuts to
Europe!* (*He is about to push the slide in again when
the flag comes up again. Furiously, to* NICK, *while he
salutes and stands at attention, pleadingly*) Hey, Nick.
This machine is out of order.

NICK (*Somberly*): Give it a whack on the side.

WILLIE *does so. A hell of a whack. The result is the
flag comes up and down, and* WILLIE *keeps saluting.*

WILLIE (*Saluting*): Hey, Nick. Something's wrong.

The machine quiets down abruptly. WILLIE *very
stealthily slides a new nickel in, and starts a new
game.*

*From a distance two pistol shots are heard, each
carefully timed.*

NICK *runs out.*

The NEWSBOY *enters, crosses to Joe's table, senses something is wrong.*

NEWSBOY (*Softly*): Paper, Mister?

JOE *can't hear him.*

The NEWSBOY *backs away, studies* JOE, *wishes he could cheer* JOE *up. Notices the phonograph, goes to it, and puts a coin in it, hoping music will make* JOE *happier.*

The NEWSBOY *sits down. Watches* JOE. *The music begins. "The Missouri Waltz."*

The DRUNKARD *comes in and walks around. Then sits down.* NICK *comes back.*

NICK (*Delighted*): Joe, Blick's dead! Somebody just shot him, and none of the cops are trying to find out who.

JOE *doesn't hear.* NICK *steps back, studying* JOE.

NICK (*Shouting*): Joe.
JOE (*Looking up*): What?
NICK: Blick's dead.
JOE: Blick? Dead? Good! That God damn gun wouldn't go off. I *told* Tom to get a good one.
NICK (*Picking up gun and looking at it*): Joe, you wanted to kill that guy!

(HARRY *returns.* JOE *puts the gun in his coat pocket*)

I'm going to buy you a bottle of champagne.

NICK *goes to bar.* JOE *rises, takes hat from rack, puts coat on. The* NEWSBOY *jumps up, helps* JOE *with coat.*

NICK: What's the matter, Joe?
JOE: Nothing. Nothing.
NICK: How about the champagne?
JOE: Thanks. (*Going*)
NICK: It's not eleven yet. Where you going, Joe?
JOE: I don't know. Nowhere.
NICK: Will I see you tomorrow?
JOE: I don't know. I don't think so.

KIT CARSON *enters, walks to* JOE. JOE *and* KIT *look at one another knowingly.*

JOE: Somebody just shot a man. How are you feeling?

KIT: Never felt better in my life. (*Loudly, bragging, but sombre*) I shot a man once. In San Francisco. Shot him two times. In 1939, I think it was. In October. Fellow named Blick or Glick or something like that. Couldn't stand the way he talked to ladies. Went up to my room and got my old pearl-handled revolver and waited for him on Pacific Street. Saw him walking, and let him have it, two times. Had to throw the beautiful revolver into the Bay.

> HARRY, NICK, *the* ARAB *and the* DRUNKARD *close in around him.*

> JOE *searches his pockets, brings out the revolver, puts it in Kit's hand, looks at him with great admiration and affection.* JOE *walks slowly to the stairs leading to the street, turns and waves.* KIT, *and then one by one everybody else, waves, and the marble game goes into its beautiful American routine again: flag, lights, and music. The play ends.*

CURTAIN

Love's Old Sweet Song

To Richard Watts, Jr.

OF ALL THE THINGS I LOVE

I love to see the sun come smiling to the world;
I love to hear the wind go singing through a field;
I love to hear a love-bird singing in a tree,
And I love to see a lovely face light up with love for me.

CHORUS

> *Of all the things I love,*
> *I love the most*
> *Sleeping in the shade of love.*
> *Sleeping in the shade of love,*
> *I love the most, my love.*
>
> *Of all the things I love to taste,*
> *Sweetest is the kiss of love.*
> *Dreaming in the shade of love,*
> *The kiss of love*
> *I love the most, my love.*
>
> *My love, of all the lovely things,*
> *Loveliest of all is you,*
> *Dreaming in the shade of love.*
> *Sleeping in the shade of love, my love,*
> *I love the most, my love.*

I love to breathe the scent of earth and new-mown hay;
I love to taste the peach and berry ripe in May;
I love to feel the spray as I walk beside the sea,
And I love to see a lovely face light up with love for me.

THE YEARS

The years, the years, they come and go,
And go and go, and oh, my heart!
The years have gone with my heart.

The days, the days still come and go,
And I still breathe,
But oh, my heart!
The years have gone with my heart.

The years, the days, the nights
Still come and go,
And I still dream,
But oh, my heart is gone,
My heart is gone with the years.

The hours, the hours, the long, dreaming hours
Still come and go,
And I still dream.
But the light is gone from my dream,
And the love is gone from my heart!

The two foregoing songs have been published by Chappell.
Music by Paul Bowles, words by William Saroyan.

Preface

"Love's Old Sweet Song," in addition to being a theatrical entertainment, intended primarily to delight the eye and ear and the heart and mind of the beholder, is *literally* a song. The singers of the song are the few people in the play selected from the many in the world, but any who see the play are likely to be the singers of the song also, inasmuch as the song is living itself. It is an old song, but the time is our time, the people are our people, and the environment is our environment. All the sources of the song are contemporary, but still the song is the oldest song in the world, as love is the most basic emotion of life. There could be no mortality without love, and no dimension to living without song. Love is an inevitable part of the bargain of the living in the inexplicable exchange of nothingness for mortality, and poetry is man's defense against being swindled in that bargain. Any man who is an alien to poetry, no matter who he is, *is* swindled in that bargain. Instinct demands love of all who live, and good living demands imagination and faith.

The line of the play is melodic, the same as the line of a song. It is a simple play, as the song is the simplest of music's various forms. While its theme is love, in a number of variations, the play is without love-sickness, no doubt simply because I do not feel things sickly. I find the tenderest or strongest emotions of a man inextricable from everything else that is a man's: understanding, a sense of proportion, love of comedy, and intelligence. The arrival of a fresh emotion, or a fresh dimension of an old emotion, or a magnification of a constant emotion, does not, as I remember things, nullify all other emotions or qualities a man possesses. Characters in drama have been generally unrounded-out, most likely for the convenience of the dramatist, and for the security of the meaning of the play. It is difficult to have rounded-out characters in a play and to have a satisfying play at the same time, but at this stage of the game that appears to be something very essential to try for. The character of man is neither steady nor predictable. Even one whose life is limited by willfully accepted rules, such as a saint, is not free of variation in impulse, thought, or act. Man's greatness and man's insignificance are both the consequence of his being inevitably free. Nothing can limit man. And yet, with all his freedom, religion in men (and I mean primarily the inherent sense of rightness, grace, beauty, and so on) compels, usually, a noble exercise of freedom, so that murder, for instance, is always rarer than delight. The people in "Love's Old Sweet Song" are free people. The freedom they enjoy, and the freedom which carries them sometimes to disaster, is a freedom which art, with all its limits, has never been able to shift from the living to the dead. We can be grateful for this failure. Freedom is not essential: it is *inevitable*. It cannot be taken from the living without literally taking life from them. For this reason any idea, however noble or base, which depends for its strength or validity on the regimenting of life is an unsound idea, temporary, and scheduled for ultimate failure. As the limits in living are good taste, the limits in art cannot be anything more severe.

The play is simultaneously naive and sophisticated. I believe the living are simultaneously naive and sophisticated, because no matter how naive a man may be there is somewhere in him great sophistication, and no matter how sophisticated he may be there is great naïveté in him. In the nature of things I cannot understand anyone in the world as well or as fully as I understand myself, and I know this simultaneous reality of sophistication and naïveté exists in myself. It is true and inevitable. It is impossible for me not to be sophisticated. It is also impossible for me not to be naive. I cannot abandon one for the other merely to simplify things. I must therefore recognize the validity of both, and, in my own work at least, I must assume that naïveté and sophistication are simultaneous in everybody. Neither are *cultivated* in myself. Neither are unnatural. I must assume, therefore, that this condition is general.

The variations of love are great, but they are not really variations. Love is the one thing that is constant, even when the variation of it appears to be hate. In reality there is no such thing as hate. Hate is love kicked in the pants. It is love with a half-nelson on itself. The deepest and most general love is love of God, the defining of which I leave to you, as you please. Love of God includes regard of self. All the kinds of love, in fact, are regard of self. As long as

a man is alive, he is alive for himself. It is foolish to be
buffaloed by embarrassment into not accepting this truth.
In the nature of things a man cannot cease to be himself,
and therefore whatever he does, good or bad, he does for
himself. Doing good things is the ultimate selfishness, and
as love is the best of the better things, *it* is the ultimate
selfishness. I can see no reason why it shouldn't be. No
morality is worth anything that doesn't understand that all
behavior is selfish. Selfishness is correct by all standards.

The necessity to defend my work again and again is em-
barrassing to me, and yet I have no alternative. To ignore
criticism, as many writers do, I regard as an evasion of my
responsibility to my work. In fairness to my critics, I acknowledge the *partial* truth and validity of every charge
brought against my work, against myself personally, and
against my methods of making my work public. What is
lacking in their criticism is the fullness and humanity of
understanding which operates in myself, in my work, and
in my regard for others. The essence of my work is honor,
honesty, intelligence, grace, good humor, naturalness, and
spontaneity, and these things do not appear to be nicely
balanced in my critics. Consequently, it is difficult for them
to make sense in themselves of that which is complicated
and unusual for them. What should delight them because
of its honesty, shocks them. What should enlarge them because of its understanding, drives them more completely
behind the fort of their own limitations.

I will take up each of the commonest charges the critics
have made against myself and my work. In a sense the
charge of exhibitionism is a valid one. No creative activity
could possibly deny the validity of exhibitionism, and it is
a mistake to regard exhibitionism as something improper.
The implication that it *is* something improper, and something characteristic only of *my* work, is that which I object
to. The creative impulse itself is exhibitionistic. The fulfilling of the impulse is even more so. And the placing of that
which has been created before others is still more so. If you
want no exhibitionism (if that is what you choose to call
it), you want no creation. After the creation of my work, it
is true that I have been more energetic than many others
in my attack upon the problem of making my work as
public as possible. This has been necessary because my
work has been unfamiliar, and because making it public *has*
been a problem. If I did not believe in my work I would

not bring it about in the first place. Since I do believe in it, I must do whatever I am able to do to make it known to as many people as possible. It is probably my enjoyment of living and working, however, which is offensive to so many, and which they put down as exhibitionism. As I understand things, acceptance of our life is the first law of living, and enjoyment of it (and I know all about its unenjoyables) is the first necessity of artful and gracious living.

To the charge of mindlessness, it would be unkind of me to ask where is the mindfulness in the work of other men, not only of our time but of other times? Where is the mindfulness of Shakespeare, if need be? By mindlessness I believe the critics mean absence of *specific* instruction to society or the state on how to behave, and *presence* of immediate living. In the play form, among other things, there must be play. It is impossible to exclude thought or belief or faith from a play, but these things are in a play after living is in it, and they are in a play as tone, not as things by themselves. Since the theater is not an adult continuation school, those who come to the theater must be entertained before they are instructed. The difference between my thinking, it would appear, and the thinking of others is that mine operates from beginnings long ago and not from headlines and news in today's paper. What appears to the glib and superficial mind or sensibility as mindlessness is, in reality, a depth and fullness so far removed from cheap thinking that it bewilders. The critic with political bias, for instance, cannot accept my thought simply because it puts him out of work.

No ambition for the living, for the individual, for the weak and stupid and the strong and wise, is loftier than mine. No affection for the ugly and base and the beautiful and noble in man is more generous than mine. No scorn for the cruel, the miserable, the wretched, the cowardly, the insane—wherever they may occur, in the good or in the bad —is greater than my scorn. No faith in grace is steadier or more encouraging than mine. Therefore, I must take it, my work is mindless. The truth is, I am not unbalanced.

It is charged, further, that my work is formless. The form of my work is simply unfamiliar. It has very definite form. The compulsion within myself for wholeness, for balance, and for grace is so great that form is the first demand I make of my work and the first demand my work makes of me. It is probable that the critics cannot see the form for the fullness. If there were nothing in the form they would see the form, but since the form is full, they cannot see it.

It is charged further that I am crazy, an ego-maniac, a charlatan, that I will write anything to celebrate my name, that I am an enemy of the people, especially the working-class, that my intention is merely to make money and rise in the world, that I have bad taste or no taste at all, and a good many other things. These charges come from men too dull, too vulgar and too inferior for me to bother with.

WILLIAM SAROYAN

San Francisco, December 1940

Note

"Love's Old Sweet Song," like "The Time of Your Life," was produced by Eddie Dowling in conjunction with The Theatre Guild, and directed by Mr. Dowling and myself. It was first performed in Princeton, New Jersey, at the McCarter Theatre, Saturday evening, April 6, 1940. This was followed by two weeks at the Forrest Theatre in Philadelphia, beginning Monday, April 8. The play next went to Ford's Theatre in Baltimore for one week. It opened in New York at The Plymouth Theatre on West 45th Street, Thursday evening, May 2, and closed Saturday evening, June 8th, after a run of 44 New York performances.

This is the cast which opened the play in New York:

Ann Hamilton	JESSIE ROYCE LANDIS
Georgie Americanos	PETER FERNANDEZ
Barnaby Gaul	WALTER HUSTON
Tom Fiora	JAMES S. ELLIOTT
Demetrios	ANGI O. POULOS
Cabot Yearling	ARTHUR HUNNICUTT
Leona Yearling	DORO MERANDE
Newton Yearling	EUGENE FITTS
Velma Yearling	BARBARA HASTINGS
Selma Yearling	ARDELE HASTINGS
Al Yearling	THOMAS JORDAN
Henry Yearling	ERIC ROBERTS
Jesse Yearling	JACKIE AYERS
Lucy Yearling	PATSY O'SHEA
Ella Yearling	MAE GRIMES
Susan Yearling	PATRICIA ROE
Maude Yearling	CAROL ESA
Lemmie Yearling	BOB WHITE
Mae Yearling	ELEANOR DREXLER
Harry Yearling	MICHAEL ARTIST
Wilbur Yearling	GERALD MATTHEWS
Richard Oliver	LLOYD GOUGH
Elsa Wax	BEATRICE NEWPORT
David F. Windmore	ALAN HEWITT

Daniel Hough	JOHN A. REGAN
Mr. Smith	NICK DENNIS
Mr. Harris	GEORGE TRAVELL
Pass Le Noir, Sheriff	HOWARD FREEMAN
Stylianos Americanos	ALAN REED
Pericles Americanos	JOHN ECONOMIDES

The out-of-town Sheriff was Pass Le Noir, whose performance I admired so much I have given his name to the part.

THE PEOPLE

ANN HAMILTON, *44, a beautiful unmarried small-town woman*
GEORGIE AMERICANOS, *a Postal Telegraph messenger*
BARNABY GAUL, *51, a pitchman*
TOM FIORA, *another messenger*
DEMETRIOS AMERICANOS, *an American citizen*
CABOT YEARLING, *a family man*
LEONA YEARLING, *44, his wife*
NEWTON YEARLING, *19, their half-wit son*
VELMA YEARLING ⎫
SELMA YEARLING ⎬ *twins*

AL YEARLING ⎫
ELLA YEARLING ⎪
HENRY YEARLING ⎪
JESSE YEARLING ⎪
SUSAN YEARLING ⎪
MAUDE YEARLING ⎬ *their children*
LEMMIE YEARLING ⎪
MAE YEARLING ⎪
HARRY YEARLING ⎪
WILBUR YEARLING ⎪
LUCY YEARLING ⎭

RICHARD OLIVER, *an unpublished writer*
ELSA WAX, *a photographer for Life Magazine*
DAVID F. WINDMORE, *a college man*
DANIEL HOUGH, *a farmer*
MR. SMITH, *a representative of the West Coast Novelty Amusement Company*
MR. HARRIS, *his associate*
PASS LE NOIR, *a sheriff*
STYLIANOS AMERICANOS, *41, Georgie's father, a wrestler*
PERICLES AMERICANOS, *71, Stylianos' father*

THE PLACE

Outside Ann Hamilton's House, at 333 Orchard Avenue,

Bakersfield, California.
The parlor of the Americanos home.

THE TIME

Late morning and afternoon of Friday, September 15,
1939.

Act One

An old-fashioned house with a front porch, at 333 Orchard Avenue in Bakersfield, California. A large front yard, with rose bushes in bloom near the house. An orange and a lemon tree. A palm. Two eucalyptus. A cement statue of a lion on the lawn.

A homeless family goes by in the street: MAN, WOMAN, THREE CHILDREN.

ANN HAMILTON, *a beautiful and rather elegant woman in her early forties, comes out of the house, looks around, walks about in the yard, to the gate, smells and cuts several roses, singing "the years, the years, they come and go," and so on; goes up onto the porch, sits down in the rocking-chair with a love-story magazine, waiting for nothing, least of all a telegram.*

GEORGIE AMERICANOS, *Greek-American Postal Telegraph messenger, arrives, skidding, on a bicycle.*

GEORGIE: You Miss Ann Hamilton?

ANN: I am.

GEORGIE: Well, a fellow by the name of Barnaby Gaul is coming out from Boston to visit you. He sent you this telegram. Know him?

ANN: Barnaby Gaul? May I read the telegram?

GEORGIE: It's collect. A dollar and eighty cents. It's a long night-letter. Lots of people can't pay for collect telegrams nowadays, but they always want to know what's in them just the same, so I *memorize* everything and let them know. *Free.* That's *my* little gift to society. People are poor. A dollar and eighty cents is a lot of money. Know him?

ANN: I'm afraid there must be some mistake.

GEORGIE: Oh, no, there isn't.

ANN: I don't know anybody in Boston. Are you *sure* the telegram's for me?

GEORGIE: If you're Ann Hamilton, it's for you. Otherwise it
ain't. Mistakes sometimes happen.

ANN: What's that name again?

GEORGIE: Barnaby Gaul. B-a-r-n-a-b-y, Barnaby. G-a-u-l,
Gaul. We get a lot of different kinds of telegrams, but
this is the best *I've* ever seen. This telegram is about love.

ANN: Love?

GEORGIE: That's right. L-O-V-E, love. I'll recite the message
to you. It's against the rules of the company, but to hell
with the company. My sympathies are with the poor, not
the rich. To tell you the truth, I'm a radical.

ANN: Are you?

GEORGIE: Of course I'm an American, too. My father's
Greek. He used to be a wrestler. My father's *father* used
to be a tobacco-grower in Smyrna, in the old country.
We read philosophy. My name's Georgie Americanos.

ANN: How do you do?

GEORGIE: How do you do?

ANN: Won't you sit down, Georgie?

GEORGIE: That's all right. You lived in this house twenty-
seven years?

ANN: I've lived in this house all my life. My goodness, I'm
forty-four years old.

GEORGIE: You're the lady, all right. My father's been reading Greek philosophy to me for three years. Consequently, I'm intelligent. If he comes out here from Boston, like he says he's going to, will you let me come out
and look at him?

ANN: If somebody's coming here.

GEORGIE: He'll be here.

ANN: All right, Georgie, you can come out. What does the
telegram say?

GEORGIE: Can I bring my father? He likes to meet people
who've traveled.

ANN: All right, Georgie, your father, too.

GEORGE: The telegram goes like this. (*Reciting the telegram*) Boston, Massachusetts. September 7, 1939.

ANN: September 7? Today's September 15.

GEORGIE: Well, to tell you the truth, I lost the telegram. It
was in my pocket. I don't know *how* it got there. I always
put telegrams in my hat.

ANN: Good gracious, Georgie, tell me what's in the telegram, even if it *is* eight days old.

GEORGIE: Has anybody walked by in front of this house whistling *Love's Old Sweet Song* lately?

ANN: No, Georgie. Please recite the telegram.

GEORGIE: Well, let me think a minute. Get everything straight. He sure is a nut. O.K. Here it is. "If you remember me, I am the young man with the red hair who walked in front of your house twenty-seven years ago whistling *Love's Old Sweet Song*." Do you remember him?

ANN: No, I don't. Please recite the *whole* telegram.

GEORGIE: How could you forget a guy like that? He goes on to say: "You were sixteen years old at the time. You had half a dozen roses in your hand. Four red and two white. I hardly noticed you when I went by, and then I came back and said hello, and you said hello. I said what is your name and you said Ann Hamilton. You didn't ask my name. We talked a minute or so and that was all. I made a note of the number of your house and the name of the street and went away. I am now fifty-one years old and want you to know I love you." *Now*, do you remember him?

ANN: No, Georgie. Is there anything more?

GEORGIE: Plenty! There's plenty more. He says: "I am coming back to you, even if you're married and have five children." How about it? Are you? Have you?

ANN: I'm not married.

GEORGIE: Aren't you married?

ANN: No. Please finish the telegram, Georgie.

GEORGIE: Well, he says: "Get rid of everybody. Love is everything. I know, now. Nothing else matters. I will walk in front of your house again very soon and I will be whistling the same old sweet song of love." They don't usually send telegrams this way, even when they're collect. They usually try to say everything in ten words. He says: "If you remember me, speak to me. If you do not speak, I shall know you have forgotten. Please remember and please speak to me. I love you. BARNABY GAUL." That's the whole message, word for word. A dollar and eighty cents. Know him?

ANN: No, I don't.

GEORGIE: Are you Ann Hamilton?

ANN: My name is Ann Hamilton.

GEORGIE: Well, *he* knows *you*. He sent you this message all the way from Boston. You're going to speak to him, aren't you?

ANN: No, I'm not.

GEORGIE: Doesn't love mean *anything* to you?

ANN: No, it doesn't. Besides, the man's crazy.

GEORGIE: Why? Just because he hasn't forgotten?

ANN: A girl of sixteen is liable to be polite and say a few words to any man who speaks to her.

GEORGIE: This is different. You must have been very pretty at the time. You're not bad now. Don't you remember holding half a dozen roses in your hand? Four red and two white?

ANN: I've cut roses from these bushes hundreds of times. I don't remember any *particular* time.

GEORGIE: Don't you remember a guy with red hair, whistling?

ANN: No, I don't. I'm not sixteen, Georgie. I'm forty-four.

GEORGIE: Well, all I know is you mean everything in the world to this nut. This Barnaby Gaul. And by all rights he ought to mean everything in the world to you, too.

ANN: Well, he doesn't mean *anything* to me.

GEORGIE: I wouldn't be so sure about that. He may come by here and sweep you right off your feet.

ANN: No, he won't.

GEORGIE: Why not?

ANN: I'm perfectly happy.

GEORGIE: Oh, no, you're not. You can't fool me. You may be satisfied, but you're not happy. You've got to be a little *un*happy to be perfectly happy. Satisfied's one thing, and happy's another. (*Pause*) Socrates. (PEOPLE *go by*) Poor people. Homeless. No place to go.

ANN: What's he say in that telegram?

GEORGIE: That's more like it. Listen carefully. (*Reciting*) "If you remember me, I am the young man with the red hair who walked in front of your house—" (*Whistling*) Listen. (*At the gate*) It's *him*. Barnaby Gaul. He's come back to you, just like he said he would. This is the greatest love story that's ever taken place in the streets of Bakersfield, California. Speak to him.

ANN: I don't remember anybody like that.

GEORGIE: Speak to him. The man's come all the way from Boston to see you again. He's moved everything back twenty-seven years where it belongs. Say a kind word.

ANN: I don't know what to say.

GEORGIE: Say *anything*. He'll understand.

ANN (*At the gate*): Here he comes. Don't go away, Georgie.

GEORGIE: Go away? I wouldn't miss this for anything in the world.

> (*The* PERSON *who appears is a handsome man of fifty whose years are instantly irrelevant. He is, in fact, youth constant and unending. His hair is reddish, if not exactly red. His face is still the face of a young man. His figure is still that. His clothes are the casual clothes of a young man who has better things to think about. He is wearing an old straw hat, and he is carrying a straw suitcase. He is walking jauntily, and he is whistling. He notices* ANN, *stops whistling and stands*)

ANN: Good morning.

GAUL: How do you do? (ANN *and* GAUL *stare at one another a moment*)

GEORGIE: Wow!

GAUL: Your son?

ANN: Yes. No.

GAUL: A handsome boy.

ANN: He's Greek.

GAUL: A classic and noble people. You have others?

ANN: No. He's a messenger. He brought your telegram.

GAUL: Telegram?

GEORGIE: Sure. From Boston.

GAUL: Boston?

> (ANN *turns and rushes into the house*)

GEORGIE: Weren't you just whistling *Love's Old Sweet Song*?

GAUL: I was *whistling*. I don't know what it was. It's a beautiful morning. The least a man can do is whistle.

GEORGIE: Didn't you walk down this street twenty-seven years ago?

GAUL: My boy, I've never been in this town before.

GEORGIE: Ah, for the love of Mike.

> (ANN *comes out of the house, holding half a dozen roses. Four red and two white*)

GAUL: Roses! I have never seen roses more beautiful to behold. Nor have I seen anyone hold roses more beauti-

fully. Nor have I seen them held any way at all by any-
one more beautiful.

GEORGIE: It's him, all right.

GAUL: *Him?* Who?

GEORGIE: *Who?* You. Don't you recognize her?

ANN: Four red and two white.

GEORGE: She remembers *you*. Don't you remember *her?*
(GAUL *stares at* ANN) All right.

(*He tears open the telegram*)

Let me read the telegram for *you,* too.

GAUL: Telegram? What telegram?

GEORGIE: What telegram! The collect telegram from Boston.
(*Reading*) Boston, Massachusetts. September 7, 1939.

(GAUL *takes the telegram and reads it silently,
glancing at* ANN *every once in a while*)

GAUL: "I love you. BARNABY GAUL."

GEORGIE: Now don't try to tell me you're not Barnaby Gaul.

GAUL: Is *this* Bakersfield, California?

ANN: Yes, it is.

GAUL: Is *this* Orchard Avenue?

ANN: Yes. 333.

GAUL: How can I ever ask you to forgive me?

GEORGIE: You *are* Barnaby Gaul, aren't you?

GAUL: Words fail me.

ANN: Oh, that's all right.

GEORGIE: Were you ever in Bakersfield before?

GAUL: Please try to understand.

GEORGIE: Were you in Boston eight days ago?

GAUL: Forgive me. Both of you. I thought I was in Fresno.
Let's start all over again. From the beginning.

(*He takes his suitcase and hurries away*)

GEORGIE: Do you remember *anybody* like that?

ANN: I don't know how I ever could have forgotten.

GEORGIE: Are you *sure* this is the nut?

ANN: As sure as I'm breathing.

GEORGIE: Well, get ready, then. Whoever he is, here he
comes again, and this time he means it. This time he
knows where he is and *who* he is, and who you are. Don't
forget to speak to him or else he'll just walk away and
maybe not send a telegram again for another twenty-
seven years.

(GAUL *appears again, whistling "Love's Old Sweet Song"*)

ANN: Good morning.

(GAUL *stops, turns, looks at* ANN, *sets down his suitcase, hurries to* ANN *and kisses her. She drops the roses one by one*)

GAUL: Ann. I knew you'd remember. I knew you'd never forget.

ANN: I thought I *had* forgotten, Barnaby. I even believed there was no one in the world like you.

GAUL: There is, however. There is.

ANN: And then when I saw you, I knew how foolish I had been to think you would never come back. I couldn't help it, Barnaby. The years moved away, slowly and then swiftly, and always I stayed here alone, living in this house, rocking back and forth in this chair on this porch. The roses bloomed and faded.

GAUL: The poor roses.

ANN: The song died.

GAUL: The poor song.

ANN: The children I wanted were never born.

GAUL: The poor children.

ANN: Barnaby, why have you stayed away so long?

GAUL: Ann, you may remember there were wars.

ANN: Oh!

GAUL: And you may remember, Ann, there were great troubles. There were panics in which a man rushed with the crowd to no place. No place at all. And I, with the million others, ran, and ran, forgetting love, forgetting everything but the need for escape. Protection from police and disease. Hide-aways in fifty-cent rooms in large cities, in small villages. There were famines, Ann.

ANN: Oh, Barnaby, you were hungry?

GAUL: Hungry? Days, weeks, months, *years* of hunger. Hunger for bread, not love. Hunger for ease and comfort, not glory. (*He embraces her*) There were disasters at sea. Shipwreck and storm. Floods and hurricanes, and a man off-balance falling in the street. Fear and shouting. No songs, Ann. There were distances, and barking dogs. Mountains to cross, and rivers and prairies and deserts. And wherever a man stood, his heart was far away, and wherever he went, his heart was not there. There was cold and few coats. There was ice and no fire. There was fury and stupor in the heart. As you dreamed here through the years, there was pain and forsakenness. There were accidents, Ann, with a man's body embarrassed by helpless and ugly posture, the arm twisted, the leg out of joint, and the heart in fever of disgust, raging against the mice.

GEORGIE: What mice?

GAUL: Mice? Go away, boy. And the foolish people asking, Are you hurt? Hurt? My God, I have been attacked by an army of termites as big as Japanese, and marching in the same military formation. There was snow and quiet, with the eyes of men staring out from secrecy and crime. There was *hate,* with the rain drenching the streets and the wind roaring around the buildings.

ANN: Oh, Barnaby.

GAUL: There were many things, Ann, to keep me away from you, as you dreamed here through the years. I remember the thirst I knew in Kansas City, and the bar-flies driving me mad. There were small things, Ann, insects and little words. Frowns and sneers. And big things. The stairway of the hotel on fire, and a man in his bare feet. There were moments, repeated a million times, that were useless to the years. And years that were meaningless to any moment. But I knew—always I knew, Ann—that you would not forget. I've come a long way, through many things, and still your face is bright. Your eyes still young Your hand warm. Your lips soft and full. The errors that have been, I dismiss. Here, in your presence, I deny all I have known but good, since you are still by sweetness molded sweet. I here cease movement and begin dream, because here dream is real. Ann, I've traveled across half the world. (*Solemnly*) I'm tired, Ann. Now I must lie down in the sweet shade of love, and dream into the years of youth. The years of *our* youth, Ann. The years we have lost and shall now regain in the embrace of love.

(BARNABY *embraces* ANN. *They go into the house.* BARNABY *turns and throws* GEORGIE *a coin*)

GAUL: My luggage, boy.

(GEORGIE *picks up the suitcase and puts it just inside the house*)

(TOM FIORA, *another Postal Messenger, arrives and settles his bike next to* GEORGIE'S)

TOM: Telegram for you, Georgie.

GEORGIE: Telegram for *me*?

TOM: Yes, *you*. Here. Read it.

GEORGIE (*Reading telegram*): "I told you I'd get even with you some day, so how do you like that? The telegram to Miss Ann Hamilton is not real. Ha, ha, ha. Your pal, Tom Fiora." Ha ha ha? What's the big idea?

TOM: I told you I'd get even on you.

GEORGIE: *You* put that telegram in my coat pocket?

TOM: That's right. That'll teach you to play tricks on me.

GEORGIE: *You* wrote *that* telegram?

TOM: *I* didn't write it. My brother Mike did.

GEORGIE: That's what I call a low-down dirty trick, and a guy in the house there getting ready to sleep in the sweet shade of love.

TOM: Serves you right. I told you I'd get even.

GEORGIE: Well, what about that lady? What about that wonderful lady who told him I was her son?

TOM: Tell her the truth.

GEORGIE: The truth? Ah, Tom, I never did like Italians. Greeks never did like Italians. How did your brother Mike ever happen to write a telegram like that?

TOM: Mike gets all kinds of funny ideas. He cut this lady's lawn one day. She told him the story of her life. He knew she was lonely.

GEORGIE: Well, who the hell is this guy, then? He's not just *anybody*. Giving me a Canadian dime. Tom, I'm going to tell the Manager.

TOM: Go ahead. He'll fire *you*, too. Then he'll come out here and make a personal call and explain everything.

GEORGIE: No, he can't do that. It's too late to do *that*.

TOM: Come on. Let's go back to work.

GEORGIE: O.K., you rat. (TOM *goes*) If that guy breaks her heart I'm going to tell my father to get a half-nelson on him and teach him some manners. Good-by, Miss Hamilton.

ANN'S VOICE: Good-by, Georgie.

GEORGIE: Is he sleeping?

ANN'S VOICE: No, he wants to shave first.

GEORGIE: Aaah. I'll be back to see how you're getting along first chance I get.

ANN'S VOICE: All right, Georgie. And thanks ever so much.
GEORGIE: Any time at all.

(*He rides away*)

(GAUL, *with lather on his face, comes out on the porch, followed by* ANN. GAUL *sings to* ANN)

GAUL (*Singing*): I love to see the sun come smiling to the world;
I love to hear the wind go singing through a field;
I love to hear a love-bird singing in a tree,
And I love to see a lovely face light up with love for me.

CHORUS:

> Of all the things I love,
> I love the most
> Sleeping in the shade of love.
> Sleeping in the shade of love,
> I love the most, my love.
>
> Of all the things I love to taste,
> Sweetest is the kiss of love.
> Dreaming in the shade of love,
> The kiss of love
> I love the most, my love.
>
> My love, of all the lovely things,
> Loveliest of all is you,
> Dreaming in the shade of love.
> Sleeping in the shade of love, my love,
> I love the most, my love.

I love to breathe the scent of earth and new-mown hay;
I love to taste the peach and berry ripe in May;
I love to feel the spray as I walk beside the sea,
And I love to see a lovely face light up with love for me.

CHORUS

(GAUL *guides* ANN *into the house.* DEMETRIOS, *a small middle-aged Greek with a big black mustache, pushes a lawn-mower into the yard, begins to cut the lawn, suddenly notices the roaring lion, roars back at it.* GAUL *opens an upstairs window*)

GAUL: Hey. You. That grass does not need cutting.
DEMETRIOS: I am American citizen.

GAUL: Even so, the grass does not need cutting. Have you got your first or second papers?

DEMETRIOS: Second papers next month.

GAUL: All right, come back and cut the grass next month.

DEMETRIOS: Is this official?

GAUL: Official. Now get your lawn-mower and get the hell out of here.

> (DEMETRIOS *hurries away with his lawn-mower. There is a moment of peaceful silence. Then* CABOT YEARLING *and his family arrive, one by one.* CABOT *thoughtfully smells a rose and surveys the terrain.* CABOT's *family consists of* LEONA, *his wife;* NEWTON, *nineteen;* AL, *seventeen; the* TWINS, SELMA *and* VELMA, *sixteen;* ELLA, *thirteen;* HENRY, *twelve;* JESSE, *eleven;* SUSAN, *ten;* MAUDE, *nine;* LEMMIE, *eight;* MAE, *seven;* HARRY, *six;* WILBUR, *five; and* LUCY, *four.* LEONA *is pregnant. The family is accompanied by* RICHARD OLIVER, *a newspaper man who is collecting material for a book. He is an oldish, partially bald young man who is very troubled. Also* ELSA WAX, *a large, plain young woman wearing spectacles, who is a photographer for Life Magazine*)

CABOT: Leonie, here we rest.

OLIVER: But, Mr. Yearling, this is somebody's front yard.

CABOT: Don't aim to do no harm. Just aim to rest a spell. Leonie's going to have a baby soon, you know.

> (*Spreads his old blanket on the lawn and lies down*)

OLIVER: Another baby? When?

CABOT: Leonie, when?

LEONA: Two or three months, most likely. He'll be my fifteenth.

ELSA: You're aiming to stay here till the little fellow comes, of course?

CABOT: Don't know why not. (*To* AL) Here, you. What are you always reading books for? Shakespeare and things like that?

> (ELSA *takes a picture*)

LEONA: When do you folks aim to leave us?

ELSA: I can't answer for Mr. Richard Oliver here. He's

aiming to write a novel about you folks, I believe. He'll be with you for the next two or three years, most likely. I won't be half that long.

LEONA: I don't reckon we could undertake to feed another mouth, what with the children growing up and needing things all the time, and another coming.

ELSA: Mr. Oliver won't be no trouble, hardly.

CABOT: Well, it ain't so much the extra mouth to feed. It's always having somebody around asking questions. (*Knocks notebook out of* OLIVER's *hand*) It's more like never being able to lie down and sleep in the afternoon, without somebody waking up a body to ask if we know how to read or not, or if we want better working conditions. (ELSA *takes a picture of* CABOT) Or somebody else taking pictures of us all the time. We ain't publicity mad. We know we ain't society folk. If it's pictures you want, there's a world full of people who're always fussing with soap and water, keeping themselves clean and nice-looking all the time.

OLIVER: I have no intention of getting in the way. Miss Wax! If you please. The pitiable plight of these unfortunate people is not the concern of one man alone, but of the whole nation.

CABOT: *Unfortunate?* I've got my driver's license.

OLIVER: Something's got to be done for them.

ELSA: All right, *do* something. What can you do?

CABOT: We ain't asking much.

LEONA: That's so. We don't want nothing from nobody— hardly. Food. A place to sleep. A roof over our heads. Clothes. A little land to walk around in. Cows. Chickens. A radio. A car. Something like that. We aim to shift for ourselves, the same as ever.

CABOT: A handful of vines to pick grapes off of to eat. A small melon patch. Good climate. Working conditions? We aim to *hire* our help fair and square.

ELSA: I don't hardly guess this family's typical.

LEONA: Oklahomans. That's what we are. Don't belong to no religious sex. Mind our own business.

CABOT: Live and let live. When do you folks aim to let us rest?

LEONA: We like to be neighborly and all, but this following us around and spying on us don't seem just right.

ELSA: I won't be much longer. We're going to call these pictures "Life Goes to a Garden Party."

OLIVER: You're making fun of these people.

ELSA: Don't be silly. I'm not making fun of anybody, except you. Because you think these people are pathetic. Well, they're not. *You* are. Look at these people. Nothing can stop them. They've got the stubbornness and fertility of weeds. And they're not common, either. I'm a photographer and I've learned to see *into* things. Your vision is so bad, the only thing you ever see is the surface, and I don't think you see that very clearly. For all we know one of these kids is a genius. (*Looking at* AL) This fellow *looks* like a genius: he reads Shakespeare. (*Looking at* NEWTON) On the other hand they may all be idiots. But how do we know the world isn't supposed to be inhabited by idiots, instead of silly people who want to get everything organized—like you?

OLIVER: You're a Fascist.

CABOT: Talk! Talk! Talk! That's all I hear, ever since you intellectuals started following us around.

OLIVER: I'm trying to *help* you people. With my novel, I hope to improve migratory agricultural labor conditions.

CABOT: Conditions are all right. I'm a little tired, that's all. I brought this family all the way from Muskogee, Oklahoma, in seven weeks, in a broken-down old Ford that cost sixty-seven dollars and fifty cents.

OLIVER: It's not a question of a broken-down old Ford—

(HENRY *hits* OLIVER *with a stick.* OLIVER *falls, and three boys leap on him*)

CABOT: No kicking, now! Fair and square! No gouging! No biting!

(BARNABY GAUL *opens an upstairs window*)

GAUL: What's going on around here? Ann. Are these people relatives of yours?

ANN: I've never seen them before.

GAUL: Don't worry. I'll get them out of here in two minutes.

HENRY: Oh, yeah!

(*Three boys run into the house.* GAUL *appears with the boys hanging on him*)

GAUL: Ann, come out here. For the love of God, save me.

(*He falls to his knees*)

ANN (*Appearing*): Barnaby! What's the matter?

CABOT: Here, you kids. Henry. Jesse. Get off that boy. Get off him before I come over there and break your arms.

(HENRY *and* JESSE *release their holds on* GAUL. *He rises to his feet*)

GAUL: What're all you people doing in this front yard?
CABOT: We aim to rest a while and catch our breath.

(HENRY *leaps on* GAUL's *leg*)

GAUL: You aim to rest a while and catch your breath? (*To* HENRY) Get away from me, you bashi-bazouk! (*To* CABOT) Call off your children.
CABOT: Henry. Leave the boy alone.
GAUL: My God! You're not all one family, are you?
CABOT: All excepting him and her. He's a writer, and she's a photographer.
GAUL: All the others yours?
CABOT: More than half of them are. Every one of them's my wife's, though.
GAUL: Well, it's been pleasant chatting with you. Now clear out of here. Go on up the street somewhere a couple of blocks.

(*He starts to enter house, singing "Of All the Things I Love"*)

CABOT: We ain't aiming to go no further just now.
GAUL: When are you aiming to?
CABOT: After Leonie has the baby.
GAUL: After Leona has the baby. When will that be?
CABOT: That won't be for a couple of months.
GAUL: A couple of months? My God!

(*He moves to go*)

ANN: Barnaby!
GAUL: I can't stand noise and confusion and crowds of people in my private life.
ANN: Barnaby! You're not *going*?
GAUL: I'm not staying.
ANN: I've already waited for you twenty-seven years. You just arrived.
GAUL: Ann, you've got the most beautiful spirit in the world, but I can't hang around a house that's surrounded by Indians.
LEONA: Oklahomans.

GAUL: Same thing. (*To* ANN) I can tell you now, and truth-fully, that I shall never forget you.

ANN: You're angry and excited, Barnaby. You don't know what you're saying. (GAUL *goes*) Barnaby! Don't go! Wait for me! Let me get my hat and coat. I'm coming with you. Barnaby!

(*She runs after him*)

HENRY (*At the upstairs window*): The whole house is ours.

(*Everybody rushes into the house*)

OLIVER: But, Mr. Yearling, you'll get in trouble. This is still private property. Of course *after* the revolution—

CABOT: Ah, to hell with the revolution.

AL (*Alone, on the steps*): What am *I* doing here? I don't belong to this man and this woman. I'll go away. I'll be truly alone, as every man must be. Good-by, my father. Good-by, my mother. Good-by, my sisters and my brothers.

(JESSE, *in one of* ANN's *hats, comes out and sees his brother going away*)

JESSE: Al! (AL *stops, turns*) Where are you going?

AL: Nowhere. Jesse, go on back!

JESSE: No. I know you're going away. I'm going with you. I don't want to be alone.

AL: Jesse, go on back! You can't go with me.

JESSE (*Grabs his brother around the waist*): No. I *won't* go back. I *am* going with you.

AL: Jesse! Listen! I can't take care of you. I don't even know if I'll be able to take care of myself. Now go on back.

JESSE: Al, please take me with you. Please.

AL: I can't, Jesse. Now go on back!

(*He pushes* JESSE, *turns and runs*)

JESSE: You're a hell of a brother!

(JESSE *sits down in front of the cement lion. Suddenly he stretches out on the lawn, face downward.* ELSA *comes out of the house.* OLIVER's *hat and portable typewriter follow. Then* OLIVER, *who stumbles out and falls on the ground, pushed by* CABOT *and* NEWTON)

CABOT: You stay away from us with your God-damn propaganda. We voted for Roosevelt.

(CABOT *and* NEWTON *go back into the house*)

OLIVER: I don't know how I'm going to be able to write this and give it social significance. (*Gets to his feet*)

ELSA: Don't be foolish. You just write what you wanted to write in the first place, and forget all these little complications.

OLIVER: I'm disappointed.

ELSA: You've been betrayed. How dare they have personalities of their own? It would be a little cruel if one of the brighter children wrote a novel about *you*. One of them might, you know.

OLIVER: Sometimes it seems impossible to be of help.

ELSA: Be of help to who? No one wants to help anybody but himself.

OLIVER: I can't figure you out.

ELSA: You can't even figure out those simple people in the house. How do you expect to figure me out?—A Vassar girl!

OLIVER: The trouble with you Vassar girls is, you've got no faith.

ELSA: And the trouble with you unpublished writers is, you *have*. Faith belongs to the great only. Foolish people aren't entitled to faith. They make trouble with it, for themselves and for everybody else. They gather their feebleness into crazy mobs that don't understand anything except to *insist*. If you want the world to be better, be better yourself.

OLIVER: Shut up!

ELSA: What?

OLIVER: Shut up! That's what! I don't want to hear any more of this chit-chat.

ELSA: You know it's the truth.

OLIVER: Shut up, I said! I love you!

JESSE: Ha-ha-ha!

(OLIVER *studies* JESSE. JESSE *studies* OLIVER. OLIVER *takes some money out of his pocket*)

OLIVER: Here! Here's half-a-dollar.

(JESSE *takes the coin*)

JESSE: What for?

OLIVER: Get yourself an education and be like me.

JESSE: You two going along?

OLIVER: Yes. And to help *you* with *your* novel, I'm going to marry her. (*To* ELSA) That's right.

JESSE: Are you coming back?

OLIVER: No, I'm not.

JESSE: Why?

OLIVER: Because I don't like you.

JESSE: Couldn't you make it seventy-five cents?

OLIVER (*Starts to bring out more money. Changes his mind*): No! Why should I?

JESSE: Ah, come on. Just two bits more.

OLIVER: No!

JESSE (*Picks up a rock and gets set to throw it*): Two bits.

OLIVER: You throw that rock, and I'll break your neck.

ELSA: Richard, be careful!

OLIVER: Shut up, I said. I can take care of myself.

JESSE (*Making a line with his foot*): Cross this line and see what happens.

OLIVER: It so happens, I'm going the other way.

JESSE: Well, you better if you know what's good for you.

OLIVER (*Turns to* ELSA): What's more, we'll have kids, too. The God-damnedest punks in the world. Don't talk. You've said everything. To hell with the people in the house! Let God take care of them, the same as ever. To hell with art! To hell with propaganda! To hell with you! I love you, so shut up and let's try to live.

(JESSE *watches them go, then rushes into the house. Inside the house there is a great commotion. The children are singing "My Country 'Tis of Thee."* GEORGIE *arrives on his bike, listens, and runs to the lower window*)

GEORGIE: Hey. Cut out that racket.

(HENRY *comes out on the porch in one of* ANN'S *dresses*)

Who are you? What are you doing in that dress?

HENRY: I'm a society lady!

(*He does a bump*)

GEORGIE: Society lady? Where's Miss Ann Hamilton?

HENRY: Who?

GEORGIE: Miss Ann Hamilton.

HENRY: Annie doesn't live here any more.

GEORGIE (*To* CABOT *in upper window*): What are you people doing in this house?

CABOT: We aim to rest a while and catch our breath.

GEORGIE: Where's Barnaby Gaul?

HENRY: You mean that fellow with the straw hat? He went away.

> (SELMA, *one of the twins, comes out and studies* GEORGIE)

SELMA: Hello!

GEORGIE: Where's Miss Hamilton?

SELMA: She went with the man. We're living here now.

GEORGIE (*To* HENRY): Get away from that wheel!

SELMA: You aiming to come back and pay us another visit some time?

GEORGIE: This house don't belong to you people.

SELMA: I hope you're aiming to come back.

VELMA (*The other twin, comes out and studies* GEORGIE): Hello!

GEORGIE: Hello, nothing!

VELMA: What's your name?

GEORGIE: Never mind what my name is. You people get out of this house!

VELMA: *My* name's Velma.

GEORGIE: What do I care what your name is? You people are house-wreckers.

WILBUR: No, we're not.

VELMA: I'm sixteen. How old are you?

GEORGIE: What do I care how old you are? You people are mice.

WILBUR: No, we're not.

GEORGIE: You folks get out of this house. It belongs to Miss Ann Hamilton and Mr. Barnaby Gaul. It belongs to *true* love.

> (VELMA *and* SELMA *come toward* GEORGIE. *He pushes down on the pedal of his bike and rides off. The big boy,* NEWTON, *breaks out of the house, holding half a loaf of French bread, a piece of cheese and other miscellaneous items of food*)

NEWTON: The whole house is full of things to eat. I got mine.

(*The* TWINS *hurry back into the house.* HENRY *follows them. There is great noise in the house, then silence*)

(GAUL *returns to the house, gets his suitcase, and tries to escape.* ANN *catches up with him at the gate*)

ANN: Barnaby! You've come back.

GAUL: Dear lady, you shame me. Your poetic words pierce me like arrows. I am sweetly wounded by your devotion! I would be the lowest of the low to leave you here in this garden of disorder, except—except, I repeat—that there are things stronger even than love, if one can only discover them. I am *not* your man, except when I am. That is the truth, and the truth is hard. Forgive me, dear lady. The lies I tell are never for the purpose of hurting others. There is murder in such lies. In mine there is birth. I say only what others wish me to say. I have said what you have wished to hear. Gentle deceit is best for the moment, but for the year, truth is best. Stay, I beg of you. Do not leave yourself. To be vagrant, dear lady, you must be swift. Stay. I shall remember you. I promise. Good-by, dear lady.

(GAUL *goes.* LEONA *comes out on the porch. There is noise and confusion in the house.* ANN *walks slowly after* GAUL)

CURTAIN

Act Two

Several hours later, about two in the afternoon. Everything has quieted down. CABOT YEARLING *is on the lawn in front of the house, sleeping in the shade.*

LEONA *is rocking in* ANN'S *rocking-chair on the porch. Miscellaneous* CHILDREN *are at miscellaneous games.*

The scene is bright and somnolent. Cries of "Ice Cream" from far away.

The TWINS *come out of the house, each in one of* ANN'S *dresses, each wearing high-heeled shoes, each powdered and rouged.*

MR. SMITH *and* MR. HARRIS, *walking by in the street, pause a moment to notice the girls.*

VELMA: Look, Ma. We bathed, too.

LEONA: Hear that, Cabot? They bathed, too.

SELMA: Look, Pa. Look at *me!*

CABOT: Selma, you look like a picture actress. Leonie, why don't you dress up, too?

LEONA: Now, Cabot!

VELMA: There must be ten or eleven more dresses in the closet, Ma.

CABOT: Why, sure, Leonie. Does a woman good to dress up fancy once in a while. Any men's clothes in there?

SELMA: No men's clothes, but lots of dresses.

CABOT: Go on inside, Leonie, and get into some pretty things.

LEONA: Well, all right, Cabot. (*She goes into the house*)

VELMA: We're going to walk around town, Pa.

CABOT: Well, all right. Be careful.

VELMA (*To* SELMA, *lifting her dress*): Are my stockings straight?

SELMA (*Lifting her dress*): Uh-huh. Mine?

VELMA: Uh-huh. Well, come on.

> (*The* GIRLS *walk away.* CABOT *gets up on an elbow to watch.* MR. SMITH *and* MR. HARRIS *walk by in the street, following the girls*)

CABOT: I'll be losing them girls soon. Get married, or go on the stage, or meet somebody, or something. They grow up and leave you. They grow up and go away. First they're little children you can hardly recognize, and then all of a sudden they're women. It's moving pictures that does it. Moving pictures. They was always the nicest children I ever knew. Sweet and thoughtful and courteous. Now, they're women. It's moving pictures! Clark Gable and all them different men coming into their lives. All those heroes jumping on horses all the time, saving people from drowning, winning wars. All them good-looking men putting their heads close to women, talking confidentially. Reciting poetry. Whispering in their ears. I remember a picture where the fellow *bit* her ear. *Bit it!* All them well-dressed men with millions of dollars, doing all kinds of brave things. You can't hardly blame the children. They don't know there ain't any people like that. They get impatient to grow up, so they can meet moving picture millionaires. I've been through ten states, and I've never seen anybody like Clark Gable, fixing everything up everywhere. I've seen 'em in one state the same as in another, working, or tired, or worried, or sick. It's moving pictures, making promises they can't keep. I'll be losing them girls soon. I can see it in their eyes. No matter what a man does, it just seems like he's always going to lose something. It scares a man. Gives him a lonely feeling. (*He lies back.* GEORGIE AMERICANOS *arrives on his bicycle*) Telegram for me?

GEORGIE: Telegram for you! I want to talk to Miss Hamilton.

CABOT: Ain't nobody here but us.

GEORGIE: What right have you got to move into somebody else's house?

CABOT: We aim to rest a while and catch our breath.

GEORGIE: What kind of people are you, anyway?

CABOT: Migratory workers.

GEORGIE: Well, why don't you work? Or migrate?

CABOT: Leonie can't work. She's going to have a baby. The big boy gets tired easy. The twins—they just went to town—they don't like farm work. The others are all too little.

GEORGIE: Well, why don't *you* work?

CABOT: Can't get a job.

GEORGIE: Ah. You're just no good. What made you come to California from Oklahoma?

CABOT: Dust.

GEORGIE: Dust! Where'd you get that from?

CABOT: The writer told me.

GEORGIE: You could have gone the other way. You could have gone to Kansas or somewhere down around in there.

CABOT: Nope. California.

GEORGIE: Aaaah. You people are no good, that's all. Well, you better get out of this house in a hurry, and don't forget it.

CABOT: Ain't your house.

GEORGIE: Ain't yours either.

CABOT: Ain't yours.

GEORGIE: Ain't yours either. You're taking advantage of Miss Hamilton—driving her out of her own house. You ought to be ashamed.

CABOT: We didn't drive nobody from nowhere. He just went, and then *she* just went. No use leaving the house empty.

GEORGIE: How do you expect anybody to live in a house with a million people like you hanging around?

CABOT: Sixteen people. We was in the front yard, minding our own business—

(ANN *arrives*)

GEORGIE: What's the matter, Miss Hamilton?

ANN: He's gone.

GEORGIE: Gone? Where'd he go?

ANN: I don't know. He said he was going back to Boston.

GEORGIE: Boston?

ANN: He said for me to forget him.

GEORGIE: Aaah.

ANN: I begged him to take me with him, but he wouldn't do it. I told him I'd sell the house. I told him to give me two or three days and I'd sell the house and we'd go away together, but he said he had to start going right away.

GEORGIE: How'd he go? By train?

ANN: He went running.

GEORGIE: How can a man run to Boston?

ANN: I ran after him a while, and then I couldn't run any more. Now, I don't know what to do.

GEORGIE: Listen, Miss Hamilton. He's just a good-for-nothing tramp, like everybody else around here.

CABOT: Migratory worker.

ANN: He's an itinerant merchant.

GEORGIE: Yeah? What does he sell?

ANN: Medicine. He gave me a bottle of it. (ANN *hands the bottle to* GEORGIE)

GEORGIE (*Reading the label*): Dr. Greatheart's Five-Star Multi-Purpose Indian Remedy. Good for all kinds of aches, pains and sores. Works externally as well as internally. Quiets nerves. Stimulates super-human powers in tired men. Excellent for female nervous wrecks. Cures backaches. Contains numerous secret vitamins. Good for epilepsy, toothache, social diseases, earache, stomach disorders, insanity. Aaaah, this is a lot of hooey.

CABOT: Son, let me have a look at that bottle.

GEORGIE: One dollar a bottle. Is that what he sells?

ANN: Yes. He's got a suitcase full of them. He's gone.

GEORGIE: Well, you better forget him.

ANN: Forget him? I'm going to sell this house and go to Boston.

GEORGIE: He isn't going to Boston. He'll go to some town near here somewhere: Visalia, or Hanford, or Coalinga, or some other little town where there are lots of poor, *ignorant* people in the streets who will buy his medicine.

CABOT: *Uninformed.*

ANN: Well, wherever he goes, I'm going, too.

GEORGIE: Listen, Miss Hamilton, that telegram wasn't a real telegram.

ANN: Of course it was real.

GEORGIE: No, it wasn't. That man's name isn't Barnaby Gaul.

ANN: Now, Georgie, don't tell lies just to comfort me.

GEORGIE: I'm *not* comforting you.

ANN: Georgie, I *know* the truth.

GEORGIE: O.K., then. I'll get Barnaby *Gaul.*

ANN: Will you, Georgie?

GEORGIE: Sure, I will. I'll bring him back here, if that's what you want.

ANN: Oh, I do, Georgie. Will you get him?

GEORGIE: If you'll get these people out of your house, I will.

ANN (*To* CABOT): You get out of here. Go away. (*To* GEORGIE) They won't go.

GEORGIE: Listen, you. You heard her. This is her house. Pack up your junk and get out of here.

(LEONA YEARLING *comes out of the house in one of* ANN'S *dresses*)

ANN: You take off my dress and get out of my house.

LEONA: My dress.

ANN: It's *not* your dress. I bought that dress at Gottschalk's in Fresno three years ago.

LEONA: My dress.

GEORGIE: Aaaaaaah.

(HARRY *comes out of the house with a book and lies down on the lawn*)

ANN: Georgie, help me.

GEORGIE: Listen, you riff-raff!

(THREE BOYS *appear at upper windows*)

Get out of this lady's house! Do you hear?

LEONA: You hush, child. You're just a boy. You don't understand things.

CABOT: That's right, son. You go along and deliver your telegrams. This is a matter that don't concern you.

GEORGIE: Aaaah.

ANN: I'm going into my house.

HENRY (*In upper window*): It's our house now. Loosers weepers; finders keepers.

(ANN *goes into the house*)

GEORGIE: You people leave that lady alone. You people are gangsters.

HARRY: No, we're not.

(ANN *comes out of the house*)

ANN: Georgie, they're all over the house. They've eaten everything. Broken everything. Stolen everything. And they won't go.

GEORGIE: I'll go get the police.

ANN: What'll *I* do? Where'll *I* go?

GEORGIE: You go over to my house. My father's there. His name's Stylianos. The address is 137 Vine Street. You know where that is?

ANN: 137 Vine Street. I'll find it.

GEORGIE: Tell my father everything, and wait there for me.

ANN: All right, Georgie. Thanks ever so much.

GEORGIE: Any time.

ANN: 137 Vine Street. (*She goes*)

GEORGIE: That's right. I'll get the police to come here and *make* them go away. I'll get a writ of some kind.

CABOT: *Writ?* The whole nation's behind us.

> (GEORGIE *rides off*)

> (LEONA *sits down in the rocking-chair.* CABOT *stretches out in the shade. Everything is quiet and peaceful. Then* DAVID F. WINDMORE *arrives. He speaks swiftly, but enunciates his words very carefully, so that they have the effect of sounding unreal and foreign*)

WINDMORE: Good afternoon, sir.

CABOT: Good afternoon.

WINDMORE: How do you do, ma'am.

LEONA: How do.

WINDMORE: A lovely day. A beautiful countryside. A rich and fertile valley. A benevolent warmth. A delightful pressure of air. My name is David F. Windmore. Think of wind for wind. Think of more-or-less for more: Windmore. Think of David and Goliath for David, and think of Frank for F, although the F is actually for Fenimore.

CABOT: Hear that, Leonie?

WINDMORE (*Opening brief-case*): No home life is a full home life unless included among its general activities is the special and important activity of r-r-r-reading.

CABOT: Hear that?

WINDMORE: A well-read man is a well-bred man. He is a man who can carry on a lively and intelligent conversation on any topic with anybody, and therefore his company is desirable on all sides.

CABOT: What must I do?

WINDMORE (*Bringing out a copy of Time Magazine*): *Time Magazine*—curt, clear, complete—brings to your home every Friday all the news of the world:

> (*Children running*)

Art, books, business, cinema, education, medicine, music, people, press, radio, religion, science, sport, and theater. National affairs: The President, the Congress, Labor, the States, crime, politics, and so on. World War, Poland, Germany, France, England, Russia, Finland, and the others. Military events at sea. Sinking of ships. Submarines and mines. China and Japan.

(HENRY *goose-steps, followed by* WILBUR, *arms raised in Fascist salute*)

Time marches on.

CABOT: How do they get that news? Telegraph?

WINDMORE: *Time Magazine* is assembled every week by intelligent men all over the world. Editor of the magazine is Henry R. Luce.

CABOT: Henry R. Luce. College man, I suppose. Educated.

WINDMORE: The managing editors are: Manfred Gottfried—

CABOT: Manfred Gottfried.

WINDMORE: Frank Norris.

CABOT: Norris.

WINDMORE: T. S. Matthews.

CABOT: Matthews.

WINDMORE: The *Associate* Editors are Carlton J. Balliett Jr.—

CABOT: Junior.

LEONA: Cabot, let the man talk.

WINDMORE: Carlton J. Balliett Jr., Robert Cantwell, Laird S. Goldsborough, David W. Hulburd Jr., John Stuart Martin, Fanny Saul, Walter Stockly, Dana Tasker, Charles Weretenbaker. The *Contributing* Editors of *Time Magazine* are: Roy Alexander, John F. Allen, Robert W. Boyd Jr., Roger Butterfield, Whittaker Chambers, James G. Crowley, Robert Fitzgerald, Calvin Fixx, Walter Graebner, John Hersey, Sidney L. James, Eliot Janeway, Pearl Kroll, Louis Kronenberger, Thomas K. Krug, John T. McManus, Sherry Mangan, Peter Matthews, Robert Neville, Emeline Nollen, Duncan Norton-Taylor, Sidney Olsen, John Osborne, Content Peckham, Green Peyton, Williston C. Rich Jr., Winthrop Sargeant, Robert Sherrod, Lois Stover, Leon Svirsky, Felice Swados, Samuel G. Welles Jr., Warren Wilhelm, and Alfred Wright Jr.

(GAUL *arrives and stands at the gate, a little drunk*)

The Editorial *Assistants* of *Time Magazine* are:

LEONA: Yes. Tell us who *they* are.

WINDMORE: Ellen May Ach, Sheila Baker, Sonia Bigman, Elizabeth Budelman, Maria de Blasio, Hannah Durand, Jean Ford, Dorothy Gorrell, Helen Gwynn, Edith Hind,

Lois Holsworth, Diana Jackson, Mary V. Johnson, Alice Lent, Kathrine Lowe, Carolyn Marx, Helen McCreery, Gertrude McCullough, Mary Louise Mickey, Anna North, Mary Palmer, Tabitha Petran, Elizabeth Sacartoff, Frances Stevenson, Helen Vind, Eleanor Welch, and Mary Welles.

LEONA: No more names?

WINDMORE: No, that just about winds up the editorial department.

LEONA: What were some of those nice names again?

WINDMORE: Duncan Norton-Taylor. Williston C. Rich Jr.

LEONA: Yes, yes. My name's Leona. I don't know what you could think of for Leona. Could you tell me?

WINDMORE: Oh, I'll remember it all right. Leona. It's an easy name to remember.

LEONA: Leona Yearling. What could you think of for Yearling?

WINDMORE: Yearling. That's easy, too. I'll remember it all right. Now, Mrs. Yearling, *Time Magazine,* I think you'll agree, is something you and Mr. Yearling should read.

CABOT: Is that so?

WINDMORE: The subscription rate is five dollars for one year. All you have to do is sign this form and next Friday the mailman will bring you your first copy of *Time.*

CABOT: Is that all I've got to do?

WINDMORE: That's all. We'll bill you later.

CABOT: Give me a pencil.

WINDMORE: Oh. Life will be so much more interesting for you after *Time Magazine* begins to arrive every Friday. So much more dramatic and exciting. (*Filling in the form*) Mr. Cabot Yearling. 333 Orchard Avenue. Bakersfield, California.

CABOT: That's right. Where do I sign?

WINDMORE: On this line, Mr. Yearling. Wouldn't you rather sit up?

CABOT: No. I just want to sleep a little. I enjoy sleeping in the afternoon. Here?

WINDMORE: Yes, Mr. Yearling.

CABOT (*Signing*): X——X. (*Hands the form back*) There you are, son. You haven't got a cigar, have you?

WINDMORE: No, I'm sorry, I haven't. I don't smoke.

CABOT: It don't matter, really. I just thought you might have one.

WINDMORE: Until next Friday, then.

CABOT: Next Friday.

WINDMORE: It's been a pleasure, Mr. Yearling.

CABOT: Not at all.

WINDMORE: Mrs. Yearling.

LEONA: Couldn't you just say a few more of those names?

WINDMORE: Henry R. Luce, Manfred Gottfried, Carlton J. Balliett Jr.

LEONA: My gracious.

WINDMORE: Whittaker Chambers. Calvin Fixx. Louis Kronenberger. Oh, yes, Mrs. Yearling. Laird S. Goldsborough.

LEONA: Laird S. Goldsborough.

WINDMORE: Oh, yes, Mrs. Yearling, Laird S. Goldsborough.

(*He bends over* CABOT *briskly, extending his hand*)

CABOT: What do you want?

WINDMORE: Just to shake your hand, Mr. Yearling.

CABOT: Oh.

(*He holds up his hand, which* WINDMORE *grasps and shakes violently*)

Mrs. Yearling?

(*He shakes her hand, too*)

Until next Friday, then.

LEONA: Just one more name.

WINDMORE: Well, let me see. Felice Swados?

LEONA: Felice Swados.

WINDMORE: And last but not least, my own personal gift to my clients. (*He brings out a toy horn; blows it; tosses one to* LEONA) Mrs. Yearling. (*Blows another, tosses it to* CABOT) Mr. Yearling. And now, good-by. (WINDMORE *turns to go*)

GAUL: Just a moment.

(HENRY *is running around the house. He stops and turns.* CABOT *gets to his elbow and turns.* LEONA *stops rocking.* WINDMORE *halts.* GAUL *sets up his suitcase*)

My friend, my fellow worker in the field, and, I believe but regret, my contemporary. With no intention in the world of being rude to you, or to these good and humble

people of the earth, I could not help overhearing part—
and perhaps the greater part—of that which I shall gen-
erously call your pitch.

(JESSE *puts his head out of an upstairs window*)

Step up just a little closer, please.

(WINDMORE *moves forward.* CABOT *stands up.*
HENRY *and* LUCY *and other children move forward
a little.* JESSE *climbs out of the window onto the
roof. To* CABOT)

For the purpose of the amazing demonstration I am
about to make, I must trouble you for a silver dollar. One
silver American dollar.

(CABOT *has no money.* GAUL *takes a dollar from*
WINDMORE'S *fingers*)

Thank you.

WINDMORE: For the demonstration?
GAUL: For the demonstration.
WINDMORE: What kind of a demonstration is it?
GAUL: A most amazing demonstration. Now, will you be
good enough to take a card. Any card at all.

(WINDMORE *takes a card*)

Thank you. What card have you?
WINDMORE: The Nine of Clubs.
GAUL: The Nine of Clubs. Will you place the Nine of Clubs
on the table face down. Madam, will *you* be good enough
to take a card?

(LEONA *takes a card*)

Thank you. What card have you?
LEONA: The Nine of Clubs.

(WINDMORE *reaches for his dollar*)

GAUL: One moment, please. (*To* LEONA) Will you kindly
hold the Nine of Clubs aloft? Step up a little closer,
please. On this card I will place this silver dollar. Around
the card and the silver dollar, I will place these three
candles, and I will light them. One. Two. Three.
LUCY (*Sings*): Happy birthday to you. Happy birthday to
you.
GAUL: Thank you, dear child. Now. The card is on the

table. The dollar is on the card. The three candles are burning. Step up just a little closer, please.

WINDMORE: I'm sorry. I must go. Give me back my dollar.

GAUL: Please do not interrupt. Never interrupt a pitch. At least not a high pitch. You are no doubt a Harvard man. A man only recently turned loose into the world from one of the larger and more exclusive Universities of the East: Harvard, Yale, Princeton, or Dartmouth. My association with Universities has been comparatively meager. I have only *seen* a University. A Baptist University, I believe, somewhere or other in the State of Ohio. Furthermore, you are a reader of *Esquire Magazine.*

WINDMORE: This suit was given to me by my mother.

GAUL: Your mother is a reader of *Esquire Magazine.* I read religious pamphlets, brochures on the lesser known arts, catalogues, and for relaxation the labels on bottles of various kinds, usually empty.

WINDMORE: This is nonsense.

GAUL: Nonsense? No, my friend. *You* are nonsense. I only dwell in a world of nonsense. I have neither degree nor diploma, and yet it is I, not you, who goes about with tidings of hope. I heal the wounds of people. I instruct them in courage and fortitude, not you.

CABOT: Hear that, Leonie? He's a preacher.

GAUL: No, my good friend, you are mistaken. My father was a preacher. I am a doctor. There is no other word for it. At the same time, I am more than a doctor.

CABOT: Well, Doc. What about them pains in my head?

GAUL: Stop thinking, my friend, stop thinking. I heal those mysterious ailments in the living which science itself has not been able to isolate or identify. I destroy death in the living. That is my work. Step up just a little closer, please.

(*Everybody moves forward a little. A husband and wife in the street stop to listen*)

WINDMORE: Will you please give me back my dollar?

GAUL: Not another word. Not another word. You are not one who is exempt from the illnesses it is my purpose here to cure. You are not exempt. I have returned to say a gentle word to the woman whose good heart I have hurt.

(LEONA *stands*)

You may put the card down, Madam. Ann! Ann!

CABOT: She ain't here, Doc.

GAUL: Where is she?

CABOT: She came back, Doc, but she went away again.

GAUL: I quarreled with her in the streets. I ran from her as though she were death itself. I came to plead with this woman. I came hoping she would be established in her home again. I came to see these good and honest people. (*To* CABOT *and* LEONA) Yes, you. And you. (*To* LUCY) And you. You *are* honest and you *are* good. (*To* LEONA) As the world has made you, so must I understand you, for as the world has made me, so must I be understood. Understanding you, I know that this house is yours, no less than hers. You were commanded to be fruitful, and by God you have been fruitful. No man may say the fruit you have brought forth is not the finest in the world, since it is yours, and you could bring forth no other. But it is mine, too, and mine is yours. Love is selfish. I returned hoping you would be gone.

CABOT: We aim to rest a while and catch our breath.

GAUL: I know. I know. I returned knowing that you would *not* be gone. There is nowhere for you to go. *I* can go where I please, but when there is homelessness, *I* am homeless. I am not separated from any part of life. Here in this front yard, I must wage with others the war in Europe, even. I am encumbered by you in the depths of my sleep. When there is hunger, I am hungry, and when the children weep, they are my children. (*To* WINDMORE) You have studied, no doubt, the reasons for things: for disgrace, for wretchedness, for disease and for stupor.

WINDMORE: I studied business administration.

GAUL: You would have done better to study sleep, as— (*Indicating* CABOT)—this man has. (*To* WINDMORE) *I* have studied the reasons for things: for disgrace, for wretchedness, for disease, for stupor. No man in the world knows better than I why these tragic things occur in that most miraculous and magnificent creation of the hand of God: the noble body which is man. *You* bring news of world-wide madness and horror to the living every Friday. You make of universal crime a topic for idle reading. You tell the people of foolishness everywhere, every week. That's fine. *I* bring *hope* to the people. I have here in these bottles a medicine. The

juices of certain roots and barks are extracted and boiled
together—

(HUSBAND *whispers in* GAUL's *ear*)

Is this the lady?

(HUSBAND *nods,* GAUL *slaps a bottle into his hand*)

It has never failed, my friend. It has never failed.

(HUSBAND *hands* GAUL *a dollar*)

Thank you, my friend.

(HUSBAND *and his* WIFE *leave*)

May the Good Lord bless you. This mixture, which has
an appropriately bitter flavor, cannot, I am sure, cure
anything. It can do no harm, but it can cure nothing.
What this fluid actually is only God knows. But the
taking of this fluid is the taking of faith. And with these
bottles I carry to the people that which they need most.
Faith. Do you understand?

WINDMORE: No, I do *not* understand.

GAUL: This humble medicine can restore a kind of faith as
long as the bottle is not empty. I know of no other way
in which to do anything about the wretchedness I see
everywhere I go. The regular cost is two dollars. For this
area of California only, and for this day only, the cost has
been reduced one half. One dollar for one bottle. The
bottle is yours.

(*He slaps a bottle into* WINDMORE's *hand*)

WINDMORE: I do not want it.

GAUL: You would reject Jesus, I believe.

(*He blows out the candles*)

WINDMORE: I don't need any medicine, whatsoever.

GAUL: You are the sickest man in the world.

(*He begins to pack up his suitcase*)

WINDMORE: You are a charlatan.

GAUL: There were many who said the same of the Son of
Man.

WINDMORE: What about the Nine of Clubs?

GAUL: It is still here, as you see.

WINDMORE: What about the dollar on the Nine of Clubs?

GAUL: It is gone, as you see. Drink and go away.

WINDMORE: Where is my dollar?

GAUL: *Your* dollar? Whose image is engraved upon the dollar?

WINDMORE: I don't know. I haven't looked carefully lately. But I will not drink and I want my dollar.

GAUL: Ah-ha. Just as I thought. You are not a student. I gave to Caesar long ago that which belongs to Caesar. Go.

WINDMORE: Give me back my dollar.

GAUL (*Closing his suitcase*): Go. I lose my patience. (*To* CABOT) Here is the dollar. (*He slides the dollar off the Nine of Clubs, and tosses the card away*) Purchase commodities for the children. Buy ridiculous things. This is a ridiculous world. Drink this.

(GAUL *hands* CABOT *a bottle, turns to go*)

WINDMORE: Give me back my money, you thief.

GAUL: Thief? I am a missionary. (*To* CABOT) If I find other college men in the streets, I will come back later with more money. (*To* WINDMORE) Until next Friday then.

(GAUL *goes*)

WINDMORE: Henry R. Luce. Curt, clear, complete. Laird S. Goldsborough. National affairs. Crime. Politics. Religion. Louis Kronenberger. Business administration. World War. $5.00 a year. You don't need to wait till next Friday.

(*Throws Time Magazine to* CABOT, *and goes.* CABOT *picks up the magazine, looks at it a moment, blows the whistle* WINDMORE *gave him. Then throws magazine away*)

CABOT: It don't make sense.

(CABOT *takes a drink of* GAUL's *medicine, and gets to his feet*)

LEONA (*Blowing the horn* WINDMORE *gave her*): Do you remember any of the names, Cabot?

CABOT: What names?

LEONA: The wonderful names the magazine man said.

CABOT: I forgot 'em all, Leonie. But did you ever hear a man talk the way that man with the bottles talked?

LEONA: I never heard anything like it before. What's going on in the world, Cabot?

CABOT: Leonie, I'm glad you asked me that. You see, the way things are. You know, about industry and all. One thing and another, they don't hardly ever match up equivalent or comparative.

LEONA: Why, Cabot, I never heard you talk like that before.

CABOT: Oh, sure, Leonie. I just don't meet the right people. The law of averages, don't you see, like when you take two and two, and subtract one, somehow or other it don't make no difference. Oh, I can think along with the best of them, Leonie. I *do* get the ideas sometimes. You remember the way I talked to that writer. I said all those things, where he came in about social security. Social security. Oh, sure. I said all those things. Economic stability and things like that. You remember how I said propaganda right to his face. Exploitation. You remember that. Land erosion and all those different things. Oh, I can talk to 'em, Leonie. I can talk right up to 'em. Educational systems and all those.

LEONA: My, Cabot. You do sound good to hear.

CABOT (*Takes another drink from bottle*): Oh, hell fire, yeah, Leonie. I'm not so old. Leonie, you look good. Young and beautiful—

LEONA: Oh, hush, Cabot!

CABOT: You do, Leonie. Yes, you do. Come sit by my side.

(LEONA *sits down beside* CABOT. *The big boy,* NEWTON, *comes around the house*)

NEWTON: Pa! What are you doing with that pretty woman? I'm going to tell Ma.

CABOT: Newt, this *is* your Ma.

NEWTON: Is that you, Ma?

LEONA: Yep.

NEWTON: I thought Pa was carrying on with some pretty woman again.

LEONA: Shucks, no, Newt. It's just me, bathed and dressed.

NEWTON: Did you bathe again, Ma?

LEONA: Yep.

CABOT: Smells like soap. Clean and sweet.

LEONA: Now, Cabot.

CABOT: Newt, go away somewhere. I want to talk to your Ma.

NEWTON: No. I want to listen.

CABOT: Now do as I say. Go away.

NEWTON: Why?

CABOT: I've got things to talk over with your Ma.

NEWTON: I'm tired, Ma. Can I put my head on your lap and go to sleep, like I used to?

LEONA: Newt, you're too big a boy for that.

NEWTON: I ain't.

CABOT: Now, get the hell out of here, Newt.

NEWTON: I won't.

CABOT: You get the hell out of here, or I'll up and spank you.

NEWTON: No, you won't.

CABOT (*Threatening to get to his feet*): I won't, won't I?

LEONA: Now, Cabot.

NEWTON: No, you won't. She's my mother, and I guess I got a right to rest my head on her lap.

CABOT: And I'm your father, and I guess I got a right to get up and kick your pants.

NEWTON: Ma, tell him to stop.

LEONA: Cabot, let the boy rest his head.

NEWTON: Sure, Pa.

> (GEORGIE *arrives, unseen. Gets off his bike, watching and listening. He keeps out of sight*)

CABOT: You go away, Newton Yearling.

NEWTON: Ah, Pa, I'm tired. I want to go to sleep.

CABOT: Go in the house and sleep. There's a time and place for everything.

LEONA: Let the poor boy rest his head, Cabot.

CABOT: Leonie, you're my wife.

NEWTON: She's my mother.

LEONA: Now, now.

CABOT: I won't have you spoiling a full-grown boy. Go away, Newt. Hurry, now.

NEWTON: I won't! I won't! I won't!

CABOT (*Getting up*): You won't, won't you?

> (CABOT *breaks into a trot, chasing* NEWTON. LEONA *sits alone.* WILBUR *comes out of the house, and puts his head on* LEONA's *lap*)

LEONA: My, it's good to be alive and bathed.

CABOT'S VOICE (*From behind the house*): Newt, you son of a bitch, drop that club or I'll break your arm.

NEWTON'S VOICE: Don't come any closer, Pa, or I'll knock your head off.

CABOT'S VOICE: Drop that club, Newt, and run for your life, now.

NEWTON'S VOICE: Don't you fool with me, Pa. I'll hit you down. Look out now, Pa. I'm warning you. Don't come any closer.

CABOT'S VOICE: Drop that club, I tell you, and run.

> (*The sound of human substance struck by a club is heard*) Newt!

NEWTON'S VOICE: I warned you, Pa.

LEONA: My, it's peaceful and wonderful here.

> (NEWTON *returns, drops club alongside lion, picks up* WILBUR, *lies down and puts his head on* LEONA'S *lap*. WILBUR *goes into the house*)

NEWTON: Ma.

LEONA: Newt. Where's your Pa?

NEWTON: In the back yard. I hit him over the head with a club.

LEONA: Is he hurt?

NEWTON: I think he's dead.

LEONA: Now, Newt, you shouldn't ought to have done that.

NEWTON: Maybe he ain't.

LEONA: A good son shouldn't ought to hit his Pa with a club.

NEWTON: Well, why wouldn't he let me rest my head on your lap?

LEONA: All right. Sleep now.

> (A FARMER *comes into the yard*)

FARMER: Excuse me, ma'am? Anybody around here looking for work?

LEONA: What kind of work?

FARMER: Picking grapes. That man there. I can pay him thirty cents an hour. If he doesn't want to work by the hour I can give him three cents a box. A fast worker can pick fourteen or fifteen boxes an hour. That's about forty-five cents. I've got a heavy crop this year.

LEONA: No, I guess not.

FARMER: I need help bad this year, ma'am. He looks like a big man.

LEONA: No, he gets tired easy. Go talk to my husband. He's in the back yard somewhere.

FARMER: All right, ma'am. (*Going to back of house*) I sure could use a few good hands.

NEWTON: Who was it, Ma?

LEONA: Just a farmer, looking for workers.

(*The* TWINS *return, accompanied by* MR. SMITH *and* MR. HARRIS)

VELMA: Ma, this is Mr. Harris. He's going to put me on the stage.

SELMA: Ma, this is Mr. Smith. He's going to put me on the stage, too.

LEONA: Well, that's nice. I knew you two would get somewhere in the world some day. I'm proud of you.

MR. HARRIS: You're *entitled* to be proud of these girls, Mrs. Yearling. Two or three months of instruction is all they need. After that, fame and fortune.

MR. SMITH: We'll take all responsibility for the girls, Mrs. Yearling. Don't you worry about anything.

MR. HARRIS (*Handing* LEONA *a card*): Our card. We're with the West Coast Novelty Amusement people. Branches in all major cities of the Pacific Coast. Our school's in San Francisco. We'll see that the girls are properly cared for, instructed, and protected from unsuitable companions.

MR. SMITH: You have nothing to worry about, Mrs. Yearling. Mrs. Cavanaugh will escort the girls to San Francisco, and look over them like a mother. In the meantime, we want to advance a little something to you on their future earnings. (*He counts out crisp new bills*) One, two, three, four, five. Six, seven, eight, nine, ten.

LEONA: Did you say *novelty* people?

MR. SMITH (*He makes an acrobatic flip-over*): Yes, novelty.

VELMA: Gee!

LEONA: My! It's certainly good to see something unusual once in a while.

VELMA: Isn't it wonderful, Ma?

LEONA: I'm proud of you.

MR. SMITH: We've only got a few minutes to catch the train.

LEONA: Now you take good care of them.

MR. SMITH: Oh, we will, Mrs. Yearling. Don't you worry about that.

GEORGIE: I've been waiting for you, Sheriff. Gosh! I thought you'd never get here. These are the people.

(*A* SHERIFF *in plain, untidy clothing, wearing a badge, appears*)

SHERIFF: Don't you worry, Georgie. I'll straighten out everything in a minute or two. Law and order in the Sovereign State of California.

(*The* YOUNG MEN *and the* TWINS *go*)

FARMER (*Returning*): Ma'am, I think that man's dead.

SHERIFF: Somebody been killed?

FARMER: Yes. Her husband.

SHERIFF: Who killed him?

NEWTON: I did. I hit him over the head with a club.

GEORGIE: No, he didn't!

SHERIFF: Well, how did he die, then?

GEORGIE: He tripped and fell—off the back porch—on his head.

SHERIFF: Let me make an *official* investigation. (*To* LEONA) Get your family together. (*Goes behind the house*)

NEWTON: Ma, he didn't fall. I hit him.

GEORGIE: He fell.

NEWTON (*Getting up, showing club*): I hit him with this.

GEORGIE: Give me that club. (*Takes club from* NEWTON, *hides it behind rose bushes*) If you don't want a lot of trouble, ma'am, get your family together and go away.

FARMER: He killed his father!

GEORGIE: He didn't kill anybody.

FARMER: He said he did.

GEORGIE: What do you expect a great big idiot like that to say?

NEWTON: I did too kill him.

GEORGIE: Ah, shut up!

LEONA: You be quiet, Newton Yearling. Children! Children! We're moving along.

HENRY (*Appearing*): Come on, everybody. We're on our way again.

(*One by one, the* CHILDREN *join their mother*)

SHERIFF (*Returning*): He's dead all right. Fell on his head all right.

FARMER: No, he didn't! That big fellow hit him over the head.

SHERIFF: Did you *see* it happen?

FARMER: I didn't *see* it happen, but he *said* he did it.

SHERIFF: Well, then shut up! Now, let's see. Get in touch with the Coroner and have him cart the body away.

GEORGIE: Thanks, Sheriff.

SHERIFF: Now, she can come back to her house.

FARMER: I tell you, there's been a murder!

SHERIFF (*Taking out notebook and pencil*): What's your name?

FARMER: Daniel Hough.

SHERIFF: How do you spell it?

FARMER: Ho-u-g-h.

SHERIFF: Age?

FARMER: Sixty-two.

SHERIFF: Married?

FARMER: Yes.

SHERIFF: Number of children?

FARMER: Five.

SHERIFF: Occupation?

FARMER: Farmer.

SHERIFF: What kind of a farm?

FARMER: Malaga and Muscat grapes.

SHERIFF: How many acres?

FARMER: Forty.

SHERIFF: That's all. Get out of here. (*He throws paper away*)

FARMER: I don't know what a man ever wants to be a farmer for. If I don't get workers, I'll lose my whole crop. It's murder.

SHERIFF: Get out of here. (*The* FARMER *goes. To* LEONA) Ready to go? All you people arriving from all over the country, making trouble, breaking laws, no respect for private property.

GEORGIE: Sheriff, you don't need to bawl them out, just because they're poor. They're just as good as any other people.

SHERIFF: Georgie, what is this anyhow? I get up out of a good pinochle game and come out here to try to help you. You want me to get these people out of her house, don't you?

GEORGIE: Yeah, but I thought you could do something for them. You're a big important man.

SHERIFF: No, Georgie, I'm not big. And I'm not important. I'm a Republican. (*To* LEONA *and the children*) Now clear out of here.

GEORGIE (*To* LEONA): You've got some place to go, haven't you?

LEONA: We'll just walk along to a front yard in the next block somewhere.

GEORGIE: Why do you always want to go to places where people don't want you? Go over to my father's house. 137 Vine Street.

LEONA: We wouldn't want to bother anybody.

GEORGIE: You won't be bothering anybody. Go over there, will you?

LEONA: All right, children!

(*They start to go. The* SHERIFF *follows them*)

SHERIFF: Now get out, all of you. Law and order in the Sovereign State of California.

(GEORGIE *stands watching them go.* CABOT *comes from behind the house, holding his head*)

CABOT: Leona! (*Sees* GEORGIE) What happened?

GEORGIE: Your boy hit you over the head with a club.

CABOT: Is that what that crazy Newt did?

GEORGIE: Yeah, and everybody thought you were dead, too.

CABOT: I ain't, though. Where's Leonie?

GEORGIE: I sent them over to my father's house. You go there, too. 137 Vine Street.

(CABOT *goes.* GEORGIE *sits on the steps of the house.* GAUL *arrives*)

GEORGIE (*Running up to* GAUL): Well, it's about time you came back to her.

GAUL: My God! The messenger of love again. My boy, forgive me. I have not come back to remain. I have come back to depart.

GEORGIE: Doesn't love mean anything to you?

GAUL: *Anything?* Everything.

GEORGIE: Then why have you come back to depart? Why haven't you come back to remain?

GAUL: To depart is to remain, and to remain is very often to depart. My heart will stay here.

GEORGIE: What good is your heart, if you're not here with it?

GAUL: I am a traveler.

GEORGIE: What about Miss Hamilton?

GAUL: My heart is broken. Need I tell you my heart is broken?—You, who are Cupid itself. This is her world, not mine. I am a traveler.

GEORGIE: Well, why don't you stop traveling? What do you always want to be running around for?

GAUL: I am one who seeks, and seeking all these years, I have never found until this day, and having found, I am *still* one who seeks.

GEORGIE: What do you seek?

GAUL: What all men seek and never find. One's self and one's companion. My boy, you, with your morning telegram from Boston, a city I have never so much as seen, today revealed to my companion and to myself. I am not Barnaby Gaul, but no man in the world is Barnaby Gaul more than I. Barnaby Gaul is he for whom shy and lonely love waits in shy and lonely house—this house—guarded these many years by this magnificent Abyssinian lion. You have revealed me. I am a fraud.

GEORGIE: No, you're not.

GAUL: I *am.* Be good enough to tell this woman that I came to say good-by.

GEORGIE: Go over to my father's house, will you, and talk to her? She's waiting there. 137 Vine Street.

GAUL: Forgive me. I am on my way again. Messenger, bring the good woman back to her trees and roses and songs and dreams. Bring the good woman home. *Home?*

(*Smoke and flames in the lower window*)

My God! *This* house is on fire. Run down to the corner and turn in the alarm.

(GEORGIE *goes*)

Now the poor woman has no home to come back to.

(*He goes into the house*)

Anybody in here?

LUCY (*Inside the house*): I want my Mama.

GAUL (*Reappearing with the* CHILD *in his arms*): All right. Don't cry. I'll find your Mama for you. This is a hell of a mess for a traveling man to be in. (*He goes*)

CURTAIN

Act Three

The parlor of the STYLIANOS AMERICANOS *home.
About three the same afternoon. The room is typical
of the parlors of almost all peoples of the Near East
in America. Oriental rug. An old Army rifle, crossing
a sword in its sheath, over an enormous photograph
of eleven men, ranging in age from 15 to 70, all with
mustaches of one sort or another; each in a military
uniform or part of one; each holding a gun. American and Greek flags, crossed. A big photograph of a
naked baby on a table covered with velvet. The
baby is* GEORGIE, *aged three months. Another photograph of a bride and groom,* GEORGIE's *father and
mother, standing stiffly in unnatural clothes. A piano.
A phonograph. A few large books. A map of the
world as it was about twenty-five years ago, bor-
dered with the flags of the various nations, as well
as pictures of the kings, emperors and presidents of
the time. Also two large photographs of* STYLIANOS
in wrestler's tights.

STYLIANOS *is at the center of the room, seated on
crossed legs, smoking a nargilah. He is an enormous
man of forty-one or so, thick-necked, with heavy
arms, big hands, and a naive, spiritual face.*

PERICLES, *his father, a man in his early seventies,
comes in noisily, walks about mumbling discon-
tentedly to himself, sits down and lights a cigarette.*

*The two men smoke in silence a moment, and then
begin to speak, the father in Greek, the son in
broken English.*

PERICLES: Aaaahkh, aaaahkh.
STYLIANOS: Don't worry, Papa. Everything's going to be
satisfactory.
PERICLES: Home. Home.
STYLIANOS: The whole world is a man's home.

PERICLES: *My* home is *Smyrna*. I was born in Smyrna. I want to die in Smyrna.

STYLIANOS: Papa, you are a strong man. Maybe some day we will go back to Smyrna together.

PERICLES: No. No. (*He finishes his cigarette, gets up*) The years are all gone. I have given them to you and Georgie.

(*He points to himself in the photograph.* STYLIANOS *gets up, puts his arm around his father*)

That was me, Stylianos. Aaahkh, aaahkh. The infidel Turks.

STYLIANOS: My papa. He is still fighting the Turks.

PERICLES: My son, if I had my youth. If I only had my youth. Give my love to Georgie. I will come back later, and we will sit together and remember the old country. Good-by.

(*He goes to door.* STYLIANOS *puts needle to an old Greek phonograph record.* PERICLES *listens, returns to his chair*)

No. I will stay. (*He sits down*)

STYLIANOS: That's right, Papa. You stay here. We got Smyrna here, too.

(*The doorbell rings.* STYLIANOS *shuts off the phonograph,* PERICLES *goes to the door*)

ANN'S VOICE: Mr. Americanos?

PERICLES (*In English*): Yes, come in, please.

ANN (*Coming in*): Excuse me, Mr. Americanos?

STYLIANOS: Yes, lady.

ANN: I'm Miss Ann Hamilton. I live at 333 Orchard Avenue. Your son Georgie told me to come here until the police drive the people away from my house. They won't go. They just won't budge. It's *my* house. Georgie went to get the police.

STYLIANOS: Don't worry. Everything's going to be satisfactory.

ANN: I'm so confused. It seems like I've been walking years. It's because *he's* gone. I guess I got *lost*, too. Everything's changed. A few hours ago I was happy. Then the people came. Then they wouldn't go. Then *he* went. Then I went after him. So many things have happened to me today.

STYLIANOS: Lady. Please cool down. It's not good to be so exciting.

PERICLES: What's the matter?

STYLIANOS (*Pours wine*): Papa, the lady's got trouble. (*To* ANN) It's nothing. Please sit down.

ANN: Oh, thank you, Mr. Americanos. It's wonderful people like you— I begged him to stay.

STYLIANOS: Here, lady. Please take this. It will do you good.

(*He hands drink to* ANN)

ANN: I told him to wait, and we'd go away together. I told him I'd sell the house. (ANN *drinks*)

STYLIANOS: Lady, don't sell the house now. Keep the house. Ask my Papa.—He don't know nothing. Prices are bad. Please cool down.

ANN: Oh, I'm so ashamed. He ran.—Right in the street. And I ran after him. (*Starts to rise.* STYLIANOS *holds her down*) I couldn't help it. I couldn't do anything else. I tried not to run, but I just couldn't stand still. I love him.

STYLIANOS: She's in love, Papa.

ANN: I walked here. Never in all my life have I walked that way. That's why I am so confused. I got lost, looking for him. Then Georgie—Mr. Americanos, your son is a wonderful, wonderful boy.

(DEMETRIOS *breaks into the room*)

DEMETRIOS: Hello, my cousin.

STYLIANOS: Demetrios! Out!

DEMETRIOS: How is you, Miss Hamilton? Troublous?

STYLIANOS: Out! Good-by, please!

(DEMETRIOS *goes into kitchen*)

Lady. Don't sell the house. Five years ago I paid four thousand dollars for this house. Two stories. Today I can't get thirty-seven hundred.

ANN: When I went into my house everything was ruined. I was born in that house. I don't know why he had to run. My mother and my father built that house when they were married. I didn't want people like that in my house. All Mama's things ruined. And they wouldn't go.

(ANN *takes another drink*)

PERICLES: Is she an actress?

STYLIANOS: No, Papa. The lady is not an actress. Lady, please cool down, please.

ANN: They just wouldn't go. Georgie told me to come here and wait.

> (*She brings Dr. Greatheart's bottle out of her bag, unscrews the top*)

He gave me a bottle of this. "Any time you feel miserable," he shouted—we were running down the street— "just take a swig of the stuff in that bottle. Won't do you any harm." I don't know what it is. I guess it's medicine, though.

> (*She starts to take a swig*)

STYLIANOS: Don't drink that patent medicine. (*He takes bottle*) That's not good. Drink this wine. (*Places bottle on piano*)

ANN (*Taking glass*): Oh, thank you, Mr. Americanos. A toast. To love.

> (ANN *and* STYLIANOS *drink together.* PAPA *takes bottle and drinks*)

I feel so strange. I'm scared. I used to live so peacefully. Everything was quiet and nice. Last night I dreamed of lions.

STYLIANOS: Lions!

> (*He fills* ANN's *glass quickly*)

ANN (*Drinks*): The lions ran after me, and then they became friendly. Then they begged *me* to be friendly. Lions begging *me* to be friendly. This morning, Georgie came with the telegram. And then *he* came. Barnaby Gaul.

STYLIANOS: Lions? Georgie? Telegram? Papa, don't drink that patent medicine.

PERICLES: What's the difference? She's crazy. I'll be crazy, too. (*He drinks*)

ANN: He's nice. It's so nice talking to you, Mr. Americanos. You're just like your beautiful son. At first I didn't understand anything. Boston. Barnaby Gaul. Six roses. But he didn't *remember*. I was so scared, because I thought I'd lose everything, all those years. But little by little he remembered, and then my heart— It sang and sang. Then I remembered the beautiful friendly lions.

STYLIANOS: Lady, drink more.

ANN: Thank you, Mr. Americanos. (*To* PERICLES) To love.

PERICLES (*Takes bottle*): Homeland.

(ANN *tries to repeat Greek word. They drink*)

ANN: I know something's happening. I don't know what it is. He came up onto the porch and kissed me. It was like he had kissed me every day for twenty-seven years. And when he walked through the house, I thought he'd been there all those years. One beautiful thing after another, as if I were still dreaming, but I wasn't scared any more. He sang to me. (*She sings. Stops*) I don't know what's happened.

STYLIANOS: Lady, please go into this room and lie down. Try to sleep.

ANN (*Going*): Thank you very much, Mr. Americanos.

PAPA: Stylianos!

STYLIANOS: Papa, the lady's got trouble.

(*He closes the door, sits on the floor and begins to puff at the nargilah.* GEORGIE *runs into the room*)

GEORGIE: Is she here, Pa?

STYLIANOS: Sleeping.

GEORGIE: Her house is on fire, Pa.

STYLIANOS: House on fire?

GEORGIE: They set fire to it. And that guy. He didn't leave town.

STYLIANOS: Wait, Georgie! Please cool down, Georgie.

GEORGIE: He's in the White Fawn saloon, Pa. You've got to go get him.

STYLIANOS: Georgie! *Please* cool down.

GEORGIE: Pa, he may run away.

STYLIANOS: Georgie, sit down a minute. Then we talk. Don't talk now. Just sit. Quiet!

(GEORGIE *tries to quiet down*)

Now, what's the matter?

GEORGIE (*Jumping out of chair*): Tom Fiora—

STYLIANOS (*Pushing him back into chair*): Quiet, Georgie.

(STYLIANOS *folds his arms and waits for* GEORGIE *to calm down*)

All right, Georgie, go ahead.

GEORGIE: Tom Fiora—he's another messenger—put a tele-

gram in my pocket. It wasn't a real telegram. He was
sore at me. His brother Mike wrote it. The telegram was
for her.

PERICLES: Georgie, is war in Europe?

GEORGIE: Yes, Grandpa. But this isn't about the war.

STYLIANOS: Cool down, Georgie. Speak slow.

GEORGIE: I recited the telegram to her. I talked to her. I
made her believe it was all real.

STYLIANOS: Georgie! What this telegram *say?*

GEORGIE: Here's the telegram, Pa. You read it. I don't like
to think about it any more.

> (STYLIANOS *takes the telegram from* GEORGIE.
> DEMETRIOS *enters and stands looking at telegram
> which* GEORGIE *has handed to* STYLIANOS.
> STYLIANOS *sees him and orders him out of the room.*
> DEMETRIOS *goes*)

PERICLES (*Rises*): Georgie. Is the Greeks in the war?

GEORGIE: No, Grandpa. Germany and Poland.

STYLIANOS (*Quoting telegram*): Love's Old Sweet Song.
Twenty-seven years. Six roses. Four red. Two white. Five
children. Get rid of everybody. Remember me. Speak to
me. I love you. It's very romantical, Georgie. Why you
exciting?

GEORGIE: Romantical, my eye. Don't you see, Pa, the guy
went into the house, and I thought everything was going
to be all right. But he ran away from her.

STYLIANOS: Don't worry. Everything's going to be satisfactory.

GEORGIE: How's everything going to be satisfactory?

STYLIANOS: You leave everything to me.

> (DEMETRIOS *comes into the room again. He doesn't
> speak, but looks expectantly towards* STYLIANOS)

Demetrios, out! Can't you see I've got trouble?

DEMETRIOS: Stylianos, for why you tell me "Out! Out!" I am
your cousin?

STYLIANOS: Yes, you are my cousin.

DEMETRIOS (*Going*): I am your cousin no more. I quit!

STYLIANOS: All right, Georgie. Tell the romance.

GEORGIE: I told her to wait here until I could come and
take her home. But now there's no home to take her to,
and the man's gone.

STYLIANOS: That man. What kind of man is he?

GEORGIE: I *thought* he was a great man, Pa, on account of the telegram. It's all my fault.

STYLIANOS: Georgie, when that man went into the house— (GEORGIE *nods*) I don't want you to feel bad, Georgie. It's not your fault.

GEORGIE: I started it all.

STYLIANOS: Georgie, be philosopher, please.

GEORGIE: What good is philosophy? Her house is burned down. The man's gone. How are we going to get out of this with philosophy?

STYLIANOS: Easy as peachy-pie, Georgie. I go get that man.

GEORGIE: He won't come. He's drinking. He won't come.

STYLIANOS: No? I carry him here. I make him talk to her. If she still wants him, I make him marry her.

GEORGIE: I told him everything at the fire. I told him to come here. Then I followed him to the White Fawn. He won't come.

STYLIANOS: You go for ride. You forget everything.

GEORGIE: All right, Pa. (*Starts to go*)

STYLIANOS: I go get that man.

GEORGIE: He's a big guy, and he carries a straw suitcase.

STYLIANOS: I find him, all right.

GEORGIE: Thanks, Pa. Gosh! I sure make a lot of trouble.

(*He goes*)

(STYLIANOS *does limbering-up exercises and half a minute of fancy wrestling*)

PERICLES: Bravo.

(GEORGIE *breaks into the room with a brand-new bicycle*)

GEORGIE: Look, Pa!

STYLIANOS: Georgie! Where you get that bike?

GEORGIE (*Honks horn*): He gave it to me.

STYLIANOS: Who?

GEORGIE: That guy, Pa.

STYLIANOS: You mean the man?

GEORGIE (*Setting the bike beside the piano*): Yeah. Barnaby Gaul. He rode the bike out here. He was riding like everything, zigzagging all over the place, blowing the horn, ringing the bell. (*He honks the horn and rings the bell*) He tried to ride one-handed through the hedge. You can't do that with both hands. He hurt himself, I guess, but he didn't hurt the bike. He's drunk. He's sitting on the lawn, holding his leg. I'm supposed to get him a drink of water. (*Begins to go, stops, sits down*) Gosh, Pa! I sure am a dope.

STYLIANOS: Dope? Why dope?

GEORGIE: I forgot everything, just because he gave me a lousy brand-new bike.

STYLIANOS: Don't worry. Everything's going to be satisfactory. Georgie, I gonna rassle that man.

GEORGIE: Ah, Pa. What do you want to rassle him for?

STYLIANOS: He's drunk. I gonna teach him manners.

GEORGIE: He's got manners, Pa.

STYLIANOS: Georgie, I gonna get head-lock, half-nelson, toe-hold and scissor-hold on that man.

GEORGIE: Ah, Pa, you'll ruin him.

STYLIANOS: That's all right. I be careful.

GEORGIE: Careful? He can't even stand up, I don't think. He's sitting on the lawn holding his leg, and you want to get a half-nelson on him. I'm supposed to get him a glass of water.

(*He goes.* BARNABY GAUL, *limping, comes in*)

GAUL: For the love of God! Bring me a glass of water. I'm dying.

STYLIANOS: Who are you?

GAUL (*Sits*): Nobody. A wretch. A man without a home. Neither son, nor brother, nor husband, nor father. A man without an address. A man who gets no mail. A traveler. A tourist.

(GEORGIE *brings him a glass of water*)

A failure.

(GAUL *drinks the water*)

STYLIANOS: Georgie, why is he bragging?

GEORGIE: He's not bragging. That's the way he talks.

STYLIANOS: What is your name?

GAUL: My name's Jim. I am a swindler who is himself swindled every day. Every minute.

STYLIANOS: Georgie, is this the man?

GEORGIE: Yeah, Pa. (*To* GAUL) I don't want the bike.

GAUL: I'm the man. Dr. Greatheart. A fraud. Barnaby Gaul. Never heard of Barnaby Gaul in my life. Who invented that incredible name?

GEORGIE: Mike Fiora.

GAUL: Mike Fiora! What'd he do it for?

GEORGIE: So his brother could get even on me.

GAUL: My name's Jim. Just plain ordinary Jim. Where is she?

STYLIANOS: Georgie, I gonna rassle that man.

GAUL: Rassle? Who's going to rassle who?

STYLIANOS: I gonna rassle *you*.

GAUL: Why? I'm hurt.

STYLIANOS: I gonna teach you manners. You ain't hurt.

GAUL: Manners? What's the matter with my manners?

STYLIANOS (*Limbering up*): You get ready, now. I give you chance.

PERICLES: Bravo!

GEORGIE: You can't rassle *him*.

STYLIANOS: Why not, Georgie?

GEORGIE: Suppose she still loves him?

GAUL: Yes. Suppose she still loves me?

GEORGIE: A lot of good he'll be after you get through with him. Come on, Pa. Leave him alone.

STYLIANOS: Why you come here? Tell the truth.

GAUL: I came to tell her her house is burned down. The poor woman's alone in the world.

GEORGIE: What did you do with the little girl?

GAUL: She's with the Sheriff. I tried to find her mother, but I couldn't, so I took her to the police. I told them the truth, but they wouldn't believe me. They said she was *my* daughter. They said she looks like *me*. They're keeping her until I know what to do with her. She needs Ann. And I need Ann. (*To* GEORGIE) Why don't you want the bike?

GEORGIE: I've made a lot of trouble. Just because you gave me a bike, I forgot everything.

STYLIANOS: Georgie, you go away.

GAUL: Why? Why send the boy away?

> (STYLIANOS *gestures to* GEORGIE. GEORGIE *goes into the kitchen.* STYLIANOS *gives* GAUL *a long meaningful look and gestures for him to come forward and wrestle*)

Now, Mr. Papakapoulos—

STYLIANOS: Mr. *What?*

GAUL: Mr. Arkapapoulos—

STYLIANOS: *What?*

GAUL: My dear sir.

STYLIANOS: You better try hard.

GAUL: I can't rassle.

STYLIANOS: You can't rassle! (*He lifts* GAUL *and spins him around*)

GAUL: One moment.

STYLIANOS: This airplane spin.

GAUL: For the love of God, Greek.

PERICLES: Stylianos, who is this great man?

(STYLIANOS *swings* GAUL *around to* PERICLES. GAUL *and* PERICLES *shake hands*)

GAUL: Be good enough to set me down on my feet. I can't stand height.

STYLIANOS (*Sets* GAUL *on his feet. Commanding*): Rassle!

GAUL: I'm in love. How can I rassle when I'm in love?

(STYLIANOS *gets full-nelson on* GAUL)

STYLIANOS: You not in love. Why you run away from that lady?

GAUL: I don't know.

STYLIANOS: Why you start trouble?

GAUL: I didn't know I was starting trouble.

STYLIANOS: Why you go in the house?

GAUL: She wanted me to.

STYLIANOS: She wanted you to?

GAUL: One moment, please.

STYLIANOS: This full-nelson.

GAUL: All right. Full-nelson.

(STYLIANOS *lets him go*)

I didn't know who she was. Your son told me. I didn't send her a telegram from Boston. Your son said I did. I love her. I need her.

STYLIANOS (*Getting head-lock on* GAUL): Poor lady. Handsome man like you, telling lies all the time. This head-lock.

GAUL: All right. Head-lock. I'm not Dr. Greatheart. I'm not Barnaby Gaul. My name's Jim. Jim Doherty. Even so, I love her.

(STYLIANOS *grips him tighter*)

Would you mind loosening your arm a little? Your son's going to be a great man some day.

STYLIANOS: Georgie?

GAUL: Yes, sir.

STYLIANOS: Georgie Americanos?

GAUL: Yes, sir. Georgie Americanos.

(GEORGIE *comes in*)

GEORGIE: Ah, Pa! Let him go, will you?

GAUL: Yeah. The boy's got the right idea. Let him go.

(STYLIANOS *releases* GAUL)

GEORGIE: All I wanted to do was make things a little better. Now they're worse.

STYLIANOS: No. I rassle him. Everything's going to be satisfactory. He loves her. Don't you?

GAUL: Of course I love her.

GEORGIE: If you really loved her, you'd love everybody. You can't go around loving one person and hating everybody else.

GAUL: Who said anything about hating anybody? I've always loved everybody.

STYLIANOS: How about that, Georgie?

GEORGIE: You ran away when you knew she loved you.

STYLIANOS: You trouble-maker!

(STYLIANOS *gets another hold on* GAUL)

GAUL: All right. What's this?

STYLIANOS: This Australian jaw-breaker.

GEORGIE: Leave him alone, Pa. It's not his fault.

STYLIANOS (*Releasing* GAUL): No, Georgie? Whose fault is it?

GEORGIE: I don't know, Pa. It sure is a keen wheel, though.

STYLIANOS: You love this woman, you liar?

GAUL: Of course, I love her. I more than love her. We have a child.

STYLIANOS: You got money?

GAUL: Some. I spent most of my money today.

STYLIANOS: How much you got?

GAUL: Oh, ten, eleven, twelve dollars.

STYLIANOS: Ten, eleven, twelve dollars!

GAUL: It's not a lot, but when a man's in love—

(STYLIANOS *approaches threateningly*)

One moment! Will you kindly take a card. Any card at all.

(STYLIANOS *takes a card*)

You are a wrestler, I believe. You have wrestled in the arena.

STYLIANOS: World's Heavyweight Champion Kern County.

GAUL: I, too, am a wrestler.

STYLIANOS: All right. Let's rassle.

GAUL: I do not wrestle as you wrestle, my friend.

STYLIANOS: You rassle women?

GAUL: You shame me. The card you have taken is the Nine of Clubs, I believe. Three times three is nine. You are also a member of the Greek Orthodox Church, I believe. The number three, therefore, is not meaningless to you.

(STYLIANOS *and* GEORGIE *cross themselves*)

Georgie, will *you* take a card?

GEORGIE (*Taking card*): We don't want any of your medicine.

GAUL: You don't need any of it, I believe. Now what card have you?

GEORGIE: The Nine of Clubs. I guess that's all you've got in that deck.

GAUL: No. Here. Look at the cards. All different. All different.

(GEORGIE *looks*)

You are a messenger.

GEORGIE: Yeah.

GAUL: I, too, am a messenger.

STYLIANOS: Rassler. Messenger. What else?

GAUL: I am a missionary. This elderly gentleman here, I believe, is your father?

STYLIANOS: Papa, I want you to meet—

GAUL: Dr. Greatheart. Dr. Greatheart!

(*They shake hands*)

GEORGIE: Ah, that's not your real name. What are you bluffing for?

STYLIANOS: Yes, tell the boy why you bluff. This is not poker game.

GAUL: My good man, *life* is a poker game, among other things.

STYLIANOS: Georgie, this man is philosopher.

GEORGIE: Philosopher, my eye. Don't you see, Pa, that's the

way he gathers a crowd around him, and then sells his
medicine. He makes them think something very mysterious is going to happen.

GAUL: Something mysterious *does* happen. Every time.
Your father is right. I *am* a philosopher.

STYLIANOS: What philosophy you have?

GAUL: You shall see in a moment. (*To* PERICLES) Will *you*
kindly take a card?

PERICLES: He is a Christian. I can tell from the way he
speaks.

GAUL: I beg your pardon. I do not speak Greek. It is em-
barrassing to me that I am not able to speak such a
magnificent language. You will forgive me, I am sure.

(PERICLES *and* GAUL *bow*)

What did your father say?

STYLIANOS: He said you are a Christian.

GAUL: I am.

STYLIANOS: He said he can tell from the way you speak.

GAUL: Your father is a noble man.

STYLIANOS: He used to be a peasant in the old country.

GAUL: I, too, am a peasant. (*To* PERICLES) I need not tell
you the card you have taken is the Nine of Clubs.

GEORGIE: Yeah, it's the Nine of Clubs all right. How come
everybody takes the Nine of Clubs?

(ANN *comes in*)

GAUL: Now, for the amazing demonstration I am about to
make—

ANN: Barnaby!

(GAUL *embraces her*)

Barnaby!

GEORGIE: His name isn't Barnaby, Miss Hamilton.

ANN: Oh, Georgie. How can I ever thank you?

STYLIANOS: His name is Jim.

ANN: And you, Mr. Americanos? You *did* come back,
Barnaby.

STYLIANOS: Jim!

ANN: I never want to see this town again. I'll sell the house,
and we'll go to Boston.

GAUL: Ann, your house is burned down.

ANN: What?

GAUL: Yes, Ann.

ANN: I don't care. I don't care about the house. I don't care about anything. I'm happy, Barnaby. You've come back to me.

(*Doorbell rings and the* SHERIFF *enters with* LUCY)

SHERIFF: Your daughter's been asking for her father.

(LUCY *runs to* GAUL'S *arms*)

ANN: Oh, what a beautiful child, Barnaby. Come here, darling. (*Opens her arms to child, who rushes into them*) Why didn't you tell me? Why, Barnaby, she looks just like you.

GAUL: It's nothing. Nothing at all. Sheriff, this little girl is not my daughter.

SHERIFF: She *looks* like you.

GAUL: She belongs to that family from Oklahoma. I looked all over for her mother, but I couldn't find her.

SHERIFF: She *likes* you. Don't you like *her?*

GAUL: I love her more than anyone in the world, except this woman, but I love the truth, too. I want you to know, because I want to be her father. I want to see her grow into grace and loveliness. I have never before felt the affection I feel for this woman and this child.

SHERIFF: Well, she *looks* like you.

GAUL: She's mine in spirit, at least. (*To* LUCY) You do love me, don't you, child?

LUCY: Yes. I love the way you smell.

GAUL (*Taking child in his arms*): I don't care why you love me, just so you do.

SHERIFF: Well, if I ever saw a father, there he is.

GAUL: And this woman, child? You love her, too, don't you?

ANN (*Holding out her arms to* LUCY): You love me, darling, don't you?

LUCY (*Running into* ANN'S *arms*): Yes. I love you, too.

SHERIFF: There you are. A father, a mother, and a beautiful child.

(*The doorbell rings. All the* CHILDREN *enter, followed by* MRS. YEARLING)

GEORGIE: Pa, these are the people.

STYLIANOS: Come in. Come in. (STYLIANOS *takes all the* CHILDREN *to the sofa*)

GAUL (*To* LEONA): Dear lady, here is your daughter. If the child is willing, and if you are willing—

LEONA: Well, you take good care of Lucy.

ANN: Oh, we will, we will!

LEONA (*To* GEORGIE): I just came to thank you. Children, we'll be going along now.

STYLIANOS: No, lady. You stay here. Everybody stay here. We all sit down and have supper together. Demetrios! My cousin, Demetrios!

> (DEMETRIOS *appears*)

You go get bread. Get meat. Get wine. We all gonna sit down and have supper together. Hurry up! We wait for you.

DEMETRIOS: I am your cousin again?

STYLIANOS: Yes. Everybody is my cousin.

> (DEMETRIOS *goes*)

> (*The doorbell rings and* CABOT YEARLING *comes in*)

LEONA: Why, Cabot! I thought you was dead.

CABOT: Dead? Leona, you look good. (*To* GAUL) Doc, I want to tell you that medicine saved my life.

GAUL: Thank you, my good man.

> (CABOT *goes to* LEONA)

Ann, I'm a pitchman. I sell this medicine to people. I sometimes drink it myself. I sometimes believe in it myself. Take a card, please.

> (ANN *takes a card*)

Thank you. What card have you?

ANN: The Queen of Hearts.

GAUL: The Queen of Hearts. Ann, I love you. I'll do anything I can to make you happy. I'll do anything *you* want me to do. I'll throw away my suitcase. I'm alone in the world. I hardly ever see a face twice, and I hardly ever see a face I want to see twice. I like people, but I don't like the disgrace they've fallen into. The only way I know how to do anything about it is to set up my suitcase in the streets, get behind it, and talk to them. Ann, tell me what you want me to do, and I'll do it.

ANN: I want to do whatever you want me to do, Barnaby.

GAUL: My name's Jim, Ann. You could help me a lot. I wouldn't spend so much time in saloons, Ann. I'd drink some, of course, but I wouldn't drink so much. After a while we could get a trailer, and you could stand up on the platform with me. You and the little girl. You'd just stand there, Ann. It does them good to look upon beauty. I know it does, because it does me good. We'd go from town to town. The highways are beautiful all the year around.

ANN: Jim, we're going to be so happy.

GAUL: Mr. Americanos, I shall always be grateful to you on account of this boy: this Postal Telegraph messenger who carries to the world the only message worth carrying. (*To* CABOT) My good man, I want you to be a living testimonial to the wonderful powers of Dr. Greatheart's Five-Star Multi-Purpose Indian Remedy. I want *all* of you to be that living testimonial. Now, Mr. Yearling, if you will line up the children, we will rehearse the amazing demonstration I am going to make from now on all over the country.

(CABOT *lines up the* CHILDREN)

Children, will each of you kindly take a card. Any card at all. (*He gives each child a card*) Hold the cards aloft.

(*Each card is the Nine of Clubs.* GAUL *starts to sing "Of All the Things I Love."* ANN *joins him. Finally the* CHILDREN *join in*)

(*To the audience, while the* CHILDREN *are singing*)

Ladies and gentlemen, I have here on this platform, Dr. Greatheart's World Famous A Capelle Choir, and while the children are singing this lovely little ballad, I'm going to ask you to step up a little closer. I have gathered these children from the four corners of the earth. Each child is a natural-born singer. Also each child is a genius. Beyond this platform and across the street is the world. What will happen to each child as it wanders into the world only God knows, but now each child is a genius.

(*He takes a bottle out of his coat pocket and holds it aloft*)

I have here in this bottle a medicine. The juices of certain roots and barks are extracted—

CURTAIN

The Beautiful People

To John Mason Brown

Note

The following private note tells something about this play:

SUNDAY MIDNIGHT. JANUARY 5, 1941.

A little after midnight December 31, 1940—last year—I began to write a play entitled A Cup of Kindness, *which I have just now finished. It will probably be called* Pole Star and Pyramid.

There doesn't appear to be any sadness in the play, and that is the biggest thing against it. There are a lot of other things in it, however, and maybe it doesn't need sadness, or maybe there is sadness in it, and I don't realize it yet.

The play has only one set, and only a handful of characters. Each part is good. I think it is going to turn out O.K.

The play was finally called neither *A Cup of Kindness* nor *Pole Star and Pyramid*, and it turned out that there *was* sadness in it. One important character, Harold, was added to the play, as well as one minor character, Steve. Harold, and his horn, came from Don Freeman, the artist. Steve, the homeless young man, came from Peter Xantho, stage manager of the show. Considerable literary writing was taken out of the play, some of it on the suggestion of Jed Harris. The part of Dan Hillboy was expanded because of the possibilities I saw in the talent of Farrell Pelly. In fact, almost every part in the play was expanded, once I had met the players and saw what they could do.

The play was produced by myself, with my own money, and directed by me. I think this is the only way for me to work in the theater, and I can imagine that it is possibly the only way for other playwrights to work in the theater too. If so, I hope they will have money enough to do so. The success of *The Time of Your Life* on the road and of *My Name Is Aram* in the bookstores and through the Book-of-the-Month Club provided me with just enough extra money to gamble on this play—which I was eager to do. Pat Duggan took care of the business.

Three free performances of the play were given before the opening: one for children, one for people who had never seen a stage play, and one for people who stood in line one morning to get their free tickets for the performance that evening. Three paid preview performances were given. The play did not go to another city for a try-out. There wasn't money enough; there wasn't time enough; and I didn't think there was any necessity to try the play out, except during the three free performances.

Putting on this play was the happiest experience in the theater I have known. No bosses, no pressure from investors, no fancy theories, and a decent chance to make a decent and honorable mistake.

I am aware of the play's defects. Although not negligible, they possess some dignity. I am sorry they needed to be, but they needed to be. Next time I hope there will be fewer of them.

WILLIAM SAROYAN

San Francisco, June 7, 1941

The Beautiful People was first performed at the Lyceum Theatre in New York on Monday, April 21, 1941. It closed, after 120 performances, on Saturday, August 2, 1941. The setting was designed by Samuel Leve. The play opened with the following cast: Eugene Loring as OWEN WEBSTER, Fredrica Slemons as HARMONY BLUEBLOSSOM, Betsy Blair as AGNES WEBSTER, Curtis Cooksey as JONAH WEBSTER, E. J. Ballantine as WILLIAM PRIM, Farrell Pelly as DAN HILLBOY, Edward Nannary as FATHER HOGAN, Don Freeman as HAROLD WEBSTER, and Peter Xantho as STEVE.

THE PEOPLE

OWEN WEBSTER, *a poet, scientist, son, and brother*
HARMONY BLUEBLOSSOM, *a little old lady in the summer-
time*
AGNES WEBSTER, *a saint*
JONAH WEBSTER, *a father*
WILLIAM PRIM, *a vice-president*
DAN HILLBOY, *a good companion*
FATHER HOGAN, *a Catholic*
HAROLD WEBSTER, *a son and brother*
STEVE, *a homeless young man*

THE PLACE

*The living-room, the front porch, and the yard of an old
house on Red Rock Hill, near Quintara Woods in the Sunset District of San Francisco.*

THE TIME

Afternoon and evening of a summer day.

A cornet is heard. The song is Wonderful One.

The curtain rises.

OWEN WEBSTER *is in the house alone. He is leaning over the table, concentrating on a letter. He lifts it, reads some of it to himself, folds it, puts it back into its envelope, and puts the envelope in a back pocket.*

OWEN: What's in New York—mice? We got mice right here in the house.

> (*He takes a penny from his pocket, flips it in the air, slaps it on his hand, and looks at it*)

Heads.

> (*He goes to the piano and starts to play* Wonderful One. *Soon the cornet is heard again. He stops playing to listen. The cornet fades away. He rests his head on his folded arms, then strikes all the keys of the piano, from left to right. He gets off the stool, stands on it, opens the top of the piano, and examines the strings inside. He runs a finger across the strings, from left to right, in three different movements. He climbs the piano, stands on it, and reaches up for one particular book on the high shelf. He opens the book, examines it, closes it, and puts it back*)

Just a lot of words.

> (*He comes down from the piano, and walks on the edge of the bay-window. He picks up a copy of the Saturday Evening Post, sits at the table and turns the pages*)

> (*Singing or chanting softly*)

Row, row, row your boat
Gently down the stream,

Merrily, merrily, merrily, merrily,
Life is but a dream.

> (*He stops. His attention is drawn to a particular picture*)

Amazing! Automobile!

> (*He tears the page out of the magazine, crumples it, throws it over his head onto the floor*)

> (*Sings again and turns some more pages*)

Gently down the stream.

> (*Discovers a new picture*)

Beautiful! Airplane!

> (*Tears out page, throws it away*)

Jello!

> (*Turns pages again. Reads a moment, rises*)

Elinore, he said, I love you.

> (*Eloquently*)

Literature!

> (*Pause*)

Oh, Elinore of the Saturday Evening Post, I love you.

> (HARMONY BLUEBLOSSOM *is seen coming up the hill. She looks around at the view, comes to the house, looks at the number on the house, and slowly enters the room*)

I love you, Elinore. Do you hear me?

> (MISS BLUEBLOSSOM *watches and listens, fascinated*)

I would travel to the far corners of Europe, Asia, Africa and Australia to see your shining face.

> (*He ends this eloquent recitation with outstretched arms*)

HARMONY: Young man!

> (OWEN *jumps and turns*)

Who in the world are you talking to?
OWEN: Elinore. (*Lowers his arms, embarrassed*)

HARMONY: Who's Elinore?

OWEN: Nobody. She's a dame in the Saturday Evening Post. She's the sweetheart of the nickel magazines. What's *your* name?

HARMONY: Harmony Blueblossom.

OWEN: Harmony Blueblossom! Honest?

HARMONY: Cross my heart.

OWEN: Nobody ever comes up here on Red Rock Hill. Are you lost?

HARMONY: I'm looking for a man named Jonah. Do you know him?

OWEN: Do I know him? He's my father.

HARMONY (*Looking at him closely*): Your *father?*

OWEN (*Proudly*): Sure.

HARMONY: Jonah *Webster?*

OWEN: That's right. Jonah Webster. (*Very politely*) Please come in. Won't you sit down?

HARMONY (*At chair*): Is he here?

OWEN: He isn't here *now,* but he'll be here soon. Please sit down.

HARMONY (*Sits*): Thank you.

OWEN (*Looking at her*): Blueblossom!

HARMONY: Yes.

OWEN: Wonderful! My father sure is a killer. If you're this pretty now, boy, what you must have been back there in the good old days before I was born!

HARMONY: When was that?

OWEN: Oh, I haven't been around long—fifteen years. (*Proudly*) I'm a failure.

HARMONY (*She brings out her knitting*): I don't believe it.

OWEN: It's the truth. No education, no social contacts, no political affiliations. I just loaf. (*Looking at the knitting*) What *is* all that stuff?

HARMONY: Knitting.

OWEN (*After watching her knit a moment*): Is that good?

HARMONY: Perfectly harmless. Surely you must do something other than loaf.

OWEN: Oh, I read, too. And sleep. And *think.* I do a *lot* of thinking for a punk my age.

HARMONY: Punk?

OWEN: Yeah. Loafer. Good-for-nothing. I haven't done a day's work in my life. I'm opposed to work. Aren't you?

HARMONY (*Knitting faster*): No. I believe I'm in favor of work.

OWEN: Well, that's all right—but *I'm* opposed to it.

HARMONY: If nobody worked, I have heard that civilization would— (*Scarcely daring to say the fearful word*) —collapse!

OWEN (*Leans against the table*): Ah, that's a lot of jitney propaganda.

HARMONY: I read it in The Reader's Digest.

OWEN: Who wrote it?

HARMONY: I don't remember.

OWEN: Well, whoever he is, he's a dreamer.

HARMONY: What do you mean?

OWEN: I mean that collapse stuff is a lot of hooey. Anything that collapses—for *any* reason—deserves to. If nobody worked, nothing would collapse. Everybody would look around, take it easy, find out what they *want* to do, and then *do* it. Then it wouldn't be work, it would be living, which is what we're supposed to be doing around here, I guess.

HARMONY: Yes. I believe we are supposed to be living.

OWEN: All right. (*From porch*) On a day like this—a beautiful summer day—any man who works—well, I feel sorry for him. He's not living. He's doing things he doesn't want to do. He's thinking about things he doesn't want to think about; worrying; losing his mind all the time. (*Angry*) A life has a right, hasn't it?

HARMONY (*Looking up at him severely*): Young man! Are you a Communist?

OWEN: Hell, no. They're no different from the Republicans, and the Republicans are no different from the Democrats. That's all politics. I don't believe in *little* rights and *little* freedoms. Freedom of speech and freedom of assembly. Who've they got to talk *to* or assemble *with*? I believe in freedom of freedom. Communist? I'm a poet.

HARMONY (*Challenged*): Well, you *eat*.

OWEN: Oh, sure. I *love* food. Don't you? But I fast, too, you know.

HARMONY: You do? Are you a Catholic?

OWEN: No, no—just a poet.

HARMONY: Then why do you fast?

OWEN: Why? Because there's no food.

(*He looks around the room, then disappears in the hallway*)

HARMONY: What in the world are you looking for?

OWEN (*Sticking his head out*): A mousetrap.

HARMONY: What?

OWEN (*Sticking his head out again*): A mousetrap.

HARMONY: Now, what do you want with a mousetrap?

OWEN (*Holding mousetrap*): Interesting, isn't it? Here, I'll show you how it works.

> (*Sets trap and places it at the center of the room right in front of her*)

How'd you like to be a mouse and get caught in something like this?

> (*Snaps the trap with a piece of rolled paper*)

HARMONY (*Startled*): I beg your pardon?

OWEN: I mean, it would be quite a surprise, wouldn't it? (*Showing her the trap*) One would feel very foolish. (*Rises*) My sister is always burning the traps because she's so afraid one of us is going to be cruel to something else alive. (*Sets trap again*) That's why I've got to hide them. You've got no right, she says. Owen Webster, you've got no right. (*Looking for a place to put the trap*)

HARMONY: Over in the corner. Over in the corner, boy—if you want to catch a mouse.

OWEN (*Places trap at center of room*): No—I've tried the corners. They don't fall for the traps there.

HARMONY: No mouse is going to fool with a trap at the center of a room. And where's the cheese?

OWEN: Cheese in traps doesn't fool our mice. They want cheese where it belongs—in the pantry, and traps where they belong—out in the open, where they can study them. They just study the traps. They don't crowd into them.

HARMONY: I have never heard of such mice. (*Pause*) And where has your father gone?

OWEN: Nowhere in particular. He likes to stand on a street corner now and then and talk to the people.

HARMONY: What does he talk *about*?

OWEN (*Kneeling on the chair*): Don't you know my father?

HARMONY: Not lately. You look a good deal like Jonah when I saw him last. I don't understand his talking on street corners.

OWEN: Well—sometimes he hollers, too. (*He looks down on the trap, smiling*) One of them will come out and look at the trap.

HARMONY: I don't know why a mouse would want to look at a trap.

OWEN: They're suspicious. They've been trained not to be fearful, but I suppose they'll always be suspicious.

HARMONY: Who in the world trained them?

OWEN: My sister! St. Agnes of the Mice, we call her. I believe the mice worship her.

HARMONY: *Worship* her?

OWEN: You don't often hear of mice bringing people flowers, do you?

HARMONY: Young man!

OWEN: Yeah. And last Christmas when my sister had the flu the mice got together in this room—over by the stairs there—and prayed for her. And St. Agnes got well without so much as taking an aspirin.

HARMONY: I have never heard of anything so interesting.

OWEN: Yeah. My sister says we must love them, but I think they should at least *see* a trap occasionally. Don't you?

HARMONY: Yes, I do. I'm not absolutely sure, however. Perhaps it would be best not to hurt their feelings, since they bring her flowers. (*Pause*) What sort of flowers?

OWEN: Little flowers. On her birthday the flowers had been arranged to spell Agnes. It was the sweetest sight the human eye ever saw. They ask very little, take care of their own sick, and pray for the best. It's simply a question of who lives here—the *mice* or us?

HARMONY (*With affection*): I would so like to see Jonah again.

OWEN: You ought to see him. He's a failure, too.

HARMONY: Not Jonah. (*Pause*) And what do *you* want to be when you grow up?

OWEN: Nothing. I'm a writer.

HARMONY: A *writer*? How wonderful.

OWEN: Yeah. I look at things carefully. I'm going to turn everything upside down, inside out, all the way around, and make it better—well, less worst. (*He demonstrates*)

HARMONY: I almost believe you. And your sister—of the mice—what does she do?

OWEN: She fights off boys and men. She's very pretty, and every man who sees her thinks she's the girl he's been waiting for all his life.

HARMONY: Is she *that* pretty?

OWEN: Oh yeah. I'll bet she's just as pretty as you were when you were a little girl. She rambles around all over the city, fighting 'em off all day. There's not a man in the lot, she says.

HARMONY: How strange. There used to be.

OWEN: Not any more. To look at her you wouldn't think a little girl like that would pack such a mean wallop.

HARMONY: Surely *one* of them must be worthy of more than a wallop.

OWEN: *Not one.* There isn't a man in the whole kit and kaboodle, she says. She expects a lot of human beings —especially men. They've been here long enough, she says. She won't have any traffic with people who don't understand how long they've been here and what a responsibility it is. There's no excuse for it, she says.

HARMONY: No excuse for what?

OWEN: For being the way they are—weak and foolish and fearful.

HARMONY: What a strange young girl.

OWEN: Yeah. The mice worship her. They spell her name with flowers. I suppose an undertaking like that calls for every hand.

HARMONY: Are there *several* of them?

OWEN: Several? There must be a *thousand*, at least.

HARMONY: A *thousand* mice in one house!

OWEN: Yeah. No *rats*, mind you—just little mice. Of course a house is a pretty big proposition, and a house like *this*— well, the good Lord knows there's room enough. My sister says there's room enough *anywhere* for a little human kindness. There are certain behind-the-scene corners and areas and spaces that we could never live in —well, that's where they live.

HARMONY: And Jonah's other children—who are they?

OWEN (*He looks at the little old lady*): Haven't you got any children?

HARMONY: No, I haven't.

OWEN: My father's got three. Me, my sister, and my brother Harold. (*Pause*) Only he's in New York.

HARMONY: New York!

OWEN: Yeah. New York, New York. Do you know how many miles away New York is?

HARMONY: No, I don't believe I do.

OWEN (*Dramatically*): Three thousand three hundred and thirty-three miles.

HARMONY: What's he doing there?

OWEN: Search me. He's nineteen years old, though. He's

got a mind of his own. He's got a cornet, too. (*He stands back, listening, and again the cornet is heard from far away*)

HARMONY: What are you listening to, young man?

OWEN: My brother. Harold. Playing the cornet.

HARMONY: Do you mean to say you can hear him *now*?

OWEN: Perfectly. Three thousand three hundred and thirty-three miles is a long way, but I can hear him. I know he's blowing that cornet *some* place in New York.

HARMONY: Oh, tush, tush, young man!

OWEN: Tush, tush? Honest I can hear him. Right here in this room, I used to play the piano and he used to sit over there in that chair and play the cornet. You know, you don't miss a fellow much until he goes to New York. That's the city that makes you miss people more and more. (*The solo ends*)

HARMONY: Is it?

OWEN: Oh, yeah. That's some city.

HARMONY: Have you ever been there?

OWEN: Only in my sleep. The other night I was there and I saw him standing on a corner. I went up to him and I said, Come on home. And do you know what he said?

HARMONY: No, I don't.

OWEN: He said, I've got to make my fame and fortune first. I've got to make a million dollars.

HARMONY: A *million*?

OWEN: Yeah. That's what he said.

HARMONY: Now, what would he want with a million dollars?

OWEN (*Comes forward*): I'm glad you asked me that, because that's exactly what I asked *him*, and do you know what he said?

HARMONY: I'm not *sure*.

OWEN: Well, he said he wanted a million dollars to throw away.

HARMONY: *Throw away*?

OWEN: That's right. Put it in a big truck, drive around town and throw it away. The stuff's no good, he said—throw it away!

(HARMONY *looks at the boy, trying to figure him out, as the boy throws the money away*)

HARMONY: Of course it was a dream.

OWEN: Sure. But it's true, too.

HARMONY: You're fifteen, your brother in New York is nine-teen, and how old is your sister—St. Agnes of the Mice?

OWEN: She's seventeen. You ought to see her. You ought to see my brother in New York, too. I've got a *letter* from him. Only it's a month old. I'll read it anyway. (*Pause, solemnly*) Here's what he says. (*Sits on table*) Dear Shakespeare. He's always kidding me about being a writer, you see. Shakespeare, Byron, Keats, Shelley, Burns, Milton—and sometimes just to get me sore he calls me Longfellow.

HARMONY: You don't *like* being called Longfellow?

OWEN: Who would? He wrote Hiawatha, didn't he? (*Chant-ing*)
On the ocean's shining surface,
On the wide-extending billows,
From the dark sea rose a hero,
Rose a hero from the sea-swell.

And so on and so on for years and years.

HARMONY: I rather like Hiawatha, young man.

OWEN: Well, if you like it, that's different. But he calls me Longfellow when he wants to get me sore. I'm a poet, not a sewing-machine.

HARMONY: What does your brother say in the letter?

OWEN: Dear Shakespeare, he says. This is the biggest city in the world. There are nine million people here. It sure feels different, not knowing anybody. I miss you, and Saint, and Father, and Dan, and Father Hogan—and the mice, too. I play the cornet every chance I get. I feel fine. Don't worry about me because everything is fine, but when the next pension check comes please send me two or three dollars—general delivery. I don't need it, but send it anyway, just in case. So long. Harold. (*Pause*) He's been in New York nine months. You know, that's a long time. This is the last letter we got from him. To tell you the truth, we're all worried, but we act like we're not. My father worries most. Well, maybe Saint does. I'm not sure.

HARMONY: Why did he go to New York?

OWEN: I guess because he's nineteen—I don't know. (*He turns his attention to the trap*) One of them will come out and look at the trap.

HARMONY: Don't you suppose they'd be a little timid about coming out—with so much talking going on?

OWEN: I don't know why they should. (*Pause*) Maybe if we sit quietly for a moment—and wait?

HARMONY: Perhaps it might *encourage* one of them.

OWEN: O.K.

> (*Sits on floor. They sit quietly, smiling at one another. They look at the trap, around the room, into corners, and everywhere. The old lady lifts her feet off the floor*)

(*Whispering*) Are you fond of mice?

HARMONY (*Softly*): Not particularly. Are you?

OWEN (*Softly*): Only insofar as they reveal still further the magnificence of Almighty God. There's a thousand of them at least—somewhere in the wood. (*Aloud*) No rats, mind you, just little mice. Give them a chance, my sister says. If God gave them a chance, we've got to give them a chance, too.

HARMONY: I never looked at it that way.

OWEN: That's the way my sister looks at it, and the mice are grateful too. (*Rises*) They go all over, looking for things for her.

HARMONY: I don't believe it.

OWEN: It's the truth. The whole thing is practically a small religion. There's a heart beating in those little animals. (*Sits on table, folding his legs*) Only last week, as I got on the Number Seventeen Street Car, I saw one of them sitting on the cow-catcher.

HARMONY: Incredible. Are you sure it was one of your mice?

OWEN: Positive. We exchanged glances.

HARMONY: Where was the mouse going?

OWEN (*Gets off the table*): I don't know for sure, but when *I* got off at Third and Market, the mouse was still there, sitting on the cow-catcher. We exchanged glances again. I suppose it went down to the waterfront, to one of the boats down there.

HARMONY: The boats! I understand that's where mice pick up diseases. The most dreadful diseases imaginable.

OWEN: A *cold*, maybe.

HARMONY: No—*dreadful* diseases. Malaria, bubonic plague, yellow fever, leprosy, and all sorts of other horrible diseases.

OWEN: Not *these* mice. They don't pick up anything that isn't worth while.

HARMONY: And where did *you* go?

OWEN (*Quickly, sporty-like*): I dropped in at a gambling joint I visit once in a while. I bet the horses whenever it appears to be the smart thing to do. Well, I went into Joe's and bet fifty cents on the nose of a two-year-old named Tree—because that's also the name of a book I have written—but she got a bad decision in a photo-finish. It was a six-furlong sprint and the jockey knew both his race and his mount. Jockey Infante. He held her back until the far turn; eased her gently into contention; went to the rail; turned her loose, and began to shout. He didn't use the whip. He just shouted, and Tree moved from fourth to third, from third to second, and then you could *really* see her heart. In fifteen seconds she closed *seven* lengths. I knew I had the right horse. *Tree.* (*Pause*) It was a photo-finish, but they gave it to the favorite, Hatchet.

HARMONY: You lost?

OWEN: Well—fifty cents, but it wasn't that. It was simply that I'd named my book Tree.

HARMONY: What is your book about?

OWEN (*Clearly, but casually*): Tree.

HARMONY: Trees?

OWEN: No. *Tree.* One.

HARMONY: Well, what do you say about it?

OWEN: I don't say anything *about* it. I just *say* it. *Tree.* You've seen a tree, haven't you? Here. (HARMONY *goes to doorway*) That's a tree right there. (*The tree lights up*) I planted it myself seven years ago, right after we moved to this house. I had an idea we'd be staying. This house has got the best view in San Francisco.

HARMONY (*Returns to chair*): Of course I've seen a tree. What else do you say?

OWEN: That's all. That's only *one* of my books. It's one of my favorites, of course, but I've got others, too.

HARMONY (*Sits*): The whole book is just the *one* word?

OWEN: Just the one.

HARMONY: What does it mean?

OWEN (*Impatiently*): *Tree.* That's all. T-r-e-e. Well, I wasn't in Joe's ten minutes, and then I was broke and back on the Number Seventeen Street Car, headed home. Well, *when* I got home my sister was right here in this room as quiet as a human being could be, so of course I knew something was up. What do you suppose that mouse had brought her?

HARMONY: The mouse on the cow-catcher?

OWEN: Yeah. The one that went down to the waterfront while I was in Joe's betting on Tree. What do you suppose he came back with—for my sister?

HARMONY: Surely not something—*huge*.

OWEN: No. He brought her an almond.

HARMONY: An almond?

OWEN: Yeah, an almond. All the way from the waterfront. He got home *sooner* than I did. An almond—all the way from the waterfront. Well, who can you feed on an almond? I went for the trap, but my sister said, You've got no right. It's not the almond, it's the effort and the kindness.

HARMONY: But isn't that stealing?

OWEN (*Officially*): Miss Blueblossom, the mice of St. Agnes do not steal. My sister is opposed to theft and murder. In *any* form. I will not have any stealing, she says, and I will not allow any murdering. That's why she's always burning the mousetraps.

HARMONY (*Getting her bag ready*): Well. (*She stands*) I'm afraid I must be going. Thank you very much, young man, for receiving me.

OWEN: Please don't go. If you'll wait just a *moment* longer, we'll see one of the mice.

HARMONY: Young man. I am an old woman. It's been pleasant listening to you. You *are* convincing, you know —but I came to call on your father—Jonah Webster. I have not seen him in—well, thirty years, I believe, but in *you* I see him again. He was *then* not quite as young as you are now, but you are, I have no doubt, his son, and he is your father. He had a mind as wild as yours.

OWEN (*Impressed and not offended*): Yeah. That's him. He'll be here soon, just like I been telling you. He's out on a street corner somewhere, talking to the people. Wait a little longer. He'll be glad to see you. I don't even know you and I'm glad to see you.

HARMONY: You're very charming. Please tell Jonah I called. Miss Harmony Blueblossom.

OWEN (*Following her to the door*): Oh, I'll tell him all right. I'll tell him you didn't get married. He'll be awfully flattered. But I wish you'd wait.

HARMONY (*At the door*): And thanks again for your delightful fairy-tale about the mice.

OWEN: Fairy-tale? You don't think I was making that stuff up, do you?

HARMONY (*Smiling gently*): Good-by, young man.

OWEN: Good-by— (*She goes*) Old lady. (*He stands on the porch until she disappears. Turns back to the room, and suddenly becomes excited. Runs after her*) Hey! Old lady! The mouse! The mouse! It's come, just like I said it would.—Hey! The mouse! Old lady! (*He comes back on the porch. Suddenly points at the trap*) I *saw* him. He was right there, looking at the trap. I *told* her if she'd wait a minute, she'd see him. (*He enters through the window, stands over the mousetrap for a moment, looks at the piano. In the distance the cornet is heard playing.*) People don't believe anything any more—not even old ladies. (*He sprawls on the windowseat and is about to go to sleep*)

CURTAIN

About an hour later.

Small flowers on the floor spell the name Agnes. OWEN *is flat on his back, sound asleep. His sister* AGNES—St. Agnes of the Mice—*comes into the yard, quietly and sorrowfully. She is a handsome girl in haphazard clothes. Her legs are bare—a healthy brown from long walks in all kinds of weather. She goes to the window and looks at her sleeping brother, then enters the house. She sees the trap on the floor, picks it up and throws it in the fireplace.*

AGNES: You've got no right. (*She stands near* OWEN) Owen. (*She shakes him*)

OWEN (*In his sleep*): Is that you, Saint?

AGNES: Wake up, Owen. Wake up. (OWEN *sits up*)

OWEN (*Quickly, as he wakes*): What's the matter? (OWEN *shakes his head, then smiles foolishly*) Oh, hello, Saint. I thought it was you. (*Stretches sleepily, suddenly notices the flowers and leaps*) Hey, Saint—look! (*He points dramatically, going to the flowers*) A-g-n-e-s, Agnes. St. Agnes, the Little Sister of the Mice. (*He turns to his sister, smiling foolishly. Her face is troubled*) What's the matter?

AGNES (*Quietly*): You ought to be ashamed.

OWEN (*Innocently*): Why?

AGNES: How could you put a trap out when they're so full of sorrow?

OWEN: I didn't know they were full of sorrow. What are they full of sorrow about?

AGNES: One's lost. (*Stands quietly by the piano*)

OWEN (*Snaps his fingers*): That's why one of them didn't come out. (*Pause, reflecting*) Sure. But after she *left*, one of them came out.

AGNES (*Sadly*): After *who* left?

OWEN: We had a visitor. An old lady. I wanted to entertain her so I put the trap out. (*Goes to her*) What's the matter?

AGNES (*Softly*): I met a man. (*Sadly*) Well, a *boy*.

OWEN: Well, what's the matter? Are you sorry you hit him?

AGNES: I didn't hit him. (*Sits*) We just walked and talked. That's all.

OWEN: Ah, what's the matter?

AGNES: Well, I like him. He's not nearly what I thought I'd find, but I like him.

OWEN: Well, that's fine. It's nice to like somebody. *Anybody.* (AGNES *puts her hands over her eyes*) Hey! What are you bawling about?

AGNES: I *like* him.

OWEN (*On one knee*): Is that the way it makes you feel?

AGNES (*Slowly*): It makes you feel sick, like a whole world sick, and nothing to do about it, but to like him, more and more with every breath you take. All we did was walk and talk. We didn't even talk *sense.* I came home, feeling pity for everything. Not love—*pity.*

OWEN (*Rises and touches her arm*): Ah, Saint. Don't feel bad. Look at your name—in flowers. I told the old lady about them, but she didn't believe me. Are you sure he's *lost?*

AGNES: He's been gone a week.

OWEN: Where'd he go?

AGNES: He went to St. Anne's.

OWEN (*Angrily*): St. Anne's? Well, it's a nice state of affairs when one of our mice gets caught in a church trap and we can't even *set* a trap in our own house.

AGNES: What the church is pleased to do about mice is no affair of ours. (*Rises*) Owen? (*Pause*)

OWEN (*Objecting*): How am I going to find a mouse in a church?

AGNES: Just go there and look around. He may not be caught, he may be lost—trapped in some small room.

OWEN (*Takes hold of a chair*): Are you sure that's what it's all about?

AGNES: Yes, I am. They're all crying.

OWEN (*As he tries to balance the chair on his head*): Well, let 'em cry. What'd they expect—fun? Things end. They change. They spoil. They're hurt. Or destroyed. Accidents happen. (*Releases chair and catches it*) Without these things, there could be no—no felicity. You ought to know that. Eventually even a tree ends. One at a time, each of them ends, but there are always *trees.* And that's the reason: because eventually each of them ends. If you're going to teach them things, teach them *every-*

thing. I suppose it's an improvement for them to be crying over *one* mouse that's dead or lost, but sooner or later everybody's got to know that death is with us from the first breath we take. (*Pause*) Are they crying *hard?*

AGNES (*Simply*): Yes, they are.

OWEN: I guess he's *dead.*

AGNES: Maybe he isn't. Maybe he's only hungry and weak —caught in a room he can't get out of. Please hurry, Owen.

OWEN (*Ready to go*): All right. If he's alive and in the church, I'll find him. I'll bring him home.

> (JONAH WEBSTER, *a little drunk, arrives singing in French:* L'Heure Exquise *by Reynaldo Hahn. He disappears into the house, followed helplessly by* AGNES, *and returns in a moment with a bottle of Scotch and a glass.* JONAH WEBSTER *is a big, powerfully built man in his early sixties. There is something of the poet about him, and something of the fool—who is fool by choice. He seems young, almost boyish, simultaneously full of humor and love and noble anger. He is as carelessly dressed as his son and daughter. He pours a drink, is about to toss it down, then suddenly stops. He looks first at* OWEN, *then at* AGNES, *then at the flowers, and then all around the room*)

JONAH: Spectacles and satellites, what's the tragedy? What's troubling this space? I feel commotion in the air, as though great and tender values were the object of some brutal assault. (*Quietly*) What tragedy is it?

AGNES: No *tragedy,* Father.

OWEN: She met a boy she likes.

JONAH (*Loudly, and with some delight*): Time reckoning of bone and blood, is this true?

AGNES (*Broken-hearted*): Yes, it is, Father.

JONAH (*Convinced*): Pole star and pyramid!

AGNES (*By the chair*): Won't you sit down, Father?

JONAH: Sit down? In this celestial zenith of sweet and holy disorder? (*Eagerly*) It *is* sweet, is it not?

OWEN (*Casually*): She's pretty sore about the whole thing.

JONAH: By the changing heavens, speak English, boy. Do you mean *angry?*

OWEN: Well, angry, then.

JONAH: Of course she's angry. Forfeiture and exchange are

bound to make one angry, *since one is likely to be swindled.* Where is he? Let me behold him.

AGNES: He is not *here.*

JONAH: Where is he, then?

AGNES: I don't know.

JONAH: Well, *who* is he?

AGNES (*Softly*): We happened to meet on our way out of the Public Library. He held the door open for me. (*Quickly*) I could have held ten doors for his one, but *he* held the door for me. We walked along together and talked. I don't know who he is.

JONAH: Does *he* know who *you* are?

AGNES: I'm nobody, Father.

JONAH: As the sun rises and sets, you *have* given over.

OWEN: She was crying a minute ago.

AGNES: Owen! (*She turns away*)

JONAH (*Reprimanding* OWEN): Hold on. Pole star and pyramid! You know, I hope, that decent pride collapses into animal sickliness when it compares its poise with the insecurity of humility. Flaunting is arrogance, not strength.

OWEN: I wasn't flaunting anything. I just thought you ought to know, that's all.

JONAH: I *knew.*

OWEN: Well, how should I know you knew?

AGNES: *Did* you know, Father? Is it so plain?

JONAH (*Smiling at the flowers*): And these flowers, Saint? Another valentine from the mice?

AGNES: They're unhappy.

OWEN: One of them has been gone a week.

AGNES: He went to St. Anne's.

OWEN: I'm going there to look for him.

JONAH: By the adoration of the lamb, that's the least we can do. Go then, and on your way back, buy a wide variety of provisions.

OWEN: A wide variety of provisions?—with what? (*Pulls a pocket inside out*)

JONAH: With *what?* With money. (*He produces a check out of his pocket*) The pension check has come. (*Reading the check*) Pay to the order of Wilbur M. Stonehedge twenty-four dollars and thirty-seven cents. (*To* OWEN) Have you a pen?

OWEN: Father, that check's been coming for seven years now.

JONAH: Let *me* fix the meridian. A pen, please. (OWEN *goes to the fireplace shelf for a pen*) I was here when the *first* check came. I am aware of the chronology involved.

OWEN (*At the table, with pen*): That check isn't for us, and never has been.

JONAH: Spectacles and satellites, of course it's for us.

OWEN (*Handing his father the pen*): It's *addressed* to Wilbur M. Stonehedge.

JONAH (*Impatiently*): By the moon's geocentric parallax, the man's dead! (*Pause*) And we're not. (AGNES *at his right*, OWEN *at his left*, JONAH *puts his arms around them*) Now I shall fix the meridian. (AGNES *goes out on the porch steps and sits there*. JONAH *endorses the check, speaking as he writes*) Wilbur M. Stonehedge. Revolving property! The man worked hard for thirty or forty years. Was duly retired on a pension. Came home to live—here, in this house. (*Simply*) And died. (*He hands the check to* OWEN)

OWEN: Yes, sir.

JONAH: Soon after his burial, by the principle of the fixed period, I rented this house for myself and my children, and the check continued to come. If it's not for us, who is it for?

OWEN: Nobody, I guess.

JONAH: Then run along and fetch the mouse home.

OWEN: Yes, sir—if I can find him.

JONAH: And on your way back, be sure to buy a wide variety of provisions. A little of everything. We shall spend an hour or two eating and drinking. After that, we shall put a fire in the fireplace and sing. Meat, bread, wine, cheese, greens, a pie, and anything else that occurs to you. If you see Dan, send him along with the provisions. (*Takes another drink*)

OWEN: Yes, sir.

JONAH (*Softly*): And send something to your brother in New York.

OWEN: I don't know where he is. Where shall I send it?

JONAH (*Impatiently*): Send it to New York. He's there somewhere. Send him some money, that's all.

OWEN: Yes, sir— (*Begins to go, stops*) Oh, yes. An old lady called to see you.

JONAH (*Irritated*): Old?

OWEN: Yes, sir.

JONAH (*Swiftly*): Then say no more about it.

OWEN: She was a very nice old—lady.

JONAH (*Holding the speech off—and pointing at him*): Quiet, by the sun's retreat through constellations, I am reminded enough of my years by *you.*

OWEN: Yes, sir. (*Runs out, and jumps off the porch*)

AGNES (*Sadly*): Please try hard, Owen. Look *everywhere.*

OWEN: Don't worry. If he's *there,* I'll find him.

JONAH: We'll be waiting for you.

OWEN (*Stops*): Her name is Harmony.

JONAH: *Whose* name?

OWEN: The old lady's. Harmony Blueblossom.

JONAH: Blueblossom! (*Pause*): Never heard of her.

OWEN: Sure you have. She's a little old lady. She *knits.* (OWEN *runs off*)

JONAH (*Shouting*): I don't know anybody who knits.

> (*He stands a moment, looking toward the door, perhaps trying to remember who* MISS BLUEBLOSSOM *might be. Looks at the flowers on the floor, smiles, turns to* AGNES. *She faces away, looking into the distance, at the sunset.* JONAH *goes to the piano and plays softly.* AGNES *enters the room.* JONAH *stops playing, turns toward her. The sunset deepens*)

Saint. (AGNES *turns*) What did you read at the Public Library?

AGNES: The encyclopedia—about hummingbirds.

JONAH: Oh, they're wonderful.

AGNES: Yes, they can fly backwards. They're funny, too. They fight great big birds. (*Pause, suddenly*) But I could have held ten doors for his one.

JONAH (*Easily, as if he were talking about nothing*): How did it happen? Did you reach the door exactly when he did?

AGNES: Not quite exactly. He was there first.

JONAH: Was he waiting?

AGNES (*By the doorway*): I'm not sure. The door's a big glass door that I never noticed before. And I never noticed before that with all the room in the world a space could still be made. If he wasn't waiting, he was there, with the space for me.

JONAH: Did he smile?

AGNES: No—he almost cried, and then I almost cried, too. He didn't need to stand there that way, and neither did

I, but that's what we did. I could have turned and walked away quickly. I *had been* walking quickly, but now I couldn't move. I wanted to, I guess, but I just couldn't. He was too alone, and then I was, too—and we just had to stay together.

JONAH: Where did you go?

AGNES (*Puts her arms around his neck*): First we went out on the steps of the library, but we just stood *there*, too. We got in the way of some people who were in a hurry. About eleven of them. They didn't like us. *Both* of us. They turned around and looked at us. There were other people coming and going, too, and we were still in the way. When we got out of their way we were facing the same direction—we weren't facing each other. We were together.

JONAH: Did you speak to him?

AGNES: Not at first. I couldn't think of anything to say. I didn't think I'd be able to speak English even—and I suppose I didn't, after we *did* talk—what we said was so foolish.

JONAH: Did you run with him suddenly, perhaps?

AGNES (*Kneeling*): Run? We could barely walk. He kept bumping into me and I kept bumping into him, and he kept saying excuse me and I kept saying oh that's all right. He stumbled, too, and said something about his shoes.

JONAH: What did he say?

AGNES: He said they didn't fit.

JONAH: He's a good boy, Saint.

(WILLIAM PRIM *arrives, stands at the open door, listening intently*)

AGNES: I know he is, but now I don't understand anything. I began to see! I didn't used to *see*. The street cars going by had people in them suddenly. There have always been people in street cars, but now they were beautiful people. I never saw people that way before. They were still sad and funny and worried-looking, but now they were beautiful, too. We walked through the park and looked at everything together. It's not the same as looking at things alone. We looked at the pigeons, as if they had just come down from the sky. As if there had never been birds before. As if they came to be with us.

JONAH: Pigeons are good to behold, Saint.

AGNES: Oh, they're beautiful. They know people. They live in buildings.

JONAH: How many of them were there?

AGNES: Oh, a sky full—a thousand, I guess. They circled around and around. He pointed at them and said pigeons. I knew they were pigeons, but when he said they were —I *liked* him. And I knew what he meant, too.

JONAH: What *did* he mean, Saint?

AGNES: I can't say what he meant, but I *know* what he meant. He didn't mean pigeons. He couldn't mean pigeons and say it so sadly. It was the same with everything else, too. Everybody in the street that we passed was new. They were like *him*. I felt sorry for them. I thought love would be another thing—not pity. Is pity love?

JONAH (*Rises*): He's a good boy, Saint.

AGNES (*Angry, rises*): He's bewildered and shy and full of terrible sorrow, and his shoes don't fit.

JONAH: But his feet within them do. (*He turns and notices* PRIM, *whom he believes to be a door-to-door salesman*) Not today. Some other time.

PRIM: Oh. (*He goes*)

AGNES (*Slowly, as if she were seeking the words*): I've waited every day—to meet one person in the world—who wouldn't offend me—and now that I've found him—instead of being heedless—and strong—and full of humor— he's sad. He could be barefooted for all I care, if he wouldn't be sad—because now I'm sad, too. (*With youthful anger*) I won't allow it. Pity's no seed to throw among the living. It's for mice, whose littleness rejoices with it. I can't believe to live—to *really* live—is foolish or impossible. (*In soft voice*) Is it impossible, Father?

JONAH: No, Saint. Not for you; not for me; and not for your brothers.

AGNES (*Solemnly*): We're not apart from the others, Father. I *thought* we were, but we're not. We are *they*, and they are us. I know that now. I don't want the foolish life. I'll learn to live all over again, but if I can't live the life I know is mine to live, if everything is to be meaningless and foolish—

JONAH: Saint! It *isn't* meaningless or foolish. (*It is now early evening*)

AGNES (*Almost angry, turning away*): But I can't forget

him. Why am I so afraid I'll never see him again? (*Almost breaking down*) Will I see him again, Father?

JONAH: He's not lost, Saint.

AGNES: He *looked* lost. I don't even know who he is.

JONAH: Whoever he is, he'll be here in this room before the world comes to an end. Will you be glad to see him?

AGNES (*Sits*): I don't know.

JONAH: *You* must decide, Saint.

AGNES: I guess I'll be glad, then. (*Pause*)

JONAH: And will you look for him? (AGNES *looks up*) Will you go out into the streets and look for him? (*She looks at her father*) Will you go everywhere in the city looking for him? (*She rises, looking away*) He can't get far, Saint. His shoes don't fit. Will you *look* for him?

> (AGNES *moves to the door. There she stops momentarily, moves to the porch, then suddenly hurries away down the hill and disappears, suggesting a bird in joyous flight*)

> (JONAH *picks up one of the flowers, looks at it, smiling, and then goes back to singing in French*)

CURTAIN

JONAH *is at the piano playing softly.*

AGNES *comes home, holding a flower. She drops it inside the room, at the door. She hurries into the house.* JONAH *stops playing and turns.*

WILLIAM PRIM *returns. He is a neatly dressed little man of fifty or so.*

He checks the house number, comparing it with the number he has on a small piece of paper. He comes up on the porch and is about to enter, when he notices the flower on the floor. He picks it up, smiles, and puts the flower in his lapel. At the open door he knocks. JONAH *turns and looks at him.*

JONAH: All right. Come in.

> (PRIM *enters the room without saying a word. He goes to the table the hard way, takes off his hat, lays it on the chair. Places his briefcase on the table and begins to take out a number of envelopes, papers, and documents with seals and ribbons on them. Suddenly he stops, his attention drawn to something fascinating in his briefcase. He looks for a moment, then looks again as he lowers his head. He takes out a small toy whistle. He smiles at the toy, lifts it to his lips and blows it. The whistle makes a sorrowful little sound*)

JONAH (*Loudly*): Cool, clean chemistry, man, is *that* what you're selling? Here's a dime. Give me that whistle.

PRIM (*Protesting*): Oh, no—that's my own. (*He looks at the whistle proudly*) A souvenir of a voyage to Mexico eleven years ago. (*Remembering the voyage, while* JONAH *looks on somberly*)

JONAH: Oh, I see.

PRIM (*Speaks in a hushed, shy, courteous whisper, but with great emphasis*): Yes. There was the second officer

—a man named Gabbage. A schoolteacher from Calistoga
with a very large nose. A young man named Collins who
was interested in bull fighting. A *Mrs. Sedley* of society.
And myself—(*Realizing his presence there, as he smiles*)
Of course. Dinner was quite an event every evening, but
one night—the third night out—there was a celebration—
an *actual* celebration—the choicest food, the very best
wine, music, singing, speeches—*friendly* speeches, spon-
taneous, unrehearsed, and with no subject. Dances—ah!
(*Pause, while he smiles*) A celebration *truly.* In the
finest sense of the word. Mrs. Sedley, a most cultured
woman, was very friendly to me.

JONAH (*Pleased*): I'm delighted.

PRIM: A memorable experience (*Sadly*) from which I have
salvaged this souvenir. (*He blows the whistle again. Remembers the happy occasion a moment longer, and then
puts the whistle on the table*) But there is work to be
done. I have here—

JONAH (*Moving in*): Yes, by the science of seafaring, what
are all those papers?

PRIM (*Going over the papers, and examining them one by
one*): Well, this is the—(*Mumbling*) The third party of
the third part— (*In his natural voice*) And this is— And
this— In short, we were under the impression that you
were alive.—But *this*—(*Picks up another paper*)—an
obituary which has come to our notice—reports your
death and burial. Consequently, we are no longer
obliged to continue the monthly pension payment—in the
sum of— (*Looks for something else on the table, finally
remembers it is in his pocket. He brings forth a small
wrinkled paper from which he reads*) Twenty-four dollars and thirty-seven cents, every month, twelve months
per year. (*Replaces paper in his pocket*) In the event of
death, you see the pension becomes automatically null
and void—null and void. (*Sincerely*) I'm sorry. (*Turns
to his papers*)

JONAH (*Loudly*): We stand in the orbit of a superior
planet.

PRIM (*Not quite able to understand. Looks at* JONAH, *then
up and around*): Thank you. (*He replaces the papers.
The whistle is the last item. He smiles again, blows it,
then with determination places it in his briefcase and
finally is ready to leave*) It's been a pleasure.

JONAH: As you say, then.

PRIM (*Offers his hand to* JONAH, *who takes it*): Good-by.
JONAH: Good-by.

> (*They bow to each other.* PRIM *goes out, but stops on the porch, not able to straighten out everything in his mind.* AGNES *enters, looks at her father, then goes to the mantelpiece over the fireplace and fills a glass with wine.* PRIM *returns. He comes forward toward* JONAH. *Looks all around* JONAH, *still not able to understand*)

PRIM (*Eagerly*): Isn't there a mistake?
JONAH (*Casually*): No, I believe not. I believe everything is quite in order.
PRIM (*Very much relieved*): I thought so myself. (*Delighted*) Of course. (AGNES *brings the glass of wine forward, notices* PRIM, *offers him the drink.* PRIM *is ready to accept, but must with regret refuse*) No, thank you. I never partake of intoxicating beverages. (AGNES *offers the wine to* JONAH, *who drinks it and returns the glass to her. She puts the glass back on the mantelpiece.* PRIM *looks at* AGNES, *turns to* JONAH *intimately*) I have a daughter of my own. Seventeen years old. (*He offers his hand to* JONAH *again, who takes it again*) Good-by. (*They bow to each other. He bows to* AGNES)
OWEN (*From a distance*): I found him! I've got him, Saint!

> (OWEN *hurries to the porch and into the room.* AGNES *runs out to meet him.* PRIM *follows* AGNES, *stops by the doorway*)

AGNES (*Looking out*): Where is he?
OWEN (*Stopping, just inside the room*): Here. In this paper.

> (PRIM *follows him to the center of the room*)

JONAH (*To* OWEN): By the map of the stars, what the devil happened to you?
OWEN (*Putting the paper on the floor and getting down on his knees*): He was up in the steeple. (*To* AGNES) Here he is, Saint. Safe and sound. I knew I'd find him. (AGNES *is turned away*) Hey, Saint.
AGNES (*Coming forward*): Is he all right? (*On her knees*)
OWEN: All right? He's in better shape than ever. Tell 'em to stop crying. Tell 'em the lost sheep has been returned to the fold.

PRIM (*Looking at the crumpled paper*): What's in that paper?

OWEN (*To* JONAH): Who's that?

JONAH (*Casually*): The man who made the voyage to Mexico.

OWEN: Oh. (*To* AGNES) Well, Saint, take a look at him. (*He opens the paper a bit*)

JONAH (*With delight*): Wee sleekit, tim'rous beastie!

PRIM: Is it a mouse?

AGNES (*Sadly*): But it's not one of *our* mice. (*She goes toward door*)

OWEN: Sure it is.

AGNES (*Turning*): No, it isn't.

OWEN (*Leaping to his feet*): Well, it was the only mouse in the whole church. (*Rises*) Saint, I'm not going to take him back up to that steeple. That's no place to live anyway. I don't know *what* he's been eating. He *looks* like one of our mice.

AGNES: He isn't, though.

OWEN: Well, maybe they'll like *him* just as much as the one that's lost—or dead. What's the difference? This is a nice mouse. How'd he ever get way up there in that steeple?

PRIM (*To* JONAH): It's a mouse, isn't it?

JONAH: A shaft of lightning in the cloud.

PRIM: What's the matter with it?

JONAH (*Explaining*): It liveth.

PRIM: Oh, it's alive, then.

JONAH: The same as thou—or I.

PRIM (*Smiling*): Well, look at that—perfectly alive.

OWEN (*To* AGNES): Well, aren't you glad? You're always complaining about the traps. Well, here's a mouse from the *steeple* of St. Anne's—living alone up there; no friends, no fires, no people with their crumbs and cheese, no songs or music—only the bells. Aren't you glad, Saint?

AGNES (*On her knees again*): I'm glad, Owen. Only that's a *proud* mouse.

OWEN (*Delighted*): Is it?

AGNES: That's a mouse that doesn't like other mice.

OWEN (*Sincerely*): Say—that's swell. No fooling, Saint?

AGNES: That's a mouse that isn't afraid, either.

PRIM (*Like a child*): What are you going to do with him?

AGNES: *I'll* take him back to the steeple.

OWEN (*Rises, objecting bitterly*): *No*. I'll keep him.

AGNES (*Rises*): You have no right.

OWEN: What do you mean? (*To* JONAH) If I set a trap because the house is full of mice, she says I have no right. (*To* PRIM, *as he points his finger*) If I go all over St. Anne's looking for a mouse that's supposed to be one of our mice, and find *another* mouse instead—and a proud one, too—and want to keep him, she says I have no right *again*. (*To* AGNES) Why not?

AGNES (*Determined*): He's going back.

OWEN (*Giving up*): All right, there he is. You can do anything you want with him. Where's my paper? (*Takes his pad and crayon from fireplace*) I'm going to write another book. (*He looks at the mouse*) Mouse. (*Loudly, as he points*) There he is. Mouse. (AGNES *goes to window*)

JONAH: Pole star and pyramid, when are you going to write a book with *two* words?

OWEN: When I *know* two of 'em. (*Writing on a large tablet*) I've got to find out about nouns before I move to verbs. You've got to be careful about verbs, otherwise you'll get things all mixed up—even worse than they are already. *Is. That's* a verb. I've got to be careful when I use a word like that. (*Pause, shaping the earth with hands*) *Is.*

PRIM: Is what?

OWEN (*Angrily and loudly*): What do you mean, *what?* Is, that's all. *Is.*

PRIM: Oh.

OWEN (*Showing the tablet to* JONAH): There—another book.

JONAH (*Takes pad and examines it. In a loud voice*): Moose? Moose and mouse are not the same, boy.

OWEN: Oh. I've got to learn to spell some day. (*Sits. He corrects the spelling. To* PRIM, *suddenly, scaring him*) What sort of a voyage was it?

JONAH (*To* PRIM): Tell the boy about the voyage.

PRIM: Oh, yes. (*Delighted, rises*) Well, we left San Francisco at five o'clock in the afternoon. A beautiful day. My wife and daughter were on the dock, waving and *crying*. My daughter was six at the time, and my wife—was pretty well along in years.

AGNES (*At window*): I'll take him back after supper when I go for a walk.

OWEN: To the Public Library?

AGNES (*Angry*): Owen!

PRIM: I waved back of course, and *cried* a little, too. It was so wonderful having them on the dock, with me on the boat—bound for Acapulco, adventure and romance. Well, we sailed out of the harbor, through the Golden Gate, and on out into the beautiful sea.

AGNES (*Looks in the paper, excited*): He's gone!

OWEN (*Hurriedly opens the paper*): He's gone all right. Well, maybe he's gone back to the church.

AGNES: He mustn't go among the other mice.

OWEN (*Angry and offended*): Why not?

AGNES: Well, he mustn't, that's all. I know why.

OWEN (*Shouting*): Well, what did you let him get away for, then?

AGNES (*Controlling her voice*): You needn't shout. I can shout as loud as you. I can't help it if he ran away.

PRIM (*Bewildered, on knees*): Did the mouse go?

JONAH: There have been greater tragedies.

PRIM: What was the matter with it?

JONAH: The same. It liveth.

PRIM: Oh.

OWEN: I did my best, that's all I know. He's probably gone back to the steeple anyway, where he belongs. (*To* PRIM) Then what happened?

PRIM (*Confused*): When?

OWEN: When you got out on the beautiful sea.

PRIM (*Rises, goes to table*): Oh, yes. Well. Here. I'll show you. (*He opens the briefcase and begins bringing out the papers and envelopes again*)

OWEN (*To* JONAH): What's he looking for?

JONAH: By the changing heavens, a whistle!

PRIM (*Pausing to read a document with a seal on it*): In the event of death, you see, the pension becomes automatically null and void. (*Pause, as he puts the paper back into the briefcase*) Null and void. A routine procedure, of course— (*He stops suddenly, horror-stricken*) Oh, dear.

OWEN: What's the matter?

PRIM: I believe something alive is in the palm of my hand. (*Excited*) Oh, goodness.

OWEN: What's the matter *now?*

PRIM: I believe it's moved up my shirt sleeve. (*Confused*) Dinner was quite an event every evening, but one night— (*He wiggles his left shoulder, while everybody watches with fascination*) —there was— (*He wiggles his right shoulder*) —a celebration. Mrs. Sedley—

JONAH: Wonderful!

PRIM: It was the happiest experience of my life. (*Pause*)

I *do* believe something rather large is crawling about on me.

OWEN (*Anxiously*): How many feet has it got?

PRIM: Let me see. (*He wiggles, counting on his fingers*) Three.

OWEN (*To* AGNES): Three? Was that a three-legged mouse?

PRIM (*Correcting himself*): No. Four.

OWEN: It's the mouse all right.

AGNES (*To* PRIM): You must hurry right down to St. Anne's.

PRIM: Who?

AGNES: *You.*

PRIM: But *why?* I'm not a Catholic. I'm a Methodist.

AGNES (*Trying to hurry him out*): It's five blocks down the hill. You must hurry up into the steeple.

PRIM (*Severely*): I beg your pardon?

AGNES: Hurry now, before it's too late. Run! (*She hurries him out of the open door*)

PRIM (*In the yard*): Run? I haven't run in years.

AGNES: Well, you simply *must* run now.

PRIM: Very well, then. (*He runs across the yard and down the hill*)

OWEN: Is he running?

AGNES: Yes, he is. (*Pause*) No, he isn't. (*Shouting to* PRIM) Run—run!

PRIM (*From a distance*): The mouse—it's gone.

AGNES: Are you sure?

PRIM (*Closer now*): Yes, I am. It ran down my leg.

AGNES: He's lost the mouse. (*Returning to the room*) The mouse simply doesn't *want* to go back to the church. It wants to stay here, with the other mice.

OWEN: Well, all right, then, let the poor mouse alone.

PRIM (*Returning to the room and standing at the table, as before*): Well, there we were, alone on the top deck.

OWEN: Who?

PRIM: Mrs. Sedley and myself—on the voyage to Acapulco. (*He takes up his briefcase again*) Here. I have a souvenir of the occasion right here. (*To* JONAH *suddenly, eagerly*) Was it a mouse?

JONAH: It was not a part of thyself crawling.

PRIM (*Suddenly shocked*): Oh, dear. (*He collapses into* JONAH's *arms.* JONAH *lets him down easily, to lie on the floor*)

JONAH: Pole star and pyramid!

AGNES: I'll get him a glass of water.

OWEN: What's the matter with him?

(DAN, *an old drunkard, comes in carrying a basket full of groceries*)

DAN: Here's the provisions, Joe. (*He sets the box on the table*)

JONAH (*Delighted*): It's about time you arrived. Now we'll sit down to a royal feast.

DAN (*Noticing* PRIM): What's the matter with *him?*— Drunk?

(OWEN *goes to the basket of groceries and starts to examine them.* AGNES *returns with a glass of water, tries to get* PRIM *to drink, fails, drinks the water herself.* DAN *shakes* PRIM)

Get up, man. Pull yourself together. It's alcohol that's made the war. Alcohol and weak men, such as yourself. (*Holding* PRIM *up*) Stand up, man. Here. Let me take you to the kitchen for a glass of water. Sooner or later, like I've been telling 'em thirty years, alcohol is going to destroy the human race. (*To* PRIM) And a little mouse of a man like you, drinking intoxicating beverages. Come along, man. You'll be the ruin of the race.

(*Everybody follows* DAN *and* PRIM *into the kitchen*)

CURTAIN

After supper, about two hours later. Beyond the windows is visible a beautiful clear night, with moon and stars.

The three men come in from the interior of the house.

PRIM: Again let me say, thank you, thank you for a most happy evening. The food could not have been finer. The conversation—could not have been—finer. The singing could not have been—finer. The speech-making could not have been—finer. (*In a stronger voice*) As for the company—

DAN: The company could not have been finer.

PRIM: Yes, Dan. I shall never forget this wonderful evening. It has been most memorable.

JONAH: I'm delighted you have been happy. Come by any time at all.

PRIM (*Sincerely thrilled*): May I?

JONAH: I shall be disappointed if you don't.

DAN: But don't drink. Just keep a sober head on your shoulders and everything is going to be all right.

PRIM (*Sincerely*): Thank you, Dan. It's friends like you who carry a man through.

DAN: Ah, it's nothing. Any sober, God-fearing, home-loving man would have done the same.

PRIM: Thank you, Dan. (*To* JONAH, *as he pats his brief-case*) Well, I have everything in order. The check will continue to come on schedule of course, but *hereafter* the sum will be ten dollars more.

JONAH: By the law of fertility and timekeeping, I am deeply grateful.

PRIM (*Modestly*): It's nothing. The company can well spare it. As vice-president, I have the authority to do so.

DAN (*Impressed*): *Vice-president?*

PRIM: Oh, yes, Dan. (*He extends his hand to* DAN, *who shakes it vigorously*)

DAN: You're going to be all right, don't you worry about

that. A little sip now and then for the stomach, but nothing more. Can I help you to the street?

PRIM: No, thanks, Dan. I'm quite all right. (*To* JONAH) I shall never forget this evening. (*He extends his hand.* JONAH *takes it warmly*) Good-by, Mr. Stonehedge.

(PRIM *goes.* JONAH *and* DAN *stand by.* PRIM *waves. They wave back*)

DAN: Stonehedge? Joe, a weak man like that should never touch a drop.

JONAH: Now, Dan, I've been dry long enough. Fetch the pretty bottle and we'll sit down to a quiet little game of casino.

DAN: It's the disgrace of the weak that makes the noble life of the strong so full of sorrow and misery. (*Bringing out a big beautiful bottle of wine and two glasses*) It's the terrible disgrace of the weak.

JONAH (*As he looks out at the sky*): Then pour a drink, Dan, to the sweet smiling face of the universe.

DAN: We'll take a cup of kindness yet, with none of the little vice-presidents around.

JONAH (*Shuffling a deck of cards idly*): Then pour it, Dan, while you and I are still alive.

DAN (*Pouring*): The little vice-presidents who stumble and fall in every parlor. The little men with the wonderful official documents.

JONAH: Then drink it down, Dan.

DAN (*Lifting his glass*): Then down it is, Joe. (*They drink together.* DAN *smacks his lips, then belches*)

JONAH (*As he pushes his glass forward again*): By the changing heavens, Dan, then pour again, and cut the cards.

(DAN *cuts the cards, and* JONAH *deals. They take their hands and begin to play. They talk and drink as they play*)

DAN: It's the weak make the wars, Joe. (*Pause, as they play*) And Harold—what's the word from *him?*

(JONAH *looks away in silence. After a moment the cornet is heard playing in the distance*)

JONAH (*As the cornet stops*): He's well, Dan.

DAN: Then God protect him.

(FATHER HOGAN *of St. Anne's comes in. He is a heavy-set cheerful-faced man in his early sixties.* DAN *gets up quickly and hangs his head*)

HOGAN: Good evening, Jonah!

JONAH: As the sun rises and sets, Father Hogan! (*Taking* HOGAN's *arm*) Come, sit down and sip a glass of wine, young man.

HOGAN: I'm no younger than thyself—and we're both old men, and maybe old fools. (*Shouting*) Dan, for the love of God, sit down!

DAN (*Leaping*): Yes, Father. (*He sits down as if obeying a command*) Just a drop for my stomach, as the good Lord's my witness. (*He points upward, toward the good Lord*)

HOGAN (*Shakes his head*): Dan, you don't understand. I *believe* you. I've always believed you. You needn't imagine that every time you speak I regard what you say as a lie. I *don't*, Dan. I believe you. (*Softly*) So why don't you?

DAN: I *do*, Father. I believe every word I say. *Every word.* Nobody in the world believes more than Dan Hillboy.

JONAH (*Shouting warmly at* HOGAN): Come you, now, sit down and sip a glass of wine. (DAN *gets a chair*) You need not be a vigilant Christian *every* minute. Sit down, Hogan.

HOGAN: Let me stand a moment, Jonah. Is there a drop for *my* stomach?

JONAH: Dan, a glass for Father Hogan.

DAN (*Fetches a glass with the happiness of a retriever*): Aye, we'll take a cup of kindness yet.

JONAH: Then pour it, Dan.

DAN (*Brave and loud*): Aye, a cup of kindness among men of the good brotherhood. (*Offers glass of wine to* FATHER HOGAN) Father? (FATHER HOGAN *takes the glass*)

HOGAN (*Waves them to sit*): Sit down, boys— (*He sips, then very seriously*) Jonah. (*He sighs and stops*) Your son Owen came to the church this afternoon—for the first time in his life.

JONAH: I've no quarrel with the church. Why shouldn't a son of mine go to St. Anne's?

HOGAN: His behavior in church was most irregular.

JONAH: *Irregular?*

HOGAN (*Noticing* DAN *with his hand on his glass, wanting*

to drink but ashamed to do so): Go ahead, Dan, *drink* it. I know it's for thy stomach.

DAN (*Trying to rid himself of his sense of guilt*): I was just going to, Father. I was just going to. (*Lifting his glass*) To the good brotherhood, Father.

HOGAN: Very well, Dan.

DAN (*To* JONAH *as he drinks*): Joe?

JONAH: Then, drink it down, Dan.

> (DAN *nods and drinks, behaving very much like a boy who has been forgiven and is beside himself with joy.* JONAH *gets up, speaking to* HOGAN)

Sit down, now.

> (*He takes* HOGAN *by the arm and makes him sit at the table.* JONAH *remains standing*)

Cool, clean chemistry, man, tell us what the boy's done. Get to the point, so we can drink in peace. What's he done?

HOGAN (*Sits down*): Jonah, he was found running about the church, upstairs and down, and was asked by Father O'Mara what he was doing. He replied that he was worshiping, and continued to run about with Father O'Mara following as well as he was able to. Father O'Mara called Father Lewis who asked the boy what he was seeking. He replied that he was seeking the lost lamb, as any good Christian would. Father O'Mara and Father Lewis, both young men, were confused and, I suppose, a little upset. They returned to their studies, but soon after heard a terrible commotion in the church itself, like the opening of the heavens. It was the boy, *inside* the pipe organ. (*Very emphatically*) He'd *fallen* in.

JONAH: He was looking for a mouse.

HOGAN (*Shocked*): A mouse?

JONAH: One of our *own* mice. His sister had sent him. Half in jest and half in earnestness, she has been watching over the mice of this house for many years now, with the result that we have named her St. Agnes of the Mice.

DAN (*Drinking*): Aye—St. Agnes of the Mice.

JONAH: Now, you and I know mice are insensible creatures and cannot respond to affection and kindness. Well, it appears *she* did not know, and that they *did* respond—in a way.

HOGAN: I don't understand.

JONAH: Father Hogan, if I do not encourage the imaginations of my children, I also do not hinder them. With her faith in the mice grew her faith in herself. As that faith grew, intelligence and humanity grew, and with these things came a greater and deeper expectation of others, of *all* the living. And, naturally, the possibility of deep disappointment, which may eventually become disillusionment, or even contempt. I think I'll soon know, since only this afternoon she met a boy whose reality moved her to pity for the whole world. Which is, of course, the beginning of true humanity.

DAN (*Drinking*): Aye, the true humanity.

JONAH: Her brother sometimes puts flowers out for her, here on the floor, as though they were from the mice, and once when she was very ill, he stayed up all night, grumbling to himself. Actually he was praying for her. When she was better again, he told her the *mice* had prayed for her. Because *she* had watched over *them*. It's no matter to me what pattern faith or humor may take. She came home this afternoon broken-hearted, and told him so by pretending the *mice* were crying because one of them had been lost—at St. Anne's. Your church. That's why he was there this afternoon. I suppose he ruined the pipe organ. Well, I'll pay for it—little by little.

HOGAN: On the contrary, the pipe organ has been out of order for some time. It's in better condition now than it ever was.

JONAH: Well, that's fine. He probably pushed something into place.

DAN (*Holds glass out*): Aye, it's the truth.

JONAH (*Standing*): Then, drink to it, Dan. (*Pause*) I wouldn't be able to speak of these things to anyone but you and Dan here, because the poor faithless minds of the others I know would make the meaning foolish instead of simple and true, as it is. (*Pause, trying to explain*) Every life in the world is a miracle, and it's a miracle every *minute* each of us stays alive, and unless we know this, the experience of living is cheated of the greater part of its wonder and beauty.

DAN (*Drinking*): Aye, the wonder and the beauty of it.

JONAH: I sometimes stand on street corners and talk to people, as you do inside the church. My only disciple is Dan here, but he's a good one. But my *church* is the whole blooming universe, and mice are as much a part of its magnificence as men, if they only knew. We are alive with all other things alive, from the mite to the whale. Pole star and pyramid, man, I tell them the same things on street corners that you tell them inside the church. (*Pause*) From my heart to the pole star is the straightest line in the world, and as the star moves, so moves my heart—and yours, and Dan's and everybody's.

DAN: Aye, the wonder and the beauty of it. (*He sips*)

JONAH: The image of the pyramid to the human mind is the image of our grace as men. The slaves who built the pyramid—the thousands of them over the hundreds of years—did not know the majesty of the thing being made. But the *image* of that thing began where it ended—in the living human mind. The line goes from one to the other: from the heart to the star, and from the star to the pyramid, and from the pyramid *back* to the heart. From *one* thing to *all* things. They're all *one*, to be seen as a whole majesty, or not to be seen at all. I choose to see, since I am by nature a religious man.

DAN: Aye, and I, too. (*He drinks*)

HOGAN: I know that, Jonah.

JONAH: It's not enough to make a record of the world—it's necessary to change it! And you cannot begin to change it from the *outside*. The image of the good must first be real to the *mind* before it can inhabit substance and occupy space. My world is myself and my kinship with all other things. And my delight is my children. We are exactly the same as all other people, but I know we live better than the rich and better than the poor, because the values which make rich and poor are without image or reality, and the real values are the only values *we* recognize and cherish. We live faithfully, and sometimes, by the standards of the world, mischievously, or even dishonestly. A check for twenty-four dollars comes here every month for a man who has been dead seven years. We have no idea who the man was, but he's dead, and each month we have sent the money back, spending it. My youngest—the boy who ran about in your church this afternoon—gambles, and sometimes, I must say, wins. *Again* we send the money back. Even in the eyes of the world, we *would* be better, gladly and gratefully, if the world itself would be, but since it *isn't*, we refuse to exchange our values for its values. I know—and I have taught my children to know—that all things of matter must be only the *image* of the *real*. The pyramid must not be the waste of a million lives, but the poetry of *every* life.

DAN: Aye, the poetry. The wonder and the beauty of it.

(*He sips, listening drunkenly.* AGNES *runs up onto the porch*)

AGNES (*Whispering*): I found him, Father. And we walked again and talked, and he's coming here tomorrow to meet you. He's shy and afraid—but I've found him.

JONAH: Of course you've found him, Saint.

AGNES: And I don't feel sad anymore. I feel the same, but I feel happy now. His name's John.

JONAH: It's a good name.

AGNES: I want to go out and walk and look at everything again, because now I understand.

JONAH: You needn't tell me, Saint. Tell the night. Tell the little children who aren't sure and the old people who've forgotten.

(AGNES *kisses* JONAH's *forehead. She goes to* DAN, *kisses him on the forehead, then to* FATHER HOGAN *and kisses him on the forehead. Then quickly turns and runs. The three men are silent a moment.* JONAH *goes to the window, then turns*)

Did you *see* her, Father Hogan? Did you see her, Dan?

DAN (*Very drunk*): Aye, and a finer lass never breathed. (*He buries his head on his arms, wearily*)

HOGAN: I'm glad the boy came to the church this afternoon. His presence there, for the first time in his life, now has meaning, and I'm grateful, even if he was only looking for a mouse.

JONAH (*Standing*): No, not a mouse. For the *image* of the living heart's shyest, most kindly smile. (*Pause, solemnly*) The absence of their brother has taught them—and myself, too—the preciousness of one another. One's son, one's daughter, one's neighbor—and the stranger, brotherless and homeless. (*Almost pathetically*) We've been worried, Father. Oh, we know he's all right—we know nothing can happen to him, because he's good—but we can't help it. He wanted to go, so *I* wanted him to go. Now, I've lost faith, because I believed goodness was a coin for exchange more powerful than any coin minted

by any government—the *only* coin. (*Pause*) I'm no longer
sure. (*Angry but softly*) If anything happens to my son
—if the world destroys him or anything *in* him, which *all*
men should have— (*Bitterly*) I shall be the most corrupt
of men. (*He goes to the piano—sits—his back turned to
them*) It was good of you to come tonight, Father.
I needed you to talk to. My children must not know that
what I have taught them may be useless in this world.

HOGAN (*Simply*): I understand, Jonah.

> (JONAH *in silence turns to the piano, as if to play.
> He strikes several chords softly, then stops. He
> stands, moves to archway, and leans there, turned
> away*)

> (*Rises, goes to* DAN. *Places his hand on* DAN's *shoul-
> der*)

I'll take you home, Dan. Can you walk?

DAN (*Lifts his head*): Walk? Dan Hillboy? Of course I can
walk. (*He tries to stand, falls back, makes a real effort,
falls back again. He looks up pathetically into* HOGAN's
face, almost weeping) I'm drunk, Father.

HOGAN: Shall I leave thee, Dan?

DAN: Wait, Father. I'll walk beside thee. It's my head—the
years I've lost. The swift, sweet years that passed me by.
I was turning a corner, Father, and then all of a sudden
the years were gone. I've told Joe, Father. He knows.
He believes me.

HOGAN: I believe you, Dan.

DAN (*Amazed at the waste*): A *street* corner, Father. But
ever since, on a night like this, the years come back.
They come back to the breathing of my boyhood, and
want *me* back, where I belong. (*Calling bitterly*) Dan
Hillboy! Lean, young Dan—with his muscles hard and
his belt tight and his shoes hitting the sidewalk like the
feet of the Lord of Life. Now, I walk with a stranger—a
weak, pathetic fool who's stolen the name of my life.
(*Swiftly and with anger*) I was the good companion of
them all, and they knifed me. (*He clutches his heart*)
They ganged up on me in the dark night as I came by
whistling and hitting my shoes against the sidewalk, and
they fell upon me. But they'll never kill *me*. As long as
there are nights like this night in the world, Dan Hillboy
will be there, young and hard, in the street of life. The

murderers won't be there, Father, but Dan Hillboy—
he'll be there. Where a man's born, he'll live, and Dan
Hillboy was born in the immortal world. (*He stops, looks
around pathetically*) I'm sick, Father. I'm sick of the
waste. I'm sick of the lies I tell myself.

HOGAN: They're not lies, Dan.

DAN (*Looking up at him*): Do you believe me, Father? Do
you believe me?

HOGAN: I believe you, Dan. Come. Stand up, and we'll go
out and look into the sky.

DAN (*Standing*): Aye, Father, I'll walk beside thee.

> (OWEN *comes running in with something in his
> clenched fist. He stops short, looks around, trying
> to understand what's the matter.* JONAH *turns and
> looks at the boy. As he smiles, the boy begins to
> smile*)

JONAH: Pole star and pyramid, boy, she's found him. He
goes by the name John.

OWEN (*Pleased, then suddenly*): Oh. I forgot to give you
the change from the check. (*He hands* JONAH *a fistful of
coins*) You'll be wanting a coin to jingle soon.

JONAH: Spectacles and satellites, have you kept something
out for gambling?

OWEN: I've got something kept.—You know what I've got
here? A little frog! I found him! I'm going to write
another book.

JONAH (*Puts his arm around the boy. He notices* DAN *and
HOGAN waiting*): I'll be home soon. (*He takes* DAN'S
arm) Come along, Dan. We'll walk down the hill to St.
Anne's—and Harry's Bar.

DAN: Aye, Joe. St. Anne's, and Harry's.

HOGAN: And I'll buy thee a drink, Dan.

> (*The three men go, as* OWEN *watches. He then
> opens his fist and looks closely at what he's got in
> his hand*)

OWEN: Now. Hop and let's have a look at you. Come on,
now, hop. Hop!

> (*The frog hops and lands on the floor.* OWEN *gets
> down on all fours and looks into the eyes of the little
> frog*)

Can you see me? Can you hear me?

(He goes to the window and tosses the frog out. Then turns to the piano. From a distance the cornet is heard again. He tries to get closer to the music. MR. PRIM *comes in shyly)*

PRIM: Your father said I could come by any time at all. Can I come by now?

OWEN: Sure. Sure. Glad to have you.

(He goes on listening. At the window, he sits. HARMONY BLUEBLOSSOM *comes in. She stands, amazed, staring at* PRIM*)*

HARMONY *(To* PRIM*)*: Jonah?

PRIM *(With his customary bewilderment)*: How do you do?

HARMONY: Surely you're not—Jonah?

PRIM: Jonah? Who's Jonah?

HARMONY *(To* OWEN*)*: Young man. This man is not your father, is he?

OWEN: No, but he's a *good* man. He sends the pension check. He made a voyage to Mexico once, too. *(He continues to listen. The cornet is heard closer)*

HARMONY *(To* PRIM*)*: Is that so?

PRIM: Oh, yes. It was the most wonderful experience of my life. *(The cornet comes closer)*

OWEN *(Suddenly, desperately)*: Miss Blueblossom—are you sure you don't hear a cornet?

HARMONY: What's that?

OWEN: A cornet.

HARMONY *(Listening)*: Of course I hear a cornet. Someone's playing a cornet.

OWEN *(To* PRIM*)*: Tell the truth, now. Do *you* hear a cornet?

PRIM *(Listening)*: Why, yes, of course. *(*OWEN *stands, as if in a trance.* HARMONY *looks at him intently)*

OWEN *(To himself)*: He's coming up the hill, through the woods where we used to play. *(Takes his tablet to the table, sits and writes) Two* words: My brother.

PRIM: Are you his mother?

HARMONY: No. Not exactly. Almost.

PRIM: Almost? Oh, it's wonderful to be here.

*(*AGNES *runs into the house.* OWEN *and* AGNES *look at one another, hoping the cornet is real this time)*

HARMONY: St. Agnes of the Mice!

PRIM: Oh, yes. One of the mice got *on* me. *On* me.

> (AGNES *and* OWEN *move to archway, listening.*
> *Everybody stands still. Nobody speaks. The cornet*
> *comes very close, and then* HAROLD *appears. He is*
> *playing the cornet. Walking behind him is a small*
> *young man,* STEVE, *who is smoking a rolled cigarette.*
> *In front of the steps, the solo ends, and* HAROLD
> *stands staring at the place. He enters the house.*
> OWEN *pushes* HAROLD'S *chair forward for him.*
> HAROLD *sits,* STEVE *in back of him*)

HAROLD: Hello, Saint. Hello, Shakespeare. (*Points at* STEVE)
This is Steve. He hasn't got a home. (*To* STEVE) Didn't
I tell you? Isn't it exactly like I told you?

> (*In quick succession, first* JONAH, *then* DAN, *and*
> *then* FATHER HOGAN *arrive, and stand looking at the*
> *miracle, speechless but smiling*)

JONAH (*Whispering*): Pole star and pyramid! Play it again,
boy. Play it again.

> (HAROLD *begins to play the cornet again.* STEVE
> *places a battered black stovepipe hat over it, and*
> *watches with admiration.* OWEN *goes to* HAROLD *and*
> *sits on the floor.* AGNES *takes the stovepipe hat off*
> *the horn and places it on* HAROLD'S *head.* PRIM *and*
> HARMONY *move in, watching. All look at* HAROLD *as*
> *he plays. The curtain comes down and quickly goes*
> *up again as* HAROLD *is still playing*)

CURTAIN

Hello Out There

Preface

This play was written early in August, 1941. It was produced at the Lobero Theatre in Santa Barbara on Wednesday, the 10th of September, 1941, as the curtain-raiser to George Bernard Shaw's *The Devil's Disciple*.

Before this play was written I had spent almost four months loafing. When I came home from New York after having produced and directed *The Beautiful People* I decided not to work for a while and if possible to get out in the sun. I hadn't gotten out in the sun in years. I hadn't had any time to get out in it. I had always planned to get out, but I had always had the bad luck of getting a story or a play going just when I wanted to quit work and start loafing, and I had always stayed with the story or play until it had been written. Then I had planned to rush right out and get in the sun, only to run headlong into another story or play, and I had always gone to work and written this one, too. That is the only way I have ever been able to take care of anything that wanted to be written. Beginning any time of the day or night I have gone to work and written it —all at once if possible, but if not, as soon as possible. I have never given myself time to sit down and not have anything else on my mind.

I am as excited about writing as I was when I was a kid, but I have not yet been able to write anything expressly for the purpose of making money. This is so because I am an amateur. I have given away any number of pieces especially written on specific themes, but I have written these pieces because the themes have been challenging and because I have not been able to resist them. Furthermore, I have never had any limitations imposed on my writing other than my own. Every new piece I see in a magazine makes me happy, and every new book that comes from the presses is something to behold with wonder, awe and amazement. I shall probably never get over the delight of writing and being published.

Even so, a good deal of my interest is away from writing, and for years now I have been planning to spend a winter somewhere in the woods, camping and hunting, but have not done so; I have planned to spend a year driving all over America slowly, with especial interest in out-of-the-way towns, but have never done so; I have planned to take a leisurely trip around the world, and have never done so; I have planned to go back to work on a vineyard for a winter, and have never done so; I have planned to read all the books I have always wanted to read, and have never done so; I have planned to study the works of every composer of the world, the music of all the people of the world, and the songs of all the folk of the world, and I have never done so; I have planned to take a year out to learn from actual painting how to paint, and I have never done so; I have planned to learn to read and write Armenian, and perhaps translate the works of my favorite Armenian writers, and have never done so; I have wanted to buy an expensive microscope and study the forms of the smallest of things, and have never done so; I have planned to perfect my new theater—a globe device with the basic colors and forms capable of creating an inexhaustibly varied drama of objects and colors and relationships, accompanied by their related sounds—and have never done so; I have planned to walk from San Francisco to Mexico City, and have never done so; I have planned to ride a bicycle from San Francisco to New York, by way of El Paso, New Orleans, Jacksonville, and Oceana, and have never done so; I have planned to marry the most beautiful woman in the world and bring up a family, and have never done so; I have never met her—how could I do so? I have planned to read the Bible and the books of all other religions, and have never done so; and I have planned to buy a hundred acres of fertile land with a stream running through it, have the house I have always wanted built on it, and on the land plant as many kinds of trees as I can get hold of, and watch them grow, and I have never done so.

I have also planned to get out in the sun and get rid of the urban pallor which has become my normal complexion, and until this summer I have not done so. But this summer I managed to make it. Of course I was temporarily sidetracked in this ambition by the writing of the play *Jim Dandy*, by the reading and correcting of manuscript and proofs of two books, by a simultaneous hunger for loafing in San Francisco dives, and by cards, horses, and dice. But finally I got away and went to Fresno and got out in the sun.

During the four months after my return from New York I went to Fresno four times—the shortest visit being a three-day visit, and the longest being a one-month one. Gradually the pallor gave way to a fairly deep tan, but nothing like the tan of Young Corbett, with whom I went fishing a number of times at Mendota and Friant.

Young Corbett runs the best saloon in my home town. The sun is very close to the earth in Fresno, its rays very direct and penetrating, the heat very great and magnificent, but if you expose yourself to all this suddenly, you are apt to get cooked. I know, because that is what happened to me every day until Corbett explained that you had to rub yourself with a mixture composed of two parts olive oil and one part vinegar. After that, instead of getting cooked every day and not being able to sleep all night and having the skin peel off after a week or so, taking the color with it and bringing out a fresh layer of pallor, the sun-color moved in slower and deeper and stayed there. But I got out into the sun, just as I had planned, and I had a lot of fun watching Corbett try to catch a fish, which he never did. Later, though, he got a big one off the coast of Santa Cruz, and to prove it he had the photograph printed in the papers. I hadn't talked to Corbett since we had sold the *Fresno Evening Herald* together, along about twenty-five years ago, when Buzz Martin was our boss and pal, Mr. York in charge of street sales, and Mayor Toomey, a big, easy-going man who made a special trip to the sand-lot at Kern and L Streets to give an informal talk to the newsboys of the town. This man, Mayor Toomey, is the first important man in the world I didn't dislike on sight. He came to the sand-lot, the kids all gathered around, and he stood there and talked to them. He didn't make a speech and he didn't say anything momentous, but his coming down that way, bothering with a gang of hoodlums, made me like him and remember him as a great man. Maybe he wasn't really great, but as I *remember* it he was. I don't think Corbett remembered me as well as I remembered him, but after loafing around together a while it was practically the same as in the old days. After having been the best fighter of his time in his division, I found him great-hearted, easy-going, boyishly eager about fishing and getting out to the country, full of high spirits, a fair singer of popular ballads, and a good drinking companion. I had found few places as pleasant to loaf around in, anywhere in the world, as my home town, no bar with a better atmosphere than Young Corbett's, and no company more pleasant than his.

By the end of July I figured it was time for me to go back to San Francisco. After I got home this play was one of the first things I wrote.

Now, having a play on the same bill with a play by the one and only, the good and great, the impish and noble, the man and superman, George Bernard Shaw, is for me an honor, and I think a most fitting thing. While I have never read *The Devil's Disciple*, and while the only play of Shaw's I have ever seen has been *Saint Joan*—and I saw that from the last row of the gallery from whence it was a pageant and not a play, since I could hear nothing said—I have long known of Mr. Shaw, read his plays and prefaces, and loved him. I admire heroic effort. Accomplishment I love. What I am about to say is no invention, and I am putting it down for whatever it may be worth to the historian of literature and for the student of influences of men on men, and because it is true and must therefore be made known. As a boy, charging pell-mell through literature, reading everything I could lay hands on in the Public Library of Fresno, I found many men to whom I felt deeply grateful—especially Guy de Maupassant, Jack London, and H. L. Mencken—but the first man to whom I felt definitely related was George Bernard Shaw. This is a presumptuous or fatuous thing to mention, perhaps, but even so it must be mentioned.

I myself, as a person, have been influenced by many writers and many things, and my writing has felt the impact of the writing of many writers, some relatively unknown and unimportant, some downright bad. But probably the greatest influence of them all when an influence is most effective—when the man being influenced is nowhere near being solid in his own right—has been the influence of the great tall man with the white beard, the lively eyes, the swift wit and the impish chuckle. I have read Schopenhauer at the age of twelve with no bewilderment and no contempt for his contempt for the world and its strange inhabitant, and no contempt for the strange inhabitant himself. I have read writing without regard for the name or quality of the writer—just writing, just print, just books. I have read Mark Twain and Walt Whitman. I have read the Russians,

Chekhov, Andreyev, and Gorki. I have read Sherwood Anderson and Carl Sandburg, Gertrude Stein and Ernest Hemingway. I have read Ibsen and Oscar Wilde. I have read *Poetry Magazine* and any of the little magazines I have been able to find in the second-hand book-stores of Fresno. I have read anything and everything—Ambrose Bierce and Bret Harte, and books in French and German and Spanish without being able to understand any of it, simply because they were books and because something was being said, even if it was in a language I did not know. I have read books about the behavior of mobs—*The Mob* by Le Bon, if I remember rightly, was one—about crime in children, and about genius in them, about the greatest bodies of things, and about the littlest of them. I have been fascinated by it all, grateful for it all, grateful for the sheer majesty of the existence of ideas, stories, fables, and paper and ink and print and books to hold them all together for a man to take aside and examine alone. But the man I liked most and the man who seemed to remind me of myself—of what I really was and would surely become—was George Bernard Shaw.

When, at the age of eighteen, I was night manager of the Postal Telegraph office at 21 Taylor Street in San Francisco I remember having been asked by the clerk there, a man named Clifford, who the hell I thought I was. And I remember replying very simply and earnestly somewhat as follows: If you have ever heard of George Bernard Shaw, if you have ever read his plays or prefaces, you will know what I mean when I tell you that I am that man by another name.

Who is *he*? I remember the clerk asking.

George Bernard Shaw, I replied, is the tonic of the Christian peoples of the world. He is health, wisdom, and comedy, and that's what I am, too.

How do you figure? the clerk said.

Don't bother me, I said. I'm night manager of this office and when I tell you something it's final.

H. L. Mencken's *Prejudices* and George Jean Nathan's suave and lively spoofing had a fine effect on me, too. I liked the men who were most like bad boys, having fun all the time, playing pranks, talking out of turn, acting up, making fun of fools and frauds, ridiculing the pompous and phoney, howling with laughter or sitting by after ruining the works and being dead-pan and innocent about the whole thing—and beyond all this being very wise and very serious, and knowing how to write—knowing that you couldn't be serious and dull at the same time and still be effective. Mencken's stuff made me bust out laughing in the Public Library. Sometimes it even made me jump up out of my chair and walk around the place whispering things at people I didn't know.

This is not the place or time, however, for me to go into detail about the men and writing and ideas which have influenced my life and writing.

All I know is that it is right for a one-act play by William Saroyan to serve as curtain-raiser to a play by George Bernard Shaw. To show you the importance of this, the inevitability of it in fact, let me reveal how, finally, this event came to be, and how close it came not to be. Let me reveal the series of accidental and fortuitous events—all of them always closer to not taking place than to taking place —which finally, one by one, resulted in this most appropriate and inevitable circumstance.

When I stepped out of the sun of Fresno and came home to the gloom of San Francisco, although I felt the time was ripe for the writing of something good, nothing presented itself to me. Therefore, I made no effort, but spent my time loafing, playing pin-ball games for hours, sitting around in little bars, listening to juke-box music, drinking and talking. After three days of this I sat down one night at two o'clock in the morning with the intention of typing a title and a few ideas I didn't want to forget. But I did not get up until I had written this play. I had been drinking a good deal, but I was not drunk. There are nights of such drinking. Instead of getting drunk a man gets sober. He gets very sober. That was how it was that night. I didn't know at the time that I had a play to write, but I must have had it to write, because I wrote it.

The very writing of the play was an accident, even if it was an inevitable one. Of course we all know that accidents are compelled. I know this from having read in my Public Library days an essay about the mystical behavior of Hindus, and from having watched this matter carefully, and considered it from one year to another. I know accidents are avoidable. Even when I was the fastest messenger in Fresno, and the one who took the most chances, I had very few accidents, and these were only mild. I was once forced to knock down a brewery horse by butting it with my head because I was going too fast and couldn't stop and the horse was blocking the alley down which I was racing. While racing down the alley I had reasoned that if somebody stepped out into my path I would have no trouble going through with no harm to him or to myself; if an automobile crossed this path I would pace my speed to swerve around it and go on my way; if something immovable blocked my way I would lift the whole front part of the bicycle, fall backwards, and probably hurt my back but not be instantly killed; and if something moving slowly appeared in my way and I could not pace around it I would—at this point, while I was going about twenty miles an hour, a brewery horse appeared and completely blocked the alley, moving much too slowly. My head butted the horse in the side, the horse exhaled, its front feet buckled and it went down. I was a little scared—especially of the horse, which was very big —but I wasn't hurt.

There were some other accidents. Chains broke on me a couple of times while I was sprinting and sprawled me out on the pavement. A cop intentionally caught my arm at the elbow as I shot through between him and a truck, spinning me around and almost ruining my bicycle. And a couple of bad drivers ran into me from behind and knocked me off my bicycle. Each of the accidents could have been avoided. I know it. The one involving the horse could have been avoided but only if I was willing to agree not to speed, and I wasn't. The chains that broke had been weak and should have been attended to. The cop was a dog anyway; I knew it, and I could have avoided the accident by not challenging him and thinking I could get away with it. And the people who drove their cars into my bike should never have been credited with wakefulness by me. I had overestimated them and I had been recklessly optimistic. But the accidents could have been avoided.

Getting the title of the play was an accident too. A clown friend of mine named Stanley Rose one night on a street corner in Fresno began calling out as if he were in the wilderness— Hello out there! Hello out there! I liked the sound and enjoyed the absurdity of it, but immediately forgot all about it.

Next, it was an accident that I went to the revival of *Anna Christie* in San Francisco; an accident that I met the director of the play, John Houseman; an accident that he asked if I had a one-act play; an accident that I had one, *this* one, just written; and an accident that I promised to put it in the mail for him the next day. It was no accident that I did, though.

On the other side of things, to begin with I had no idea what other plays would be presented with my play. I imagined they would be new plays by one or another of the several American writers of plays. It turned out that there would be only one other play, and that this play was *The Devil's Disciple* by George Bernard Shaw. But this was also an accident. It seems that Mr. Shaw was allowing no further productions of his plays until after the war. The production of this play had just barely got under the wire, but under the wire is under the wire, and my work has finally appeared on the same bill with the work of George Bernard Shaw.

Such progressions as these are important to record. It shall seem to some critics most frightful of me to associate my name with George Bernard Shaw's, but let me simplify everything by making known very clearly that if it matters which of the writing men I have felt close to, and by whom my writing has been influenced, that man has not been Ernest Hemingway, as Mr. Edmund Wilson seems to feel, but George Bernard Shaw. Now, if Mr. Shaw and Mr. Saroyan are poles apart, no comparison between the two, one great and the other nothing, one a genius and the other a charlatan, let me repeat that if you must know which writer has influenced my writing when influences are real and for all I know enduring, then that writer has been George Bernard Shaw. I shall in my own day influence a young Shaw or two somewhere or other, and no one need worry about that.

Young Shaw, hello out there.

WILLIAM SAROYAN

San Francisco, January 1942

CHARACTERS

The Young Gambler
The Girl
The Husband
Another Man
The Wife

Scene: a little jailhouse in Matador, Texas.

There is a fellow in a small-town prison cell, tapping slowly on the floor with a spoon. After tapping half a minute as if he were trying to telegraph words, he gets up and begins walking around the cell. At last he stops, stands at the center of the cell, and doesn't move for a long time. He feels his head, as if it were wounded. Then he looks around. Then he calls out.

YOUNG MAN: Hello—out there! (*Pause*) Hello—out there! (*Long pause*) Hello—out there!

(*A* GIRL'S *voice is heard.*)

THE VOICE: Hello.

YOUNG MAN: Is that you, Katey?

THE VOICE: No—this here is Emily.

YOUNG MAN: Who?

THE VOICE: Emily.

YOUNG MAN: Emily who? I don't know anybody named Emily. Are you the girl I met at Sam's in Salinas about three years ago?

THE VOICE: No—I'm the girl who cooks here. I'm the cook. I've never been in Salinas. I don't even know where it is.

YOUNG MAN: You say you cook here?

THE VOICE: Yes, I do.

YOUNG MAN: Well, why don't you cook something good?

THE VOICE: I just cook what they tell me to. (*Pause*) You lonesome?

YOUNG MAN: Lonesome as a coyote. Hear me hollering? Hello out there!

THE VOICE: Who you hollering to?

YOUNG MAN: Well—nobody, I guess. I been trying to think of somebody to write a letter to, but I can't think of anybody.

THE VOICE: What about Katey?

YOUNG MAN: I don't know anybody named Katey.

THE VOICE: Then why did you say, Is that you, Katey?

YOUNG MAN: Katey's a good name. I always did like a name like Katey. I never *knew* anybody named Katey, though.

THE VOICE: *I* did.

YOUNG MAN: Yeah? What was she like? Big girl, or little one?

THE VOICE: Little.

YOUNG MAN: What sort of a girl are *you?*

THE VOICE: Oh, I don't know.

YOUNG MAN: Didn't anybody ever tell you? Didn't anybody ever talk to you that way?

THE VOICE: What way?

YOUNG MAN: You know. Didn't they?

THE VOICE: No, they didn't.

YOUNG MAN: They should have. I can tell from your voice you're O.K.

THE VOICE: Maybe I am and maybe I ain't.

YOUNG MAN: I never missed yet.

THE VOICE: Yeah, I know. That's why you're in jail.

YOUNG MAN: The whole thing was a mistake.

THE VOICE: They claim it was rape.

YOUNG MAN: No—it wasn't.

THE VOICE: That's what they claim it was.

YOUNG MAN: They're a lot of fools.

THE VOICE: Well, you sure are in trouble. Are you scared?

YOUNG MAN: Scared to death. (*Suddenly*) Hello out there!

THE VOICE: What do you keep saying that for all the time?

YOUNG MAN: I'm lonesome. I'm as lonesome as a coyote. (*A long one*) Hello—out there!

(*The* GIRL *appears, over to one side. She is a plain girl in plain clothes.*)

THE GIRL: I'm kind of lonesome, too.

YOUNG MAN (*Turning and looking at her*): Hey— No fooling? Are you lonesome, too?

THE GIRL: Yeah—I'm almost as lonesome as a coyote myself.

YOUNG MAN: Who *you* lonesome for?

THE GIRL: I don't know.

YOUNG MAN: It's the same with me. The minute they put

you in a place like this you remember all the girls you ever knew, and all the girls you didn't get to know, and it sure gets lonesome.

THE GIRL: I bet it does.

YOUNG MAN: Ah, it's awful. (*Pause*) You're a pretty girl, you know that?

THE GIRL: You're just talking.

YOUNG MAN: No, I'm not just talking—you are pretty.

THE GIRL: I'm not—and you know it.

YOUNG MAN: No—you are. I knew Texas would bring me luck.

THE GIRL: Luck? You're in jail, aren't you? You've got a whole gang of people all worked up, haven't you?

YOUNG MAN: Ah, that's nothing. I'll get out of this.

THE GIRL: Maybe.

YOUNG MAN: No, I'll be all right—*now*.

THE GIRL: What do you mean—now?

YOUNG MAN: I mean after seeing you. I got something now. You know for a while there I didn't care one way or another. Tired. (*Pause*) But I'm not tired any more. Hello out there.

THE GIRL: Who you calling now?

YOUNG MAN: You.

THE GIRL: Why, I'm right here.

YOUNG MAN: I know. (*Softly*) Hello out there!

THE GIRL: Hello.

YOUNG MAN: Ah, you're sweet. (*Pause*) I'm going to marry you. I'm going away with you. I'm going to take you to San Francisco. I'm going to win myself some real money, too. I'm going to study 'em real careful and pick myself some winners, and we're going to have a lot of money.

THE GIRL: Yeah?

YOUNG MAN: Yeah. Tell me your name.

THE GIRL: Emily.

YOUNG MAN: I know that. Tell me the rest of it.

THE GIRL: Emily Smith.

YOUNG MAN: Honest to God?

THE GIRL: Honest. That's my name—Emily Smith.

YOUNG MAN: Ah, you're the sweetest girl in the whole world.

THE GIRL: Why?

YOUNG MAN: I don't know why, but you are, that's all. Where were you born?

THE GIRL: Matador, Texas.

YOUNG MAN: Where's that?

THE GIRL: Right here.

YOUNG MAN: Is this Matador, Texas?

THE GIRL: Yeah, it's Matador. They brought you here from Wheeling.

YOUNG MAN: Is that where I was—Wheeling?

THE GIRL: Didn't you even know what town you were in?

YOUNG MAN: All towns are alike. It doesn't make any difference. How far away is Wheeling?

THE GIRL: Sixteen or seventeen miles. Didn't you know they moved you?

YOUNG MAN: How could I know, when I was out—cold? Somebody hit me over the head with a lead pipe or something. What'd he hit me for?

THE GIRL: Rape—that's what they *said*.

YOUNG MAN: Ah, that's a lie. (*Amazed, almost to himself*) She wanted me to give her money.

THE GIRL: Money?

YOUNG MAN: Yeah. If I'd have known she was a woman like that, I'd have gone on down the street and stretched out in a park somewhere and gone to sleep.

THE GIRL: Is that what she wanted—money?

YOUNG MAN: Yeah. A fellow like me traveling all over the country, trying to break his bad luck, going from one poor little town to another, trying to find somebody good somewhere, and she asks for money. I thought she was lonesome. She *said* she was.

THE GIRL: Maybe she was.

YOUNG MAN: She was *something*.

THE GIRL: I guess I'd never see you, if it didn't happen, though.

YOUNG MAN: Oh, I don't know—maybe I'd just mosey along this way and see you in this town somewhere. I'd recognize you, too.

THE GIRL: Recognize me?

YOUNG MAN: Sure, I'd recognize you the minute I laid eyes on you.

THE GIRL: Well, who would I be?

YOUNG MAN: Mine, that's who.

THE GIRL: Honest?

YOUNG MAN: Honest to God.

THE GIRL: You just say that because you're in jail.

YOUNG MAN: No, I mean it. You just pack up and wait for

me. We'll high-roll the hell out of here to San Francisco.

THE GIRL: You're just lonesome.

YOUNG MAN: I been lonesome all my life—there's no cure for that—but you and me—we can have a lot of fun hanging around together. You'll bring me luck. I know you will.

THE GIRL: What are you looking for luck for all the time?

YOUNG MAN: I'm a gambler. I don't work. I've *got* to have luck or I'm no good. I haven't had any luck in years. Two whole years now—one place to another. Bad luck all the time. That's why I got in trouble back there in Wheeling, too. That was no accident. That was my bad luck following me around. So here I am, with my head half busted. I guess it was her old man that did it.

THE GIRL: You mean her father?

YOUNG MAN: No, her husband. If I had an old lady like that, I'd throw her out.

THE GIRL: Do you think you'll have better luck if I go with you?

YOUNG MAN: Yes, of course. It's no good searching the streets for anything that might be there at the time. You got to have somebody with you all the time. You got to have somebody who's right. Somebody who knows you, from way back. You got to have somebody who even knows you're wrong but likes you just the same. I know I'm wrong, but I can't help it. If you go along with me, I'll be the best man anybody ever saw. I won't be wrong any more. You know when you get enough money, you *can't* be wrong any more—you're right because the money says so. I'll have a lot of money and you'll be just about the prettiest girl in the whole world. I'll be proud walking around San Francisco with you on my arm and people turning to look at us.

THE GIRL: Do you think they will?

YOUNG MAN: Sure they will. When I get back in some decent clothes, and you're on my arm—well, Katey, they'll turn and look, and they'll see something, too.

THE GIRL: Katey?

YOUNG MAN: Yeah—that's your name from now on. You're the first girl I ever called Katey. I've been saving it for you. O.K.?

THE GIRL: O.K.

YOUNG MAN: How long have I been here?

THE GIRL: Since last night. You didn't wake up until late this morning, though.

YOUNG MAN: What time is it now? About nine?

THE GIRL: About ten.

YOUNG MAN: Have you got the key to this lousy cell?

THE GIRL: No. They don't let me fool with any keys.

YOUNG MAN: Well, can you get it?

THE GIRL: No.

YOUNG MAN: Can you *try?*

THE GIRL: They wouldn't let me get near any keys. I cook for this jail when they've got somebody in it. I clean up, and things like that.

YOUNG MAN: Well, I want to get out of here. Don't you know the guy who runs this joint?

THE GIRL: I know him, but he wouldn't let you out. They were talking of taking you to another jail in another town.

YOUNG MAN: Yeah? Why?

THE GIRL: Because they're afraid.

YOUNG MAN: What are they afraid of?

THE GIRL: They're afraid those people from Wheeling will come over in the middle of the night and break in.

YOUNG MAN: Yeah? What do they want to do that for?

THE GIRL: Don't *you* know what they want to do it for?

YOUNG MAN: Yeah, I know all right.

THE GIRL: Are you scared?

YOUNG MAN: Sure I'm scared. Nothing scares a man more than ignorance. You can argue with people who ain't fools, but you can't argue with fools—they just go to work and do what they're set on doing. Get me out of here.

THE GIRL: How?

YOUNG MAN: Well, go get the guy with the key, and let me talk to him.

THE GIRL: He's gone home. Everybody's gone home.

YOUNG MAN: You mean I'm in this little jail all alone?

THE GIRL: Well—yeah—except me.

YOUNG MAN: Well, what's the big idea—doesn't anybody stay here all the time?

THE GIRL: No, they go home every night. I clean up and then I go, too. I hung around tonight.

YOUNG MAN: What made you do that?

THE GIRL: I wanted to talk to you.

YOUNG MAN: What did you want to talk about?

THE GIRL: Oh, I don't know. I took care of you last night. You were talking in your sleep. You liked me, too. I didn't think you'd like me when you woke up, though.

YOUNG MAN: Yeah? Why not?

THE GIRL: I don't know.

YOUNG MAN: Yeah? Well, you're wonderful, see?

THE GIRL: Nobody ever talked to me that way. All the fellows in town—they—(*Pause*.)

YOUNG MAN: What about 'em? (*Pause*) Well, what about 'em? Come on—tell me.

THE GIRL: They laugh at me.

YOUNG MAN: Laugh at *you?* What do they know about anything? You go get your things and come back here. I'll take you to San Francisco. How old are you?

THE GIRL: Oh, I'm of age.

YOUNG MAN: How old are you?—Don't lie to me! Sixteen?

THE GIRL: I'm seventeen.

YOUNG MAN: Well, bring your father and mother. We'll get married before we go.

THE GIRL: They wouldn't let me go.

YOUNG MAN: Why not?

THE GIRL: I don't know, but they wouldn't. I know they wouldn't.

YOUNG MAN: You go tell your father not to be a fool, see? What is he, a farmer?

THE GIRL: No—nothing. He gets a little relief from the government because he's supposed to be hurt or something—his side hurts, he says. I don't know what it is.

YOUNG MAN: Ah, he's a liar. Well, I'm taking you with me, see?

THE GIRL: He takes the money I earn, too.

YOUNG MAN: He's got no right to do that.

THE GIRL: I know, but he does it.

YOUNG MAN (*Almost to himself*): You shouldn't have been born in this town, anyway, and you shouldn't have had a man like that for a father, either.

THE GIRL: Sometimes I feel sorry for him.

YOUNG MAN: Never mind feeling sorry for him. (*Pointing a finger*) I'm going to talk to your father some day. I've got a few things to tell him.

THE GIRL: I know you have.

YOUNG MAN (*Suddenly*): See if you can get that fellow with the keys to come down and let me out.

THE GIRL: Oh, I couldn't.

YOUNG MAN: Why not?

THE GIRL: I'm nobody here—why, all they give me is fifty cents every day I work here—sometimes twelve hours. I'm nobody here.

YOUNG MAN: Get me out of here, Katey. I'm scared.

THE GIRL: I don't know what to do. Maybe I could break the door down.

YOUNG MAN: No, you couldn't do that. Is there a hammer there or anything?

THE GIRL: Only a broom. Maybe they've locked the broom up, too.

YOUNG MAN: Go and see if you can find anything.

THE GIRL: All right. (*She goes.*)

THE GIRL (*Returning*): There isn't a thing out there. They've locked everything up for the night.

YOUNG MAN: Any cigarettes?

THE GIRL: Everything's locked up—all the drawers of the desk—all the closet doors—everything.

YOUNG MAN: I ought to have a cigarette.

THE GIRL: I could get you a package maybe, somewhere. I guess the drug store's open. It's about a mile.

YOUNG MAN: A mile? I don't want to be alone that long.

THE GIRL: I could run all the way, and all the way back.

YOUNG MAN: You're the sweetest girl that ever lived.

THE GIRL: What kind do you want?

YOUNG MAN: Oh, any kind—Chesterfields or Camels or Lucky Strikes—any kind at all.

THE GIRL: I'll go get a package. (*She turns to go.*)

YOUNG MAN: What about the money?

THE GIRL: I've got some money. I've got a quarter I been saving. I'll run all the way. (*She is about to go.*)

YOUNG MAN: Come here.

THE GIRL (*Going to him*): What?

YOUNG MAN: Give me your hand. (*He takes her hand and looks at it, smiling. He lifts it and kisses it*) I'm scared to death.

THE GIRL: I am, too.

YOUNG MAN: I'm scared nobody will ever come out here to this God-forsaken broken-down town and find you. I'm scared you'll get used to it and not mind. I'm scared you'll never get to San Francisco and have 'em all turning to look at you. Listen—go get me a gun.

THE GIRL: I could get my father's gun. I know where he hides it.

YOUNG MAN: Go get it. Never mind the cigarettes. Run all the way.

> (THE GIRL *turns and runs. The* YOUNG MAN *stands at the center of the cell a long time.* THE GIRL *comes running back in. Almost crying.*)

THE GIRL: I'm afraid. I'm afraid I won't see you again. If I come back and you're not here, I— It's so lonely in this town. I'll stay *here*. I won't *let* them take you away.

YOUNG MAN: Listen, Katey. Do what I tell you. Go get that gun and come back. Maybe they won't come tonight. Maybe they won't come at all. I'll hide the gun and when they let me out you can take it back and put it where you found it. And then we'll go away. Now, hurry—

THE GIRL: All right. (*Pause*) I want to tell you something.

YOUNG MAN: O.K.

THE GIRL (*Very softly*): If you're not here when I come back, well, I'll have the gun and I'll know what to do with it.

YOUNG MAN: You know how to handle a gun?

THE GIRL: I know how.

YOUNG MAN: Don't be a fool. (*Takes off his shoe, brings out some currency*) Don't be a fool, see? Here's some money. Eighty dollars. Take it and go to San Francisco. Look around and find somebody. Find somebody alive and halfway human, see? Promise me—if I'm not here when you come back, just throw the gun away and go to San Francisco. Look around and find somebody.

THE GIRL: I don't *want* to find anybody.

YOUNG MAN (*Swiftly, desperately*): Now, do what I tell you. I'll meet you in San Francisco. I've got a couple of dollars in my other shoe. I'll see you in San Francisco.

THE GIRL (*With wonder*): San Francisco?

YOUNG MAN: That's right—San Francisco. That's where you and me belong.

THE GIRL: I've always wanted to go to some place like San Francisco—but how could I go alone?

YOUNG MAN: Well, you're not alone any more, see?

THE GIRL: Tell me a little what it's like.

YOUNG MAN (*Very swiftly, almost impatiently at first, but gradually slower and with remembrance, smiling and* THE GIRL *moving closer to him as he speaks*): Well, it's on the Pacific to begin with—ocean all around. Cool fog and sea-gulls. Ships from all over the world. It's got seven hills. The little streets go up and down, around and all over. Every night the fog-horns bawl. But they won't be bawling for you and me.

THE GIRL: Are people different in San Francisco?

YOUNG MAN: People are the same everywhere. They're different only when they love somebody. That's the only thing that makes 'em different. More people in San Francisco love somebody, that's all.

THE GIRL: Nobody anywhere loves anybody as much as I love you.

YOUNG MAN (*Whispering*): Hearing you say that, a man could die and still be ahead of the game. Now, hurry. And don't forget, if I'm not here when you come back, I'll meet you in San Francisco. (THE GIRL *stands a moment looking at him, then backs away, turns and runs. The* YOUNG MAN *stares after her, troubled and smiling. He sits down suddenly and buries his head in his hands. From a distance the sound of several automobiles approaching is heard. He listens. Several automobile doors are slammed. A wooden door is opened with a key, then slammed, and footsteps are heard in a hall. Walking easily, almost casually, and yet arrogantly, a* MAN *comes in. The* YOUNG MAN *jumps up suddenly and shouts at the* MAN, *almost scaring him*) What the hell kind of a jail-keeper are you, anyway? Why don't you attend to your business? You get paid for it, don't you? Now, get me out of here.

THE MAN: But I'm *not* the jail-keeper.

YOUNG MAN: Yeah? Well, who are you, then?

THE MAN: I'm the husband.

YOUNG MAN: What husband are you talking about?

THE MAN: You know what husband.

YOUNG MAN: Hey! (*Pause, looking at* THE MAN) Are *you* the guy that hit me over the head last night?

THE MAN: I am.

YOUNG MAN (*With righteous indignation*): What do you mean going around hitting people over the head?

THE MAN: Oh, I don't know. What do you *mean* going around—the way you do?

YOUNG MAN (*Rubbing his head*): You hurt my head. You got no right to hit anybody over the head.

THE MAN (*Suddenly angry, shouting*): Answer my question! What do you mean?

YOUNG MAN: Listen, you—don't be hollering at me just

because I'm locked up. You *think* you're the husband. You're the husband of nothing.

THE MAN (*Draws a pistol*): Shut up!—

YOUNG MAN: Go ahead, shoot— (*Softly*) and spoil the fun. What'll your pals think? They'll be disappointed, won't they? What's the fun hanging a man who's already dead? (THE MAN *puts the gun away*) I know you've come to tell me what you're going to do. Well, you don't need to tell me. I *know* what you're going to do. I've read the papers and I know. A mob of 'em fall on one man and beat him, don't they? They tear off his clothes and kick him, don't they? And women and little children stand around watching, don't they? Well, before you go on *this* holiday, I'm going to tell you a few things. You've been outraged. A stranger has come to town and violated your pure, innocent, virtuous women. You've got to set this thing right. You're home-makers, and you beat your children. (*Suddenly*) Listen, you—I didn't know she was your wife. I didn't know she was anybody's wife.

THE MAN: You're a liar!

YOUNG MAN: Sometimes—but not this time. Do you want to hear about it? (THE MAN *doesn't answer*) All right, I'll tell you the truth, as God's my witness. I met her at a lunch counter. She came in and sat next to me. There was plenty of room, but she sat next to me. Somebody put a nickel in the phonograph and a fellow was singing "New San Antonio Rose." Well, she got to talking about the song. I thought she was talking to the waiter, but *he* didn't answer her, so *I* answered her. That's how I met her. I didn't think anything of it. We left the place together and started walking. The first thing I knew she said: This is where I live.

THE MAN: You're a dirty liar!

YOUNG MAN: Do you want to know the truth? (THE MAN *does not answer*) O.K. She asked me to come in. Maybe she had something in mind, maybe not. Didn't make any difference to me, one way or the other. If she was lonely, all right. If not, all right.

THE MAN: You're telling a lot of dirty lies!

YOUNG MAN: I'm telling the truth. Maybe your wife's out there with your pals. Well, call her in. I got nothing against her, or you—or any of you. Call her in, and ask her a few questions. Are you in love with her? (THE MAN *doesn't answer*) Well, that's too bad.

THE MAN: What do you mean?

YOUNG MAN: I mean this may not be the first time something like this has happened.

THE MAN (*Swiftly*): Shut up!

YOUNG MAN: Oh, you know it. You've always known it. You're afraid of your pals, that's all. She asked for money. That's all she wanted. I wouldn't be here now if I had given her some money.

THE MAN (*Slowly*): How much did she ask for?

YOUNG MAN: I didn't ask how much. I told her I'd made a mistake. She said she would make trouble if I didn't give her some money. Well, I don't like bargaining, and I don't like being threatened, so I told her to get the hell away from me. The next thing I knew she'd run out of the house and was hollering. (*Pause*) Now, why don't you go out there and tell 'em they took me to another jail —go home and pack up and leave her? You're a good guy, you're just afraid of your pals. (THE MAN *draws his gun again. He is very frightened. He moves a step towards the* YOUNG MAN, *then fires three times. The* YOUNG MAN *falls to his knees.* THE MAN *turns and runs*) Hello—out there! (*He is bent forward.* THE GIRL *comes running in, and halts suddenly, looking at him.*)

THE GIRL: There were some people in the street, men and women and kids—so I came in through the back, through a window. I couldn't find the gun. I looked all over but I couldn't find it. What's the matter?

YOUNG MAN: Nothing—nothing. Everything's all right. Listen. Listen, Katey! Get out of here! Go out the way you came in and run—run like hell—run all night! Get to another town and get on a train. Do you hear?

THE GIRL: What's happened?

YOUNG MAN: Get away—just get away from here! Take any train that's going—you can get to San Francisco later.

THE GIRL (*Almost sobbing*): I don't want to go any place without you.

YOUNG MAN: I can't go. Something's happened. (*He looks at her*) I'll meet you in San Francisco, Katey—because I love you, and I've got some money in my other shoe, and when you've got money you can do anything. (*He falls forward.* THE GIRL *stands near him, then begins to sob softly, walking away. She stands over to one side, stops sobbing, and stares out. The excitement of the mob out-*

side increases. THE MAN, *with two of his* PALS, *comes running in.* THE GIRL *watches, unseen.*)

THE MAN: Here's the son of a bitch!

ANOTHER MAN: O.K. Open the cell, Harry.

> (*The* THIRD MAN *goes to the cell door, unlocks it, and swings it open. A* WOMAN *comes running in.*)

THE WOMAN: Where is he? I want to see him. Is he dead? (*Looking down at him, as the* MEN *pick him up*) There he is. (*Pause*) Yeah, that's him. (*Her husband looks at her with contempt, then at the dead man.*)

THE MAN: All right—let's get it over with.

THIRD MAN: Right you are, George. Give me a hand, Harry. (*They lift the body.*)

THE GIRL (*Suddenly, fiercely*): Put him down!

THE MAN: What's this?

SECOND MAN: What are you doing in here? Why aren't you out in the street with the others?

THE GIRL: Put him down and go away. (*She runs towards the* MEN. THE WOMAN *grabs her.*)

THE WOMAN: Here—where do you think *you're* going?

THE GIRL: Let me go. You've got no right to take him away.

THE WOMAN: Well, listen to her, will you? (*She slaps* THE GIRL *and pushes her to the floor*) Listen to the little slut, will you?

> (*They* ALL *go, carrying the* YOUNG MAN's *body.* THE GIRL *gets up slowly, no longer sobbing. She looks around at everything, then whispers*)

THE GIRL: Hello—out there!

END

Final Word

But then who reads plays? Who *can?* I'd certainly like to know who has read these. And why.

WILLIAM SAROYAN

San Francisco, January 31, 1967

CLASSIC DRAMA OF THE AGES

This extensive series contains collections of important plays covering the entire range of British and European literature, prepared under the direction of John Gassner, Sterling Professor of the Yale School of Drama. Each book includes a general introduction by Professor Gassner on the drama of the period or country covered.

GREEK DRAMA   Moses Hadas, Editor   NC285 / 95¢

A brilliant collection of nine plays which display the diversity and grandeur of tragedy, the critical and satiric genius of comedy. *Agamemnon, Choephoroe,* and *Eumenides* by Aeschylus; *Antigone, Oedipus the King, Oedipus at Colonus* and *Philoctetes* by Sophocles; *Medea, Hippolytus, Trojan Women* by Euripides; *Frogs* by Aristophanes. Also included is an introduction to Greek theatre and separate prefaces to each play.

ROMAN DRAMA
Samuel Lieberman, editor & translator   NC244 / 95¢

The Rope, The Manaechmi Twins, and *Prisoners of War* by Plautus; *The Woman of Andros, Phormio* and *The Brothers* by Terence; *Hippolytus, Oedipus,* and *Medea* by Seneca are presented in new and modernized translations. A general introduction to the Roman theatre, the dramatists, and individual plays is included, as well as an essay by John Gassner, "The Legacy of Rome."

MEDIEVAL AND TUDOR DRAMA
John Gassner, general editor   QC286 / $1.25

Plays from the entire range of English drama during the medieval and early Renaissance periods. Latin texts are given in English and all plays written originally in Middle English have been modernized. *Everyman,* John Heywood's *The Four PP, Ralph Roister Doister, Gammer Gurton's Needle,* and *Gorboduc.* Bibliography.

FOUR GREAT ELIZABETHAN PLAYS
John Gassner, general editor   SC218 / 75¢

The dramatists of this period started a long and rich national tradition ranging from tragedy to comedy. This book contains: *Doctor Faustus* by Christopher Marlowe, *The Duchess of Malfi* by John Webster, *The Shoemaker's Holiday,* by Thomas Dekker, and *Volpone* by Ben Jonson. Introduction by the editor, with notes on each of the plays.

FOUR GREAT COMEDIES OF THE
RESTORATION AND EIGHTEENTH CENTURY
John Gassner, general editor   SC228 / 75¢

During this period, the only recognized sin was the sin of dullness. Here are four important works reflective of this era: William Wycherley's *The Country Wife,* William Congreve's *The Way of the World,* Oliver Goldsmith's *She Stoops to Conquer,* and Richard Brinsley Sheridan's *The School for Scandal.* Introduction by Brooks Atkinson. Explanatory notes on each of the plays.

CLASSICAL FRENCH DRAMA
Wallace Fowlie, editor   HC135 / 60¢

In this volume are five plays representing the diversity, the traditions and the style of Classic French theatre: Corneille's *The Cid*, Racine's *Phaedra*, Moliere's *Intellectual Ladies*, Marivaux's *The Game of Love and Chance*, Beaumarchais' *The Barber of Seville*. Wallace Fowlie has translated and edited the text, and provided biographies of the dramatists.

THE COMPLETE PLAYS OF ARISTOPHANES
Moses Hadas, editor   QC277 / $1.25

Lysistrata, Clouds, Frogs, Thesmophoriazusae, Birds, Plutus, Archarnians, Wasps, Knights and *Ecclesiazusae*. The introduction and preface to each play by the noted editor Moses Hadas, place the drama of Aristophanes in historical and literary perspective.

NINETEENTH CENTURY RUSSIAN DRAMA
John Gassner, general editor   SC168 / 75¢

The drama of this period introduced a quality of realism unknown in more formalistic European theatre. *The Stone Guest* by Pushkin, *The Inspector General* by Gogol, *A Month in the Country* by Turgenev, *The Thunderstorm* by Ostrovsky, *The Power of Darkness* by Tolstoy. Translated by Andrew R. MacAndrew, with an introduction by Marc Slonim.

TWENTIETH CENTURY RUSSIAN DRAMA
John Gassner, general editor   SC174 / 75¢

Five outstanding works showing the brilliant range of Russian creativity during this era. *The Three Sisters* by Chekhov, *The Lower Depths* by Gorky, *He Who Gets Slapped* by Andreyev, *The Bathhouse* by Mayakovsky, *A List of Assets* by Olesha. Translated and with an introduction by Andrew R. MacAndrew.

THE DYBBUK & OTHER GREAT YIDDISH PLAYS
Translated and edited by Joseph C. Landis
                                                     QC294 / $1.25

For the first time anywhere, an exceptional collection of Yiddish drama; five plays; *The Dybbuk, God of Vengeance, Green Fields, King David & His Wives* and *The Golem*. There is also a major introduction.

AVAILABLE WHEREVER PAPERBACKS ARE SOLD

BANTAM WORLD DRAMA

Introducing a new library of living theater—from Euripides to Osborne. This series contains authoritative editions as well as fresh modern translations of the classics and important contemporary plays. Many of the plays contain introductions and commentaries by leading critics and scholars.

☐ **NT11 TEN PLAYS BY EURIPIDES.** This volume includes all
　　95¢ of the Greek dramatist's most important plays including MEDEA, TROJAN WOMEN, ELECTRA and ALCESTIS.

☐ **ST7 THREE PLAYS.** The three most famous plays by
　　75¢ Thornton Wilder, showing him at his audacious best —OUR TOWN, THE SKIN OF OUR TEETH and THE MATCHMAKER.

☐ **HT5 CYRANO DE BERGERAC.** Here is Edmond Rostand's
　　60¢ immortal play in which chivalry, wit, bravery and love are forever captured in the timeless spirit of romance. Translated by Brian Hooker.

☐ **NT2 THE CRUCIBLE.** The world-acclaimed drama by
　　95¢ Arthur Miller, author of DEATH OF A SALESMAN. This play focuses on the problem of the Salem witch trials and guilt by association.

☐ **NT3 INCIDENT AT VICHY.** Arthur Miller's most recent
　　95¢ play, a powerful and disturbing drama of ten men locked together by their common sense of doom.

☐ **NT4 AFTER THE FALL.** Many critics have damned this
　　95¢ play as a shockingly intimate portrayal of Arthur Miller's personal life with Marilyn Monroe. Others hail it as the most electrifying drama of our age.

☐ **NT1 A VIEW FROM THE BRIDGE.** Arthur Miller's inter-
　　95¢ nationally famous play about a man doomed to self-destruction by his own guilty desires.

☐ **HT6 FOUR GREAT PLAYS BY IBSEN.** His world-renowned
　　60¢ plays for all time—A DOLL'S HOUSE, THE WILD DUCK, AN ENEMY OF THE PEOPLE and GHOSTS.

☐ **NT8 THE ENTERTAINER.** This shocking play by John
　　95¢ Osborne, author of LOOK BACK IN ANGER and INADMISSIBLE EVIDENCE, is symbolic of a ruthless world desperately hell-bent on self-destruction.

AVAILABLE WHEREVER PAPERBACKS ARE SOLD

Bantam Books, Inc., Dept. WD, Room 607, 271 Madison Ave., New York, N. Y. 10016

Please send me the Bantam Books which I have checked. I am enclosing $_____ (check or money order—no currency please). Sorry, no C.O.D.'s. Note: Please include 10¢ per book for postage and handling.

Name_____

Address_____

City_____State_____Zip Code_____
Allow two to three weeks for delivery　　　WD-1-67